Women and Culture

Women and Culture

Between Malay *Adat* and Islam

Wazir-Jahan Karim
Begum

Westview Press

BOULDER • SAN FRANCISCO • OXFORD

Dedicated to the memory of my late mother,
Begum Bismillah Munawar, who cared more
than we knew, and to Razha and the boys,
Raqib, Rashid and Nuril.

This Westview softcover edition is printed on acid-free paper and bound in library-quality, coated covers that carry the highest rating of the National Association of State Textbook Administrators, in consultation with the Association of American Publishers and the Book Manufacturers' Institute.

Copyright © 1992 by Westview Press, Inc.

Published in 1992 in the United States of America by Westview Press, Inc., 5500 Central Avenue, Boulder, Colorado 80301-2877, and in the United Kingdom by Westview Press, 36 Lonsdale Road, Summertown, Oxford OX2 7EW

Library of Congress Cataloging-in-Publication Data
Wazir-Jahan Begum Karim
    Women and culture : between Malay *Adat* and Islam / Wazir Jahan Karim.
    p. cm.
    ISBN 0-8133-8519-9
    1. Women—Malaysia. 2. Men—Malaysia— Attitudes. 3. Sex role—Religious aspects—Islam. 4. Social values. 5. Islam—Social aspects—Malaysia. I. Title.
HQ1750.6.W396 1992
305.3'09595—dc20   91-33340
                                                                                      CIP

Printed and bound in the United States of America

The paper used in this publication meets the requirements of the American National Standard for Permanence of Paper for Printed Library Materials Z39.48-1984.

10   9   8   7   6   5   4   3   2   1

Contents

Tables, Figures and Maps

Preface

Malaysia covers an area of about 130,000 square miles, encompassing the Malay Peninsula in the west and the states of Sabah and Sarawak in the north-western Borneo Island (Map 1). The two regions are separated by about 400 miles of the South China Sea. While the Peninsular Malaysia, covering 52,0000 square miles, has its frontiers with Thailand, Sabah and Sarawak, together about 78,000 square miles, border the territory of Indonesian Kalimantan. The two territories together contained a total population of 17.9 million in 1990.

The population of Peninsular Malaysia comprises three major ethnic groups, the Malays, the Chinese and the Indians. The current Malay population in the Peninsula is 56.0 per cent followed by 33.0 per cent Chinese, 10.2 per cent Indians and 0.9 per cent of other minorities. Virtually all Malays are Muslims, and they live predominantly in the rural areas of the Peninsula (69.2 per cent). The majority of the Chinese and Indians are settled in the urban centres of the country. In the rural areas, the Indian population is mainly contained in oil-palm and rubber estates and plantations. There are numerous other ethnic groups in Malaysia or in Sabah and Sarawak who are Muslims or who have recently converted to Islam, but these groups have been excluded from the study, since they deserve to be studied separately.

About four-fifths of Malaysia including Sabah and Sarawak is covered by forests and swamps but between the coast and the mountainous interior lies the agricultural zone, where plantations, estates and smallholdings produce a range of export-oriented crops, namely rubber, oil-palm, pineapple, cocoa, coconut, cloves and pepper. Padi cultivation, catering mainly for the local market, is found throughout the Peninsula with vast areas of rice concentration in Kedah, Perlis, Province Wellesley and the north-east of the Peninsula. Tin-mining, introduced in the nineteenth century by pioneering groups of Chinese entrepreneurs, was the first export-oriented non-agricultural commodity which was encouraged by the British Colonial Government. Manufactured goods were encouraged and produced only in the decades after Independence when the monopolistic control of the colonial government over major items was introduced. In Peninsular Malaysia, the expansion of the rural economy toward greater intensification and diversification of agriculture and the acceleration of manufacturing in urban centres over the last few decades has not significantly affected regional distribution of the different ethnic groups in the country. The Malays remain predominantly rural, the Chinese, urban while the Indians remain encapsulated in infrastructural transport development services and plantations. However, massive movement of the Malay rural population into ready-tailored urban waged-income employment has produced a migrant population structure in urban centres. They live at the periphery of towns and cities in village-styled residential areas or squatters.

The development of systems of social stratification, based on class and ethnicity, diffuses cultural and religious boundaries so that it is possible to say that differences in modes of thinking and living within each ethnic community are as varied as the differences amongst them. However, in certain spheres of symbolic group identification at the national level, through custom, language and religion, ethnicity becomes a meaningful force of cohesion and unity. Capitalism, modernity, political party ideology, and religion produce splitting effects within and amongst ethnic groups and the dominant theme in Malaysia of inter-ethnic rivalry between the Malays and Chinese in maintaining and extending spheres of control in politics and the economy is challenged by increasing class differences within the communities.

This book has taken a long time to complete. I began my field research in Mawang (fictitious name) in Seberang Perai in January 1981 and the first draft was prepared in December 1985. Part of this long stretch in research was spent in the National Archives in Kuala Lumpur and the University of Chicago, where much of the data was written up during my sabbatical in 1984-85. This research on gender in *adat* and Islam encompassed a major portion of a study I had undertaken under the KANITA Project (Women in Development) between 1981 and 1985 in Universiti Sains Malaysia. During 1981 to 1983, the Kanita Project was funded by the National Advisory Council for the Integration of Women in Development, and I realized the dearth of material on *adat* and Islam, in ideology and practice in the rural areas in Peninsular Malaysia. As Convenor of this Research Programme, I assigned myself the task of investigating gender relationships in custom and religion. The historical perspective seemed important, in the context of modernization, industrialization and Islamic revivalism. Could *adat*, the core indigenous values, ideals and sentiments of Malay society,withstand the onslaught of change and development, or was it to disappear as rapidly as capitalism and revivalism appeared to rearticulate the systems of economic and social relations? The answers were not so simple and a packaged theory of dependency or cultural rejuvenation did not seem to express the problem at hand. As in many other cultures in the world, women are the most visible and dramatic symbols of change, used and abused by public and private organizations and movements to demonstrate the strength and success of new ideologies and modes of behaviour. Yet the power of women visibly and invisibly remains a vital force in society. In Malay society, I was interested to know the power structures of Malay women in the past, in relation to the present and the future.

Today, industrialization and Islam appear to battle against one other for the monopoly of control over women's labour, biology and sex. Yet in early Malay history, the Islamization of the Malay states did not reduce women's power in any significant way and indeed in colonial history appeared to be a source of power for women by granting them an intellectual base for political activity. Hence, Malay women's position vis-a-vis men should be seen against the wider historical and cultural fabric of Malay society. The way in which *adat* and Islam integrate and separate over different epochs in history appeared to express differences in Malay constructs of gender. Generally a pattern seemed to emerge. Inasmuch as the power of Malay men lies in Islam and local articulations of Islamic thought vis-a-vis *adat*, Malay women's historical and contemporary value is located within the bilaterality of *adat* which, with its emphasis on seniority, parenthood, reciprocity and productivity, gives them a fair share of human and ritual resources to work on. However, the spirit of human liberation through Islam has worked for or against Muslim women and when used successfully by women came closer to traditional and newer articulations of *adat*. Eventually, Malay bilaterality in *adat* attempts to be an 'equalizer' – neutralizing counter-stream ideologies which articulate women's position differently through principles of biology, patriarchy and misogyny.

This study emphasizes culture as a vital system and process which generates different and often opposing strategies for men and women. Malay *adat* and Islam as the main ingredients of Malay culture best benefit women when they are ritually and symbolically interfused (as when women draw sunna rituals into their own sphere of social relations) and best benefit men when they are dialectically opposed (as when revivalism attempts to equate women's productivity with domesticity). In the long term, gender relationships appear to be extremely volatile, expressing the vitality of a culture struggling to maintain its own identity in history.

The peculiarity of Southeast Asian bilaterality has not been emphasized much before, but it provides interesting contrasts with West and South Asian social systems, where Islam has become accepted as a major religion and way of life. In these societies, pre-Islamic *adat* traditions are usually based in patriarchy or patriliny and Islam merely complements some of these earlier traditions. In Southeast Asian Muslim societies, bilaterality has not always allowed Islam to develop into a similar form, except in periods when revivalism reorders gender relationships in the direction of male dominance. Even so, it merely encourages cultural splitting rather than systematic restructuring. Contemporary Malay society expresses this phenomenon dramatically with its struggle for and against capitalism, industrialization, revivalism and orthodoxy.

The captions in the beginning of each text are derived from Malay proverbial sayings and *pantun* which need no explanation to those well versed with Malay culture and language. They express the themes of each chapter rather clearly. The last caption however needs some explanation. The Boat (*Biduk*) Passes (*Lalu*), Water Cress Parts – to rejoin (*Kiambang Bertaut*) is a proverbial Malay saying to indicate stability or timelessness in family and social relations – that over time, conflicts and contradictions will often occur but the basic structures remain. The *kiambang* is a floating plant of the species *Pistia Stratiotes*. In English its closest translation is 'cress' or 'lettuce' although it is often confused with the water hyacinth. It is referred to as *Apon-apon* or *Kapu-kapu* in Java and *Chauk* in Thai.

Wazir Jahan Karim

Acknowledgments

Between 1981 and 1985 I received several different grants which were integrated into the KANITA Project. I would like to acknowledge the assistance of the National Advisory Council for the Integration of Women in Development, formerly at the Prime Minister's Department, Kuala Lumpur, the International Development Research Centre and the Ford Foundation, for the period of my field-work and archival research in the National Archives. I also wish to extend my appreciation to the National Archives of Malaysia for permitting me to do most of my archival research there.

I was fortunate to receive a Fulbright Fellowship in 1984/85 which allowed me to do most of my writing at the University of Chicago. I wish to express my appreciation to several people who helped me during the period of my research and writing. My foster family in Mawang, Rokiah, Zuriah and Ma'cik Sabariah were a constant source of help to me and I could not have completed the research without their warm kindness and hospitality. My gratitude and thanks also to the rest of the women and children in Mawang and Tasek who patiently subjected themselves to my inquisition.

Finally, my thanks to several friends and colleagues who helped me by providing useful comments and ideas on the final drafts: Marshall Sahlins, Ioan Lewis, Razha Rashid, Cheah Boon Kheng and former members of the KANITA research team who directly and indirectly contributed to this research – James Lochhead, Pauline Das, Vasanthi Ramachandran, Jamilah Karim Khan and Ramli Abdullah to name a few.

W.J.K.

Map I: Malaysia and Its Neighbours

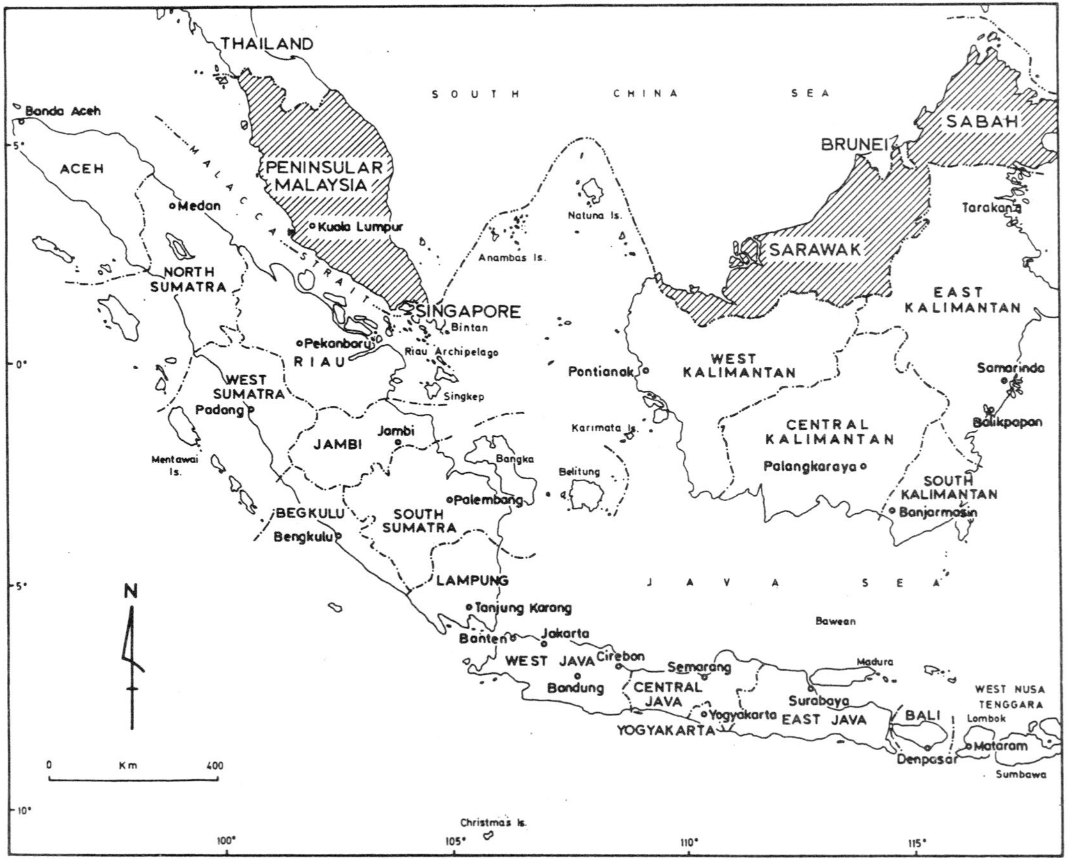

1

Gender, Culture and History

Biar mati anak, jangan mati *adat*
Better a child perish, rather than our customs die
— *Malay proverb*

Introduction

Studies of gender in the social sciences have attempted to adopt a number of different theoretical approaches, most of which serve the common purpose of providing answers to questions of women's 'power' in society vis-a-vis men.

Power is here defined as the system of arriving at decision-making in a direction which provides personal autonomy. In the context of gender relations, power is concerned with both domestic and wider spheres of activity relating to class, politics, religion and ethnicity. How men and women participate in decision-making and express autonomy within and across their spheres of activity summarizes their power relationship to one another in the short and long term.

A dominant approach in feminist scholarship in anthropology was the view that sexual asymmetry was a basic condition of man and significant through our history (Gough, 1975; Rosaldo and Lamphere, 1974; Reiter, 1975; Raphael, 1975). Since basic biological and sexual differences already existed between men and women, cultural systems merely served to interpret and elaborate upon these rules. Hence cultures only differed in the extent to which gender was used as a rule, formal or symbolic to sort out hierarchical forms of relationships between men and women.

The approach of feminist Marxists' was to relate history to gender where processes of change or transformation was seen to accompany visible forms of social differentiation based in gender (Leacock, 1981 a, b, c) Lee, 1982;

Gough, 1975; Reiter, 1975). A perspective adopted from Morgan and Engels on the emergence of rules of the sexual division of labour and from Marx on the oppression of women and men of the working classes, such writers usually made cross-cultural comparisons of gender relations in 'egalitarian' and complex industrial societies to demonstrate the progressive utilization of gender as a rule of social differentiation. Feminist Marxist scholarship in anthropology was strongly supported by economists, developmentalists and planners concerned with the effects of agriculture and industrial change on women as labour resources. Generally these researchers argued that colonization and industrialization processes had the effect of restructuring gender rules in a direction detrimental to women (Boserup, 1970; Rogers, 1980; Heyzer, 1986). Since decision-making in agriculture and industry were male-dominated or male-oriented, sexual or biological rules were utilized, diminishing women's importance in economic development. They also argued that where pre-existing egalitarian rules of gender had existed, these were ignored to ensure men a central participatory role in development and decision-making.

Presenting a contrary perspective, structuralists and symbolists argued that sex and gender were only some of the many ways of establishing modes of social differentiation and control. The complexity of structures of social differentiation in different cultures suggest that the position of women cannot be argued through universal theory. Studies by Almagor (1978), Harris (1978) and Sansom (1978) brought out some of the structural variations of subjugation and social control in non-Western societies. Hence women's power vis-a-vis men differed in form and meaning according to cultural constructs. Male hegemony in biology, class and politics developed from the cultural meanings attached to sex and gender rather than from universals of the unknown.

MacCormack and Strathern in a collection of articles employing symbolic analysis argued against the 'putative universality of the nature-culture categories' applied to women and male-female relationships (1980: vii). MacCormack in her critique of this feminist approach in anthropology argued that the 'genderizing' of anthropology should be done in the context of the relativity of ideas and morals on which anthropology was built. She stated, 'Might we then conclude that both men and women are nature and culture, and there is no logic compelling us to believe that at an unconscious level women, because of their naturalness, are opposed and subordinate to men?' (1980: 17).

This view was again taken up by Ortner and Whitehead (1981) in a collection on the symbolic analysis of gender. They argued that this 'culturalist' approach was less reductionistic than the feminist perspective (of feminist Marxism, or culture/nature biological reductionism) and more important to the development of modern anthropology, in its movement towards hermeneutics, personal psychology and Weberian relativism. However, to move away from the non-committal passive paradigm of 'early symbolism' which attempted to challenge feminism in anthropology, they argued the case for 'modern symbolism', where constructions of meaning relating to sex, women and gender could be approached within a common framework of reference, to incorporate the different perspectives of 'actors' cross-culturally. Selecting prestige systems as a framework of reference, they concluded that the cultural constructions of sex and gender tended everywhere to be stamped by the prestige considerations of socially dominant male actors (1981: 12). To elaborate, the evolution of world religions, kinship ideologies and political systems generated notions of 'social honour' and 'social value' which heightened male dominance. Hence, cultural constructions of gender relations was everywhere similar. Culture only changed the form of construction of meanings but the hierarchies that were constructed were based on sex and gender.

The approach of Ortner and Whitehead (1981) continues to be debated. Arguments for a 'constructionist' and 'deconstructionist' methodology have not all led to the popular conclusion of male-dominance. Moore argues that an investigation into the constructions of 'women' and 'men' are essential and should not be assumed. She states that 'biological difference between the sexes tell us nothing about the general social significance of that difference' (1988: 7). The construction of ethnocentrism and racism might tell us something more about women and men, since these two forces have historical and cultural origins. In racism, biology might be used as an issue of differentiation but the fact that it is utilized, manipulated and applied makes it cultural, rather than natural. In her volume, she concludes that anthropology is in a position to reformulate feminist theory because it can more successfully (compared to other disciplines in the social sciences) remove social data from Western bias and Eurocentrism. The future of feminist anthropology she states, is in a movement away from 'sameness' to 'difference' and in this women anthropologists have to realize a lack of academic cohesion when discussing issues of women's oppression.

I would like to carry this argument further by suggesting that the movement towards deconstructing women's history and the history of gender in terms of macro forces of colonialism, religious orthodoxy, fascism and globalization, cannot rid itself of Western bias or Eurocentricity if anthropologists again base their analysis on the theoretical formulations of thinkers who have attempted these reconstructions on Western data. For an anthropologist researching on gender in Muslim Southeast Asia, the absorption of the method of deconstruction is important, not so much the ideas being deconstructed. The processes of examining continuity and change is more useful than the contents which unfold.

The post-modernist disenchantment with Marxism has led writers to explore the theory and methodology of European philosophies concerned with the development of the history of knowledge and the history of ideas. Approaches linked to the constitutive nature of the process of knowledge production (Bordieu, 1980; Fabian, 1983) have repopularized most of the major works of Foucault which highlight history as processes of knowledge construction within culture. Foucault, in 'The History of Sexuality' (1978) saw historical processes as linked to the relations of power amongst unequals from which emerged hierarchies of gender. He argued that European eighteenth century culture focussed on 'specific mechanisms of knowledge and power centering on sex' (103). The power specialists of succeeding epochs continued with more effective strategies of concretizing gender, articulated in the final exploitation of women in capitalist technology.

This approach systematically links gender hierarchies to the historical construction of knowledge in Western civilization. It shows how such constructions become implanted in the minds of men and women as those with power elaborated upon this knowledge over time. On a higher level Said's 'Orientalism' (1978) specifically addresses a similar problem, of Western knowledge serving to reinforce power relations across cultures, legitimizing colonial and imperialistic policies. Foucault however explains this phenomenon as something which occurs within the processes of formation of Western culture itself — how intellectual colonialism occurs within Western society. The study of gender in non-Western cultures may address several of these interrelated academic issues. A basic area of investigation is the way in which constructions of Western knowledge have been superimposed upon indigenous non-Western knowledge systems rendering reinterpretations of relationships of gender and sex. These reinterpretations, surfacing in formal education, media, legislation and political processes may be demonstrated through articulations of opposition between the two systems or alternatively, continuity and accommodation.

A second area of inquiry is the validity of the Foucaultian model in non-Western cultures bearing in mind its Eurocentric value and application. 'The History of Sexuality' deals specifically with an interpretation of power from a Western paradigm that gender inequality is an expression of inequality generated from the tradition within. Scholars researching on women in non-Western cultures may have to critically examine the relevance of 'The History of Sexuality' to local data. The assumption that one should begin with the premise of unequal power generating gender hierarchies is not necessarily relevant in non-Western civilizations which derive a theory of knowledge from concepts and values of bilaterality; the need to maintain complementarity and similarity rather than hierarchy and opposition, the need to reduce imbalances through mutual responsibility and co-operation and the value of sharing power between supporters and followers. Bilaterality does not concern itself with relationships between the powerful and the powerless but the powerful and less powerful.

This study on Malay women is concerned with some basic articulations of power derived from *adat* and *Islam*, two systems of ideas which have contributed to the development of Southeast Asian history. *Adat* which is both intellectually and emotionally understood by the Malays and Malay-speaking populations of Southeast Asia exists with variations in concepts and interpretation throughout different Muslim and non-Muslim societies. However, consensus runs throughout the region that women's power and autonomy is derived from *adat* rather than Islam. *Adat* occupies a prominent place amongst the pan-Asian philosophies of Buddhism, Hinduism and Confucianism which have throughout history become the favourite reference books of men, for the surplus power they generate to this particular sex.

The most obvious characteristic of *adat* in the context of matters relating to land, economics, kinship and marriage is its overall pervasive norm of 'bilaterality' of reducing hierarchical differences based on gender. In relation to social rank and class, *adat* acknowledges such hierarchies but attempts to reduce their importance through reinforcing values of generosity, generalized reciprocity, co-operation and sharing. In my own ethnographic observation, the ethos of mutual consideration and social justice prevails through metaphorical language and ritual. It is obvious that the Malay ego-centred kindred system of patterning relationships underplays many modes of gender differentiation which are expressed in other Muslim communities maintained by institutions of patriliny-sexual segregation, marriage alliances, male authority and leadership, female domesticity and male-initiated divorce. Significantly, in both traditional and modern Malay society, the distribution and division of land and property do not automatically operate according to Islamic law. *Adat* and Islamic law are seen as alternative choices and final decisions are often based on customary notions of *pakat* (from *muafakat*, 'a plan of agreement') which give equal opportunities for women and men to inherit property.

Significantly further reflections reveal its equalizing or neutralizing mode, balancing on one level, relationships between men and women and on another, diverse systems of ideology which interject into contemporary life. Through *adat*, Malays view women's heightened sexuality to be as derogatory as women's diminished sexuality in Islamic revivalism. A premium is still placed on the self-assured woman who expresses her sexuality through the coveted symbolic modes of *adat*, who competes with others to attain economic and social independence and who obtains rank and power through politics or industry, without discarding traditional family and kinship values. This 'core culture' of gender relationships in the modern context is a constant reminder of the manifest and covert power of women.

The following factors, in right combination and proportion, determine differences in 'status' or 'rank' among a local Malay population. Generally, bilateral principles of ordering gender accords an inbuilt flexibility which is capable of absorbing both sexes into a common 'status' network system. In conclusion, certain basic criteria reflect the bilaterality of Malay sociopolitical relations from which are generated rules of separation of power and rank.

Generally, the importance of origins, age and seniority, personal attributes and morality very often override considerations of gender and this will be elucidated in Chapter 5 which deals with a description of village life.

1. *Age and Seniority:* determine formal and informal power or influence of both men and women though elders of the grandparental generation may gradually lose their influence when they cease to perform or participate in community rituals and functions.
2. *Matrimony:* This also applies equally to men and women although in the context of polygyny, men may acquire higher, and women lower status. However, this depends on whether male and female perceptions of polygyny are considered. When women's perceptions are considered, monogamy is favoured to polygyny. In most instances, men who acquire more than one wife are looked down upon by women, unless it appears to be absolutely necessary, for example, when a marriage is without issue. Amongst urban upper-class Malays, to whom polygyny is increasingly a phenomenon of 'conspicuous consumption', urban Malay women view the practice with distaste and often refer to it as 'female commoditization' (*membuat wanita seperti barang*).
3. *Socioeconomic Ranking:* Again, men and women with wealth, individual or family titles (acquired or ascribed), property, land, formal education and professional qualifications enjoy higher status both formal and informal, than those without. Also, these factors provide them with numerous opportunities to acquire powerful positions within the village or state.
4. *Personal Attributes :* Both men and women with charisma, leadership qualities, and amiable and friendly dispositions acquire popularity and influence, though men have a considerable advantage in utilizing these attributes for prestigious political and religious careers. In conjunction with age and marital status, charisma may grant success

in a career in religion and politics much more quickly than socio-economic ranking.

5. *Morality:* This is an extremely important attribute for both men and women and has possibly been previously underplayed by anthropologists studying Malay culture. It revolves around the notion of personal honour or *maruah* (Arabic, *muru'a*, meaning 'a sense of honour') and *nama* or social recognition. A Malay without *maruah* and *nama* is a social outcast within his or her community and may be stigmatized for life. Traits such as cowardice, insolence, greed and selfishness go contrary to Malay notions of decorum, derived from custom or *adat*. Malays, in fact, equate 'status' with honour and the newly introduced concept of *taraf sosial* (lit. 'social status') is hardly used in any sense except in formal sociological or economic publications. The concepts of *maruah* and *nama* are applied on the level of individual behaviour. To be personally dishonoured (*jatuh maruah, hilang maruah*) has lasting consequences on the individual and immediate family (nuclear or extended). It is in defence of *maruah*, in cases when a person is wrongly stigmatized, that men and women resort to acts of revenge, expressed in reciprocal actions of malice, name-slurring and witchcraft.

Adat and *Islam* as the main components of Malay culture serve to provide contradictory and conflicting statements of gender relations, particularly in areas of ritual, economic and political activity. By showing how these internal contradictions are resolved over history, at times in the direction of Islam and at other times, in the direction of *adat*, I argue that women are as able as men to exploit the cultural system to their advantage and to transmit throughout history, components of the culture which significantly support their own power and autonomy. I also attempt to demonstrate that the Islamic intellectual tradition may mystify rather than reproduce male power in more concrete ways since *adat* may permeate politicization processes and provide women with sources of latent and manifest power. Generally, this study suggests that the Foucaultian notion of power and gender may be inapplicable in cultures which concretize relationships between men and women through relationships of bilaterality. Even when Western sources of knowledge are introduced, these have to permeate a cultural base which is already laden with contradictory explanations of power between men and women. Hence in contemporary history where *adat* and *Islam* are both confronted with Westernization, gender choices may be split, with men upholding fundamentalism to reject Westernization and women upholding *adat* or Westernization depending on which provides them with a wider practical venue for autonomy and self-expression.

A post-modernist view of gender has to critically re-examine the notion of the historicity of male-dominance which has become evident in European social history. It is not so much the Foucaultian notion of the historicity of male-dominance which is important but the historical method of establishing this conclusion — the construction of gender rather than maleness as a basis for power and how this influenced the formation of local social history. This critical approach will then show that the European example is one of the many examples of 'difference'. It is not an explanation of 'sameness' or a reason to apply a new universal in anthropology.

Bilaterality in Southeast Asia

A significant amount of research on women and gender in Southeast Asia has been produced within a feminist perspective where an analysis of colonial history, change and development was systematically associated with the devaluation of women (Kahn, 1976; Stivens, 1981; Heyzer, 1986; Ng, 1987). The focus on either matriarchy or patriarchy in Southeast Asia has deemphasized the distinguishing structural feature of numerous Southeast Asian social systems which operates by rules of bilaterality, characterized by fluid, loose interlocking social networks, ego-centric ties and a diffusion of role and status concepts in relation to gender (Murdock, 1960; Winzeler, 1974; 1976). Gender relations are for the most complementary but non-hierarchical. Autonomy in work management and income allow women a monopoly over the domestic sphere and opportunities for wider public and social activity. Significantly, systems which are ideologically linked to matriarchy as in Minangkabau or patriarchy as in Batak or Balinese society demonstrate bilaterality, on the level of practical activity (H and C Geertz, 1961; Benda-Beckmann 1984; 1988; Eberhardt, 1988).

While it is evident that the indigenous milieu of gender relations rests uneasily on Indic-Buddhist and Islamic traditions in cultural history, male dominance in these areas of orthodoxy have provided women with new venues of competition for public activity. Ortner and Whitehead (1981) argue that kinship, motherhood and the mother-son bond enhances the prestige of men rather than women and that this heightens with advancing religious orthodoxy (1981: 1-128). I would argue to the contrary that this does not clearly occur in Southeast Asia and that flexibility of interpretation over prestige gives women and men sufficient leverage to operationalize power in a direction advantageous to the 'self'.

It has been suggested by Winzeler that the late and incomplete processes of state-formation in Southeast Asia is due to the prevalence of bilaterality. Processes of state formation here refer to the development of more centralized modes of political control which challenge localized systems of power relations within the indigenous population. He writes:

Societies in this region all lack the kinds of subsistence bases that are most readily linked to male-centred patrilineal forms of social organization, such as co-operative big-game hunting, large-scale animal pastoralism and dry-grain draft animal agriculture. Instead, they rely for the most part on either slash-and-burn horticulture or wet-rice agriculture, with fishing and in some cases gathering being important secondary activities; in all these, men and women tend to be more or less equally involved, both in production and processing (1976; 631).

These generalities hold true for insular Southeast Asia in particular, where kingships could not produce highly centralized forms of organization, comparable to South Asian and European states. However, it is difficult to presuppose that bilaterality preceded state-formation processes without specifying the periods in history with which the statement is concerned. For example, in Malaysia's pre-colonial history, Malay kings (raja, sultan) were created by the establishment of patrilineages with fictious genealogies produced from other descent systems outside the Peninsula. The absence of patrilineages or patrilineal systems of descent amongst the indigenous Malay population of the time suggests that Malay folk history differs from the formal constructions of the Malay state. Bilaterality was a local construct of social relations and a mode of conceptualizing relations of gender. Also the value of balance, flexibility, interchangeability and fluidity transcended higher levels of interaction based on religion, economics and politics and made it difficult for patriarchally ordered kingship systems to domesticate the masses. To expand Winzeler's argument further, I see bilaterality as a wider abstraction of kinship and gender and a popular Southeast Asia mode of conceptualizing relationships of any kind. Whether the context of reference is gender, class, religion or the state, the creation or the need to create flexible boundaries of action and interaction seems to be valued.

This argument appears to be supported by Geertz's description of Southeast Asian religion, in particular Islam:

> The peasantry absorbed Islamic concepts and practices, so far as it understood them, into the same general Southeast Asian folk religion into which it had previously absorbed Indian ones, locking ghosts, gods, jinns and prophets together into a strikingly contemplative, even philosophical animism. Modes of operationalizing dual or multi-structures seems to be the general concern of the populace, rather than the rejection or substitutions of one system for another. Hence the patriarchy of the Great Tradition could not so easily subdue the bilaterality of the masses, since each religion was adopted eclectically achieving only ritualistic and symbolic legitimacy admist the more individualistic egocentric animism (1968; 13).

The continuing role of animism, shamanism and spirit mediumship in

Southeast Asia supports this argument. Amidst the elitism of Hinduism, Buddhism and Islam in Southeast Asia, it encourages the democratization of power amongst the masses and a sense of personal autonomy in action and interaction.

Malay Bilaterality

In Malay society values of mutual responsibility and indebtedness continue to order vital relationships of rank, class and gender. Bilateral modes of social relations discourage social hierarchies derived from Western capitalism or religious orthodoxy. The *adat* system acknowledges hierarchies of age, seniority and class but simultaneously introduces informal mechanisms for balancing out social differences or reducing them. In gender, Malay value preferences describe a system where hierarchical distinctions are not easily created on the basis of biology or sex. Young unmarried women are marginalized by their age and marital status rather than sex. In the same way, male youths are excluded from many spheres of ritual activity by their 'inexperience', a product of age and single status.

By showing that bilaterality in Malay culture determines to a significant extent, the modes of expression of intersexual relationships, transcending the boundaries of biological, affinitive and primary ties into wider spheres of relations, this study also attempts to establish a conceptual framework for extending kinship theory into gender analysis. Reviewing Malay bilaterality processually, it is possible to say that women significantly influence the patterns of formation of Malay social history through social roles which are usually unaccounted for in formal history. Men are more often seen by historians to be the 'history makers and breakers' but assessing their roles from the gender point of view, they may alternatively be seen to represent more directly, the 'idealisms' of the system. Processes of creation and maintenance of formal rules, titles and courtly regalia, are designed to provide male roles with more legitimacy and distinction. Malay metaphorical statements, however, emphasize the contributions of women to social formation processes: 'Young men are the hope of the people, but young women, the pillars of the state' (*Pemuda harapan bangsa, pemudi tiang negara*) and 'If a woman, emulate Tun Fatimah, the war heroine with the truest spirit of patriotism' (*Kalau perempuan biarlah warisi Tun Fatimah, Seri Kandi yang bersemangat nasional sejati*). By advancing research on gender through indigenous value systems (in Southeast Asia, those based on bilaterality) social scientists may be forced to review and redefine Malay women's contributions to processes of formation of history and culture.

The use of the term 'bilaterality' in the wider context of social relations does not attempt to conform to former conceptualizations of kinship in social anthropology. In kinship theory, the term itself is loaded with ambiguities and it has been said before that, ideally, bilateral kinship systems do not exist. Anthropologists resort to other specific kinship terms which best describe the peculiarities of each culture. 'Bilateralism' then becomes a convenient abstraction of kinship terminology within which are produced features like 'kindred' or 'utrolateral filiation' (Freeman, 1961) common to the Iban and other Southeast Asian cultures, 'non-unilinear descent groups' (Goodenough, 1955: 71-72) akin to European and American cultures of the West, and 'ambilateral' or 'ramage' (Firth, 1930; 1957: 4-8) which best describe the social system of the Maori and Polynesia. In general, certain universalities of relationships exist in bilateral kinship systems, oriented around rules of marriage and gender that are more symmetrical and non-linear in form. In this sense, it may be more useful to use the term 'bilaterality' as a convenient abstraction to denote rules of 'balancing' or harmonizing intersexual ties and relationships. On a wider level, bilaterality is a rule of social relations in society, obscuring clear distinctions of rank and class amongst unequals. Since this study is concerned with providing a meaningful focus of conceptualization and abstraction for the study of relations of gender, 'bilaterality' will be used in the context of rules of social relations (male-female, patron-client, elite-peasant, elders-youth) rather than kinship. Generally, Malay society, which has best been described as 'bilateral', 'ego-centred' or 'kindred ordered' (Djamour, 1959; Wilder, 1982; Swift, 1965; Banks, 1983) can be said to contain a system which attempts to define gender within similar generations in terms of a set of symmetrical relationships with minimal differences in power. This system encourages interchangeability and flexibility in roles and status between men and women in particular and unequals in general.

Malay bilaterality is a convenient locus to discuss developments within the system of gender relations over time. It has previously been shown how intersexual behaviour is affected by socioeconomic developments from within and without. Barth (1973; 18), analysing Middle Eastern descent systems, attributed such shifts to politics, commenting that 'where the territorial estates at the base of these politics are removed the whole unilineal organization disappears and kinship and local life takes on a highly bilateral character'. Leach (1973: 53-55), studying English bilaterality through the Quaker families of the nineteenth century, demonstrated how economic expansion and industrialization encouraged the society to eventually develop a patrilineal structure, maintaining the bilateral ideology only through matrilateral filiation. In Malay society, it has previously been suggested that the existing Malay bilateral structure is derived from Minangkabau matrilineality which could not be sustained effectively as the Malay kingship State evolved (Taylor, 1948; Wilkinson, 1971; Hooker,

1970). These authors tended to contrast Minangkabau matriliny against the patriliny of Palembang rather than see the two systems as gradually converging into bilaterality in the course of expansion of the Malay states.

Empirical evidence demonstrates that the Malay populace did not take on the system of patrilineal descent utilized by Malay kings to produce hierarchical distinctions between peasants and the emerging royal class (Gullick, 1965; Winzeler, 1976). Significantly, Minangkabau *adat (perpatih)*, derived from Padang, probably did permeate Melaka-based Malay *adat (temenggong)* introduced in the fifteenth century. Hence, the state of Naning, under the jurisdiction of Melaka but lying at the Negeri Sembilan border, came under the influence of Minangkabau law. In the same way that patriliny was rejected by the Malay populace, matrilineal forms of organization did not emerge in the other states in Malaya after the fifteenth century. Throughout the states of Malaya, with the exception of Negeri Sembilan and Naning at the Negeri Sembilan border in Melaka, the cultural fabric of the society remained, at the least, bilateral. Peletz (1981: 31) discussing the centrality of women and marginality of men in Minangkabau society describes how this system of gender relations weakened under British colonization. The British institutionalized patriarchal decision-making patterns in Islam, including matters of land inheritance and administration.

Again, the Islamization of the Malay states from the fifteenth century did not change the bilateral component of Malay society. In the context of Malayan sociopolitical history, while bilateral features of social organization in time formed the fabric of the Malay family, kinship and community relations, patriliny and matriliny uniquely remained peripheral systems, maintained by a specific class of political elites or sub-cultural grouping respectively.

In the Malay Peninsula, bilaterality contains structures which on the level of ideology and behaviour, attempt to order relationships between men and women in more similar rather than dissimilar ways. This, however, does not imply that relationships between men and women are egalitarian as allegedly exist in foraging cultures (Leacock 1981 b and c; Lee, 1982; Morris, 1982). Significantly, the introduction of formal laws through Islam (*Syariah* Law), which render men greater advantage in matters of inheritance and property, has made this rather impossible but the continued practice of *adat* or customary law, from which Malay society has obtained its bilateral features within the domain of everyday social affairs, produces a more balanced way of sorting out sex roles within the confinement of similar age-grades and generation.

Islamic ritualization and public policy generally enable men to command more power in formal decision-making, at the level of the village or state. However, their ability to dominate the formal domains of social activity does not entirely suggest significant or radical separation of powers between men and women. This is mainly because a woman's relative inaccessibility to roles in the formal or public domains of activity in Islamic ritual does not necessarily make her 'invisible' or 'marginal'. She has access to a range of public roles which are importantly upheld by *adat*. In this sense, it is difficult to dichotomize male and female relationships in terms of the 'public' and 'private', or 'formal' and 'informal'. The kindred system maintains its significance through *adat*, and it is this relationship which has enabled the family and household unit to merge smoothly with the wider network of community and social relations, making it the most vital unit of anchoring and extending relationships, both primary and secondary. The range of public roles which are derived from the domestic domain are wide, allowing private-domestic spheres to be integrated with the public or formal. Roles which are widely spread amongst women, such as food-processing and exchange, trading, ritual and craft specialization, midwifery, religious teaching and training, do not justify 'public' or 'private' distinctions to be made. Such distinctions suggest that female specialization lacks 'public' value or cannot compete with other public roles of men.

Significantly, in the context of the Malay family-kindred structure, motherhood cannot be seen as 'private' or domestic or contributing to woman's 'invisibility' and domestication (making her in a symbolic sense seemingly closer to 'nature' than 'culture'). She is not powerless in her domesticity nor does her domesticity prevent her from seeking a more public position through traditional or modern modes of professional specialization. When conceived in its totality, motherhood enables a woman to generate further social and economic roles of decision-making which not only command formal status but also allows her to be economically independent from men. For this reason, this study does not attempt to explain the boundaries of male and female roles or behaviour in terms of conceptually opposing categories like public and private, non-domestic and domestic and formal and informal. Such distinctions only help to reproduce artificial gender distinctions which do not explain or reflect Malay bilateralism in any meaningful way.

Islam Within Different Cultural Traditions

General statements on the interrelationship between *adat* and Islam have been made. Geertz's argues that Islam is functionally political necessitating Muslims in different parts of the world to work within the orbit of local interpretations of the religion. Hence, peasant syncretism of Islam in Java may be contrasted to Moroccan scripturalism — to restore an idealized, hermetic Islam (1968: 106). Lewis (1986: 97) sees Islam as strategically useful in helping African Muslims reconstruct personal and universalistic group identity in the face of socioeconomic changes. Religious phenomenology unifies and separates many levels of social experience, from cults, charisma and spirit-possession to pan-Islamic movements.

However, if our concerns are gender relationships and the power of women vis-a-vis men, it is important to know how the two systems are constructed to produce a specific system of 'gender in culture'. The patriarchy of *adat* in the Arab-Muslim world ideally positions Islam as the liberator of female oppression (Mernissi, 1975; Dwyer, 1978; Fazlur Rahman, 1983). In Southeast Asia, however, the converse may be true. *Adat* acknowledges social hierarchies of rank in political and class terms but not in gender. In this context, Islam cannot, ideally speaking, be construed as a liberator of female oppression. Indeed theoretically, it introduces so many more ways of dichotomizing male and female relationships in domestic and public terms that it may have the adverse effect on women's position, particularly when splinters of Arab *adat* are lodged in indigenous family and kinship systems, religious cults and political organizations. Hence, an examination of gender relationships in history and context is important, vis-a-vis the extent to which Islam has influenced *adat* in sorting out gender relationships and role behaviour between men and women and conversely, the extent to which Malay *adat* with its ideals of equalizing gender, override or adjust to religious considerations. Thus, the exercise of relating 'emic' or subjective constructs of gender to two formally different traditions, necessitates analytical objectification in that the researcher sees it important to understand the history of the interrelationship between *adat* and Islam. The moot question of which system is effectively concerned with or capable of equalizing or neutralizing gender in the long term, despite their relative success or failure, in the short term, underlies the objective nature of this research. On the wider level, this concern reflects another academic exercise, the problem of understanding women's power as part of the process of development of culture.

Malay *Adat* and Islam

Generally, *adat* (from the Arab word '*adat*, plural meaning culture, refinement, propriety, humanity) refers to the total constellation of concepts, rules and codes of behaviour which are conceived as legitimate or right, appropriate or necessary. In Malay society, *adat* prescribes codes of ethics and behaviour in a range of different social circumstances or situations affecting individuals or groups. It is often related as synonymous to 'customs' (*upacara amal*) or 'culture' (*budaya*) and on the highest level of meaning suggests group cohesion and social identity pertaining to Malay

notions of ethnic exclusiveness and unity. On the lowest order of conceptualization, to think and do things in a 'correct' or 'proper' way, is to act
and behave according to *adat*. A Malay is *beradat* (with *adat*) if he or she
possesses the most important intimate knowledge of norms of Malay
culture and society.

Islam occupies a similar status in the way it seeks to encourage Malay
cohesion and unity within a multi-ethnic population. References to unity
through Islam are often expressed symbolically in the notion of the *umma*
(*umam*, pl.; lit. 'Muhammad's community'), the all-embracing sense of a
'common brotherhood' or 'co-operation amongst common believers'.
Knowledge of, and information about Islam, however, have been traditionally controlled by religious authorities or specialists, who from time
to time dictate various notions and concepts of relationships and behaviour
which are construed as being important and necessary for the vital
development of the *umma*. Thus, sources of ideas and knowledge about
Islam are formally intuitively derived rather than learned through formal
socialization processes. *Adat* is usually nurtured in individuals through
informal forces of socialization (family, elders, kinsmen, neighbours,
patrons, leaders) and for this reason, rests more comfortably on the Malays
in the sense that it is also more spontaneously understood and shared. Its
framework of ideas and influences about 'morality', 'order', and 'justice'
is 'popular' compared to Islam's formal scripturalism. It is through *adat*
that state, regional or community preferences of custom and practices
continue to be maintained and it is on these levels of social interaction
that deep-rooted sentiments of origin (*keturunan*) and community sharing
(*perkauman*), kinship and affinity (*kekerabatan dan persaudaraan*) and social
rituals (*adat istiadat*) serve to maintain and strengthen values of cohesion
and identity. In this aspect, Islam, with its more worldly provisions of
inter-ethnic affiliation, maintains the more symbolic function of cohesion,
elevating 'folk culture' to a 'great tradition'.

Within a society, formally opposing ideologies of men and women (as
in Malay *adat* and Islam) make it necessary for its members to develop
sets of resolutions or alternatives about their 'modus operandi'. The final
choices decided upon at a particular time in history define social realities
in male and female relationships. Let us review this in relation to existing
viewpoints.

The dominant view that women's position, in relation to men, is best
analysed through historical processes, has led to the conclusion that social
trends in history have disfavoured women, ultimately causing a decline
in women's 'power'. This notion of 'power' shows little concern for the
internal dialectics of defining gender relationships at different stages in
history. Newly imposed ideologies through colonization, imperialism or
legislation may reinforce pre-existing mechanisms of equalizing (as in

Malay *adat*) or unequalizing (as in Malay Islam) relationships between men and women but only a careful examination of local interpretations of conduct can help us understand some of these processes.

Ideologies which make formal references to hierarchies of gender may sometimes not be properly integrated into practical activity. The resulting system of social relations may not show significant differences between the old and new or formal and informal systems of relations. Generally, when a society is ordered by two or more ideologies which are theoretically in conflict, such developments are usually more apparent. In the long term, adjustment processes may assume many modes and levels of conceptualization and action. Relating these processes to gender, it may be difficult to draw conclusive trends of women's 'power' by merely reviewing formal developments in history. Evidence must be drawn from informal historical sources or social, economic and family histories.

The general concern to locate the importance of indigenous constructs of gender in *adat* and Islam suggests that this study is concerned with the meaning of gender in culture. However, the perspective of history shows a concern for relating some of these subjective statements of meanings with wider sociological realities. Ultimately, it is hoped that this study may encourage further research on the history of Malay gender relations which ultimately elucidates some of these processes of development of Malay culture in Southeast Asia. Reviewing the increasing literature which has emerged in the field of gender studies in Malaysia (Strange, 1981; Hing, Talib, Karim, 1984; Fatimah Daud, 1985; Ong, 1987), it is significant that most of these researchers see 'culture' as a passive construct that is pre-given or pre-defined. Yet, in history, Malay culture has produced many variants of 'society'. Power relationships between men and women have been constructed differently over history, producing different images of gender relationships over time. Despite these sociopolitical and economic variants of society, the essence of the Malay social heritage and norms of behaviour remains rooted in basic traditions of *adat* and Islam.

At a particular epoch these processes are either concerned with the 'adatization of Islam' (when *adat* is interpreted as compatible with Islam and becomes the primary mode of articulation) or the 'Islamization of *adat*' (when adat is interpreted as incompatible with Islam and Islam becomes the mode of articulation). Over history, the presence of ideologies which are structurally in conflict with one another, necessitates actors to develop specific rules of ordering and sorting out what may become problematic areas of relationships between men and women. Thus, dissonance in gender relationships, caused by opposing ideologies of men and women (as in Malay Islam) necessitates sets of resolutions or alternatives to be made and the final choices decided upon are what ultimately defines women's power in relation to men and society. The task of the researcher is to sort out these interjections of power rather than to merely assume that unequalizing mechanisms continuously erode the power structures of women. To give an example, if notions of sexual equality continue to form an important construct in Malay society, it implies that *adat* is in a continuous dialectics with Islam, a dialectics of equalizing relations against all odds.

Reviewing the dominant view that women's position in relation to men is best analysed through historical processes, researchers may have to critically review the assumption that social trends in history act to women's disfavour, ultimately causing a gradual decline in women's 'power'. The problem might be more complicated than that assumed. For example, in situations when policies or laws are introduced in favour of men and these do not result in increasing rivalry or competition between the sexes, indigenous norms and mores have probably allowed this to occur, rendering women more receptive to decisions which reflect their differential 'power'. In such systems, newly imposed rules merely reinforce pre-existing mechanisms of gender differentiation and discrimination. However, passive acceptance at one stage may lead to active protest at another. Such is the history of the blue-stocking movement in England, women's participation in trade unionism in Europe, Indian women's involvement in the Quit India Movement, and a hundred other examples in modern history. In the Muslim world, Lewis (1971) argued the case for women's spirit-possession cults in North Africa as protest movements against female oppression. When legislation serves to do the opposite, for example, disfavouring women in a more egalitarian system, dissonance may result between the old and new. A compromise position may develop, or new modes of protest, ideologically or symbolically, may surface with time. Ong (1987), in her study of female factory workers in Selangor, Malaysia, discusses 'spirit-possession' as a form of ideological resistance against capitalist discipline.

Ultimately, it is important to view culture in a general sense as the active process of creation of modes of relationships (men and women, older and younger generation, state and society) which form the basis of social relations in future history. In the Malay context, this active process is concerned with how *adat* and Islam, as the basic constructs of Malay culture, produce variants of society, with each variant maintaining its specific pattern of social relationships. Amongst other things, these variants of society define the power spheres of men and women.

The Historical Method in the Study of Gender

A major section of the book is devoted to the reconstruction of the sociopolitical roles of Malay women in history, mainly to demonstrate the way in which certain rules of politics, both formal and informal, have developed to include women as important participants of history. On a more general level, the first section of the study demonstrates the development of power relationships between men and women through earlier rules of interpretation of *adat*. *Adat* at this level articulates the Malay order of politics between state and society and the interplay of power between men and women. Since there has in fact been no previous study of this kind in Malaysia, this section of the study deals with textual analysis, a methodology which has drawn conflicting emotions in the social sciences.

Arguments of the invalidity of textual interpretation, the most obvious source of history have been put forward in anthropology for a number of reasons — distortion of social realities, subjectivity in contextual meanings, changing meanings through translations, ideological bias and personal psychological motives. However, these arguments deny the scientificity of hermeneutics and its possible contribution to the social sciences. Also, it denies a relationship between meanings derived from written forms and those derived from social action. The debate between objectivism and subjectivism in the anthropological method has not been resolved, mainly because in dealing with human behaviour and social action, it is impossible to predetermine forms and procedures of arriving at purely objective paradigms in anthropology. The study of texts in history or social behaviour in anthropology can both be subject to similar methodological problems of explanation and understanding so that it is more important to speak of objectification processes in understanding culture rather than cultural objectivity, both in the short and the long term. To echo Ricoeur's theory of interpretation with respect to texts, processes of distanciation are concerned with the variance between the spoken and written form, between the author's intention and the psychological impact processes of listening and reading, and finally between the author's intention of meanings to the original audience and the following inscribed expressions of it (1981: 14).

Ricoeur's views of distanciation can be extended to the sphere of action in the social sciences, particularly in anthropology, where speech, language and action are captured as past events — things which have happened in the presence of the anthropologist who sets out to pursue its semantic and contextual structures by discussion and analysis. Cultural phenomena which are observed in totality, in time and place, are subject to detail analysis after they have happened, where the present in the short term diffuses into the past in the long term as more and more events are interlinked and related. In the words of Ricoeur, 'the objectification of action is marked by the eclipse of the event of doing by the significance of what is done' (1981: 15).

In this sense, methodological processes and paradigms in recovering meaning in text and action cannot be clearly separated. A text can be structurally compared to action and vice-versa. Objectification lies in the way in which real meanings are recovered; through noting these processes of distanciation rather than in solely discussing the internal relations of meaning in text, in the Levi-Straussian sense. The objectivity of structuralism is manifested in the way in which contextual meanings are differentiated from more general social processes which determine their symptomatic and symbolic manifestations. Thus, the shift from semantics to hermeneutics, and from functionalism to structuralism, in fact is an attempt to control the objectification of social knowledge. The difference between text and action should be seen less as a difference between explanation and understanding than as a difference in use of research resources; both have the potential of recovering meaning in its intended form if distanciation processes are clearly defined and understood.

The pursuit of the objectification of knowledge, regardless of the research resources used, is the more important problematic of arriving at reality in the human and social sciences. Undeniably, all forms of social knowledge are subject to interpretation reflecting internal subjectivities of discipline; but if theoretical and methodological procedures can show and measure distanciation, the objectification of knowledge can be arrived at in more predictable ways.

Indeed, if the more formalist approaches in social and cultural anthropology are considered, the empirical method is probably less easily objectifiable, on account of its emphasis on performing actors, constantly sorting and resorting day-to-day as well as long term issues and problems. As Wagner (1981) suggests, and in the mood of this study, culture has both an inventive and creative feature. It 'moves' in time and space, as the members of a society attempt to come to grips with social realities. The anthropological method only allows the anthropologist the gift of creativity and invention, in subjecting the people studied into well constructed paradigms ordered for the benefit of the anthropological market. This, according to Wagner, creates a 'Wax Museum' effect, so that one can hardly refer to empiricism in anthropology as the only method of scientification of culture. As he suggests, the study of 'cargo-cults' in Australia should more realistically be conceived as a study of native responses to Western culture. In metaphorical terms, this would in the present author's opinion, include the anthropologist as part of the cargo. In its truest sense, this phenomenon is an expression of the way in which Austronesian cultures reproduce themselves, through a self-generative mode of interpretation. It is a 'native' invention of observation and participation in an experience of materialism which in a non-materialistic environment is conceived as 'God-given'.

In many instances of field experiences, the subjects which are being scrutinized for variations and diversities or similarities of behaviour, simultaneously indulge in a mental exercise of comprehending their 'world'. Their cognitive sphere knows no boundaries or limits of explanation. The resulting efforts on the part of social scientists, in particular anthropologists, to study cultures through cognitive structures of phenomenology attempt to overcome this problem but this perspective, which can be said to be an attempt to scientify subjectivism, does not completely exclude the principle of interpretation. What is perhaps important to emphasize here is that the task of social scientists should be geared towards the recovery of intended meanings in as efficient a way as possible, and that regardless of the procedures applied, subjectivity and objectivity may be near or far apart from each other depending on the rules of distanciation which are applied.

Though the first section of this study approaches Malay social history through the text, a range of former textual interpretations of these are also included to build up as comprehensive a picture as possible of Malay rules of politics in *adat* and the emergence of patterns of gender relations in state politics.

The early development of rules of gender in fifteenth-century state politics directly concerned the ordering of marriage rules of kings or sultans with women of the class of *bendahara*, the family of prime ministers or advisors to the king. In the early stages of the evolution of the traditional Malay Sultanate in Melaka, it was *adat* (in this sense, 'necessary, according to custom') for the daughters of the prime minister to marry the reigning sultan, thus creating a line of royal marriages with a 'commoner' class through matrilateral filiation. Eventually, a commoner class enjoyed the elevated status of aristocrats of the Court. As 'wife-giver' to king, the prime minister strengthened his control of the throne.

The relationship between the prime minister and king, however, produced an uneasy alliance of power, since the former could, if he so wished, withdraw women to demonstrate his autonomy, as the last *bendahara* of Melaka did, with his beautiful daughter, Tun Fatimah. Women of the *bendahara* class could also function independently, transferring their roles from consorts into heads of state, as Tun Fatimah eventually did on the death of the king. Hence, permanent lines of dissension developed within the early kinship order but it was this critical balance which probably prevented the Malay populace from emulating rules of patriliny of royal families representing the 'State'. The promotion of a value system attempting to control or reduce formal hierarchies and check the spread of patriliny marked the origins of Malay *adat* in 'society'. Simultaneously, a 'code of ethics' emerged to affirm the position of the 'State'. This was generally known as *adat-istiadat DiRaja* or 'royal rituals and regalia'. *Adat* traditions of the Malay populace de-emphasized social hierarchies, while royal state *adat-istiadat* traditions emphasized them. The dialectical situation between value preferences of the 'State' and 'society', however, did not remove opportunities for Malay women to participate directly in politicization processes and to consolidate their powers within a system which reinforced male dominance through an Indic and Islamic world view.

Within the *adat* frame of reference, women who excel in politics are featured as *Seri Kandi* (Sanskrit *Sri*, 'majesty', 'holiness', *Kandi*, 'wife of Arjuna') a combination of terms which has come to mean 'war heroines' in Malay.[4] This class of women is a popular literary reference appearing in Court historiographies, folklore and other forms of classical and popular literature. The term *Seri Kandi* symbolizes women's active participation in politics and their bravery, valour and honour in dealing with crisis relating to war, invasion, dethronement or forms of Court intrigue. Significantly, the term also encompasses a category of Malay women who excel in the martial arts and who are as capable as men in personal combat.

The emergence of other Malay states in the Peninsula and the expansion of kingships encouraged the conversion of marriage rules from matrilateral filiation with commoners to royal alliances amongst different royal families. However,though this strengthened the powers of the ruling class over the peasantry, British colonial rule and the subsequent development of the modern state system eventually enabled Malay women to participate directly in political movements directed against the British. The nationalist movement in the decades prior to independence in 1957 recapitulated the *semangat perjuangan* or 'spirit of warfare' of Malay women and saw the 'rebirth' of many *Seri Kandi* actively participating in national movements that were eventually banned for being anti-British.

Though confronted with the usual problem of unequal representation within the formal political structure (State Assemblies and Parliament), a situation also apparent in other Third World as well as Western countries, it may be said that the spontaneous granting of voting rights to Malay women as well as those of other ethnic groups, the continued nomination of women for high political posts and the general attempt by the ruling party to align women's political behaviour with rules of custom rather than Islam, seems to suggest a positive concern for women's continued participation in politics. However, it is generally agreed amongst social scientists that because of existing political party structures and rules of organization, little progress has been achieved in this direction since independence (Manderson, 1980; Karim, 1983).

Contemporary History and the Ethnographic Method

In this study, the use of historical material or historiographies covers the first three chapters of the book. The remaining chapters are based on ethnographic material obtained from participation observation and a social survey of a cluster of villages at the Kedah-Penang border, but especially, the village of Mawang where the major portion of the research was undertaken. Research in Mawang and its neighbouring village (Tasek) was undertaken from 1981 to 1985, and was stretched out in a series of field visits, lasting from one week to one month. The technique of participant observation was mainly employed. The author stayed with a *keluarga angkat* (adoptive 'fictitive' family unit) and maintained ties which were based on the network of kindred relationships extended by the 'adoptive' family.

Field research through participant observation provided rich insights to prevailing institutions of sexual division of labour, role stereotyping and socializing. It became apparent, for example, after some months of study, that marital status more than gender determined the limits of participation of men and women in decision-making processes. Amongst the youths, for example, it became apparent that although males were less restricted in their physical movements and choice of employment, they were as 'marginalized' as their female counterparts in community affairs, particularly in rituals of *adat* or Islam. With marriage and child-bearing, both men and women gained ritual advantage and joined the prestigious rank of elders.

New trends of employment of young village girls in urban jobs mainly factory work, also led to interesting observations, when viewed from a village perspective. Expectations of elders towards these young girls remained unchanged, despite the latter's rapid acquisition of modern and urban values. They were expected to behave like their female counterparts who remained in the village. Overt indications of Westernization in dressing, social behaviour, and sexual interaction were frowned upon. The *sopan-santun* of *adat* (gentility, refinement) was still the preferred mode. Islamic influences from urban centres were also radically different from Islamic socialization in the village. The control of the rural *ulama* over the younger generation in the village was replaced by *dakwa* (revivalist) leadership in towns and cities; the latter encouraged greater public display of Islam than the former, suggesting greater participation in religious activities, at least on the ritual and symbolic level of interaction. Field research enabled rural/urban comparisons and differences to be more effectively sorted out, particularly with regards to male and female activity. Generally, the combination of the historical method and anthropological research enabled gender roles in *adat* and Islam to be more efficiently studied.

Observations of Malay notions of domesticity and work revolve around the concept of *suri rumahtangga* and *pekerjaan*, formal census definitions which women understand to mean the 'unsalaried housewife' and 'waged employment' respectively. Women who place themselves in the former category may also show a high degree of participation and decision-making in farming or agro-based industries. Their ability to organize family labour in farming, to retain their own income for personal expenditure or personally preferred patterns of spending and to develop professions and occupations which are traditionally of 'high status' places them in a different category from the census definition of an 'unsalaried housewife'. Their domesticity is differently conceived when they control the monetary returns from the fruits of their labour. They then indicate that they have a *pekerjaan*, relating to farming. When they also own the farm and capital resources relating to farming, they also refer to themselves as the head of the household or *ketua rumahtangga*. Control over land, human resources and capital allows them to review their position differently from other women but even so, those who indicate that they are 'housewives' and dependent on their husband's earnings never really fully function as 'housewives' or 'dependents'. They contribute a fair share of their labour to farming or pursue supplementary sources of earnings which are not disclosed to their husbands.

Trends towards mechanization have contributed towards women's displacement in agriculture but observations of these changes should best be viewed as short term effects of labour redistribution within the rural economy. If ethnographic observations are stretched out over a few years, one can see that trends towards reemployment in both the agricultural and industrial sectors favour women more than men. Even if the earnings continue to be low, women in need continue to seek work in farming or industry rather than remain unemployed. Hence, from observation it appears that the employment cycle is more continuous in women than men.

Reviewing gender relationships in the context of urbanization, in-dustrialization and Islamic revivalism in rural areas, it appears that attempts have been made, at least intellectually, amongst religious specialists and scholars to sort out apparent differences between *adat* and Islamic law. Retrospective observations show that this has far-reaching consequences in the practice of public rituals which are of obviously Indic origin, such as the public display of the bride and bridegroom during weddings (*bersanding*), the frequency of seances and the invocation of Hindu gods in healing and curing rituals (*menurun hantu*), spirit cleansing ceremonies (*lancang kuning, puja pantai*) or worshipping of shrines (*keramat*). However, other trends can be observed in the symbolic and ritual reassertions of behaviour derived from *adat*, usually conveniently categorized within the framework of Islam, to strengthen the legitimacy of such institutions. Thus, *adat* rituals became interfused with *sunna* traditions in Islam (from *sunna* (Arabic), customary procedure, sanctioned by tradition, in particular the Prophet's sayings and doings), that is, activities which are not compulsory in Islam but if performed produce spiritual merit. A number of these *sunna* rituals continue to display magical or animistic rites so that it is difficult to conclude from this that Islam has displaced *adat* both conceptually and ritually. The converse situation seems to be more apparent.

Again observations on the effects of modernity and Westernization on gender relations requires the ethnographer to discard normal vision for diagnostic scanning procedures. Ethnographic scanning will show that the new sexuality of Malay women through Westernization or fundamentalism has produced splitting effects on Malay society, where expressions of modesty through *adat* acts as a traditional neutralizer. Its system of maintaining checks and balances in values and behaviour prevents sexual behaviour from assuming similar proportions as in the west. Hence, the malignancy in either direction is neutralized by this traditional cure. Social trends in religious revivalism or, alternatively, modernity and Westernization reflect the convergence of two trends of thought in contemporary life. The presence of two sets of ideological and social intrusions reflects the dialectical relationship between Westernization and fundamentalism. In this context, *adat* assumes a mediatory role, in providing an intimate and intuitive mechanism for reordering relationships according to the requirements of culture.

The study ultimately demonstrates the phenomenon of adaptation and readaptation of indigenous social systems to different forms of social intervention, in both the short and the long term. Ever since the early stages of the development of Malay notions of 'social order' through *adat* and Islam, many different interpretations of rules of thought and behaviour have been tested and applied. The resulting system that has emerged over many decades seems to be a combination of the most resilient norms of social relations, interpreting behaviour within and across rank, class, age and gender. Currently, Islamic values appear to be more easily adapted into the system (as Western values once were) merely because the adaptation process is *'ad hoc'*, 'symbolic' or 'situational', allowing for a variety of social choices and preferences. In this way Islam has a splintering effect on the populace, with each new mode of interpretation ruling out the other on the level of thought and behaviour. Eventually, they cancel each other out and allow *adat* to be lodged more firmly in the ritual sphere. On the macro-level in the long term, the *adat*-Islamic spectrum of ideas in Malay society represent a dynamic flexible constellation of values reproduced in different forms to suggest different meanings of relationship.

Notes

1. Islamic laws of marriage and the family come under the jurisdiction of the states rather than the Federal Government. Though they vary in their contents and interpretations they generally attempt to impose restrictions on polygyny in different ways, by requiring the written consent from the first wife, consent from

the local *kadi*, statement of income, etc. The Muslim Family and Marriage Bill for the Federal Territory of Kuala Lumpur was passed in February 1984 and, interestingly, although it attempts to integrate polygyny with Islamic fundamentalism by removing the requirement of written consent from the first wife, it introduces a more controversial dimension to the problem. It suggests that economic wealth should be the deciding factor for polygyny, subject to validation from the Syariah Court. In urban areas it can only succeed in becoming an added prestige item for successful bureaucrats and entrepreneurs, creating a parallel situation of polygyny amongst rural elites.

2. A much more detailed discussion of Malay *adat* or customary law is given in Chapter 2.

3. This salient feature of Malay social organization permeates Southeast Asian systems in general, significantly differentiating the Southeast Asian model from the South Asian.

4. A Malay/Indonesian derivative of two Sanskrit words. Note, that *Sri* in Sanskrit usually refers to exceptional qualities in men. *Kandi*, wife of Arjuna, was noted for her valour and bravery (Malay *gagah berani*), *Seri Kandi* like Tun Fatimah are also associated with patriotism (*bersemangat nasional sejati*).

2

The State in Early Malay History

Raja adil, Raja disembah, Raja tak adil, Raja dicanggah
A just King is a King obeyed, a cruel King is a King defied
— *Malay proverb*

Origins of *Adat-Istiadat* of the Malay State

This chapter discusses some salient features of *adat* in early Malay history in the context of Malay kingships and the development of indigenous political structures.[1] Generally, the study attempts to show that before the expansion of Malay states outside Melaka in the sixteenth century, marriage rules of Malay kings developed the political roles of Malay women in both a symbolic and a real way. Kingships were granted legitimacy through principles of matrilateral filiation where men assuming high titles through mythical or fictitious genealogies, married local women in order to retrench their position within the region. These processes of 'domestication' of Malay kings bridged the gap between myth and history, for 'royal' genealogies based on mythical links with former heroic king could be enacted through further symbolic and ritual procedures granting absolute sovereignty.

These procedures are essential components of *adat-istiadat* Raja ('royal customs') which involve men and women (the latter, both directly and indirectly) in public decision-making. Through these rules, women often gained further impetus to extend their sphere of influence within the structure of kingship. The consequent development of marriage alliances amongst the many kingships which later emerged in the Peninsula, altered the political significance of these marriages but by then a class of royal and aristocratic lineages had emerged to contribute to the increasingly divergent political roles of women as leaders and functionaries of the political system.

Classifications and Perspectives
of the Pre-Colonial Malay State

It has been suggested by Winzeler (1976) that the late and incomplete processes of state formation in Southeast Asia is due to the prevalence of bilaterality. 'Processes of state formation' here refer to the development of centralized modes of political control to challenge localized systems of power relations within the indigenous population. He argued that male-centred patrilineal politics could not develop within a populace where women controlled the most important sources of food production relating to wet-rice cultivation. Slash and burn horticulture, hunting and fishing were performed mostly by men. The complementary nature of male and female activity in food production was more symmetrical than hierarchical. Whether Southeast Asia had developed this particular mode of ecological adaptation before patrilineal politics became important is a point of debate but these generalities hold true for insular Southeast Asia, in particular, where kingships did not produce highly centralized forms of political organization comparable to South Asian and European states. The relationship between political and economic organization however needs to be discussed processually in relation to different time periods in the evolution and development of Southeast Asian States. As Cohen (1976: 632) comments, bilaterality in Africa 'may precede that state, develop along it or spread and develop after its appearance'. The present chapter is not so much concerned with processes of formation of the Malay state, as with the rules governing relationships of power and gender which developed along with the Malay state. However, it will be shown later that Malay women were an important economic force and that this explained the preference for *adat* rules in land ownership where bilateral principles were adopted.

It is generally upheld that Malay kings (raja, sultan) were created by the establishment of patrilineages with fictitious genealogies from other descent systems outside the Peninsula. The absence of patrilineages or patrilineal systems of descent amongst the indigenous Malay population of the time validates this view somewhat. Locating these events in Peninsular Malaysia's early pre- and post-colonial history, before the development of the modern state system introduced by the British in the twentieth century, the study attempts to analyse gender relationships through the 'bilaterality' of *adat* rules in Malay politics.

The 'traditional' Malay polity has consistently been conceptualized as a centralized state system with powers vested in various royal and chieftancy families over commoners of the peasantry class.[2] Historians, ethnologists and anthropologists have usually analysed the pyramidal three-tiered hierarchy of ruler, chiefs and commoners in structural and functional terms, emphasizing processes of legitimization of the ruling class over their subjects and the vital intermediary role of the chiefs in implementing and consolidating this power on the grassroots.

Gullick (1965) the most widely quoted writer of Malay indigenous politics, accepted the Malay king or ruler as the main source of social control over the peasantry. He saw the chiefs (*orang besar*, literally, 'big men') to be part of the ruling class that effectively maintained political cohesion within the state. In his research, he concluded that 'the subject class in the Malay states were certainly not united by the same interests as the ruling class . . . but there was an awareness of the sultan as the apex of the system' (p.137). The subject class believed, in real or symbolic terms, that 'the sultan could influence the prosperity and welfare of the state for good or ill', though it was 'an attitude blended of loyalty and a cynical awareness of their own helplessness in face of oppression' (p.137).

Milner (1982) in his work on pre-colonial Malay political structures, rejected the basis of Gullick's hypothesis by suggesting that he has presented it through static functionalism, where the concern for political institutions, systems of social control and political cohesion had removed the more fundamental concern in political anthropology for 'political culture' or, in Geertz's terms, 'the meaningful structures within political experience'. Milner's concern to examine Malay political activity in *Malay* terms, so as to reflect cultural perceptions of authority and power and political behaviour at all levels of hierarchy, prompted him to examine indigenous rather than European sources of history. Unlike Gullick who depended mainly on English, Portuguese and Dutch material for his research, Milner examined two Malay *Hikayat* (personal histories), the *Hikayat Pahang* and *Hikayat Deli* extensively. Through the *Hikayat*, he concluded that the Malays (and not necessarily only the kings) were politicized, sought honour rather than wealth, and fame rather than sanctuary. Commoners who supported chiefs and kings were politically motivated to do so and strove to achieve rewards through formal titles or spiritual merit, both of which ensured them a better position in society.

Though Milner's analysis attempted to illustrate the Malay polity as a dynamic, volatile system with channels for social mobility, he nevertheless retained its image as a centralized political system, where the Malay raja was the 'person through whom men became acquainted with the other world'. More importantly, he saw the relationship of the raja and his subjects as 'of the most intimate nature' where the subject's 'private self was his public self and the society in which that public self was embedded existed only as a projection of the raja' (p.103). In this sense, Milner succeeded in reinforcing the functional, symbolic aspects of Malay politics between the ruling and the subject class, a perspective which he considered unsuitable in the study of Malay polity. Furthermore, by being completely dependent on the *Hikayat* as a source of reference, he invariably gave more importance to the formal messages being communicated through the *Hikayat* — its value as a historiography, written for kings to immortalize their kingships. Thus, certain formal structures of the Malay polity were deliberately highlighted to express the importance and supremacy of the sultanate — the spirit of participation and co-operation between ruler and subjects, the sense of righteousness and justice of the rulers, and the ability of commoners to achieve rank and position by supporting their interests.

Milner's study did not probe into the silent anarchial messages of the *Hikayat* which may be known through distanciation between the writer's own emphasis of themes of crisis in court on the one hand and his elaborate narrations of formal court events and regalia to highlight Malay kingship on the other. Much of this message is elucidated in the regularity of citations and expressions of personal and family honour of men and women of the commoner class of *bendahara* who were upgraded to compose the core members of the royal court.[3] More importantly, this concerned the inherent structural conflicts within the Court between the family of the *bendahara* (Court Treasurer, Adviser and Premier) and the raja, expressing the delicate balance between rules of descent and influence, loyalty and honour and servitude and personal autonomy.[4] Thus, while it is important to attempt to understand Malay political structures through the Malay world view, it is equally important to recognize and differentiate between formal and symbolic notions of the Malay state, or differences in the ideology of kings and commoners. Both systems of ideas were revealed in the *Hikayat*, reflecting tones of inconsistency and incompatibility between values upheld by the king and his subjects, including members of the royal court.

In the sense that a social historian or political anthropologist may go astray by going 'all native' without understanding codes of political behaviour which are usually latently rather than openly expressed in political writings of this kind, it may also be more meaningful to utilize all existing historical material available, to attempt at a reconstruction of political ideas, concepts and behaviour that unravel the underlying 'structures' of the Malay polity. Possibly, it requires an integration of Gullick's research methodology and Milner's theoretical concerns and a combination of native and Western documented historical sources to ascertain the kind of principles ordering political behaviour. The following is an evaluation of the methodology and text of Malay sources of history, relating mainly to the *Hikayat* as a media of political writing.

The Hikayat as a Source of Malay Social History

The *Hikayat* have usually been considered unreliable or unauthentic sources of history, written by indigenous and mostly unknown Malay authors, several decades or centuries after the occurrence of the events narrated in the text. Nevertheless, these accounts of Malay history which span across centuries of events from as early as the sixth or seventh century, are increasingly being treated as valuable documents which can provide solutions to the riddles and obscurities of early events in Malay social history.

The *Hikayat* recorded events in history concerned with the exploits of kings and members of the Malay royal court. They were originally passed down by word of mouth, and eventually recorded by extremely literate members of the royal court and other unidentified scholars towards the late eighteenth and early nineteenth centuries. It was not only the delay in the recording of political events in the *Hikayat* which prompted European writers of Malay history to view such texts with much scepticism and scorn (particularly when comparisons were made with more reliable documented historiographies and oral histories from other sources), but the fact that most of the events in the text were related through magical and supernatural descriptions which served to convert facts, if not semantically at least metaphorically to fiction. Laced with magical (*kesaktian*) descriptions of the exploits of key characters and figures in the stories, the *Hikayat* appeared to draw a slim line between history and myth. Obviously, this is a real problem unless one can clearly understand that it was the written style of texts of the time, to draw upon pre-existing ideas of magic and divinity, for the consumption of the audience. The language of fantasia in kingships also succeeded in separating the kings, ritually and symbolically, from their subjects.[5]

The final criticism against the *Hikayat* was the problem of confirming the authencity of the Malay authors who were, for the most part unidentified. The *Hikayat Merong Mahawangsa* was written by a Malay author who merely identified himself as *fakir* (poor man), while the authors of most of the remaining *Hikayat* texts remained unknown. The author of *Misa Melayu*, concerned with describing Perak's pre-colonial history was, however, clearly identified as Raja Chulan ibni Raja Mansor Shah, who was said to have written the text after the death of Sultan Iskandar Shah of Perak (1756-1770).[6] This was one of the few authorised texts of the *Hikayat*, where the author was an extremely literate scholar of Malay literature with a fame in scholarship which transcended the Perak royal court to the literate gentry of the commoner class. Another is the *Salalatus Salatin* or *Sejarah Melayu* ('Malay Annals') used extensively in this chapter. It is one of the most widely quoted indigenous sources of Malay history. It was essentially concerned with recording the history of the Melaka Sultanate, from its formation to its final disintegration with the invasion of the Portuguese in 1511. The *Sejarah Melayu* was said to be written by a descendant of the Muslim Tamil branch of the Melaka *bendahara* after the collapse of the Melaka Sultanate. The author was said to be a *bendahara* Tun Seri Lanang, a descendant of the last *bendahara* of Melaka, Tun Mutahir.

Despite the scepticism expressed over the *Hikayat* by European writers like Winstedt, Wilkinson and Maxwell, it is significant that these sources of Malay history had been widely used by these very authors themselves, not so much to verify dates of events or illustrate detail chronicles of activities but to provide useful background information of the genealogies and lineages of the Malay raja or sultan and other insights into Malay cultural and social history during the pre-colonial period. For example, Wilkinson based his writings on Melaka history almost entirely on indigenous sources, particularly the Malay Annals. In one of his later writings, he concluded:

> This account of Malacca Sultanate is based almost in its entirety upon the 'Annals'. They are an anecdotal History. They avoid all dates; when they give us the length of a reign they are usually wrong. Always uncritical, they record myths and miracles as things that happened. But they give us a life-like picture of the times, reflect the mentality of the Malacca Malays, and explain to us the working of Malacca government with its curious insistence on show and ceremonial for keeping up the authority of princes and nobles. Even though they may go astray in details they tells us what the Sultanate was like. They are the best record we have. The Chinese Annals help us to date events and do little more. When we get to Portuguese and Dutch times, we get both dates and details, but we also find that the writers were kept at their work as traders and accountants and had neither desire nor time to study a race whom they regarded as faithless and perfidious (1935 b: 69).

Winstedt, who also relied heavily on the Malay Annals in his 'A History of Malaya' (1935), recognized some sources to be more useful and authentic than others, amongst these being the *Salalatus Salatin* or *Sejarah Melayu*, *Bustan-as-Salatin*, *Hikayat Acheh*, *Hikayat Merong Mahawangsa*, *Hikayat Negeri Johor*, *Tuhfat-al-Nafis*, *Sejarah Raja-Raja Riau* and *Salsilah Melayu dan Bugis*. Thus, he recognized that Malay literature, which focussed on histories and epical events, provided a wealth of information on the nature of the kingship, the cultural system of the Malays in the pre-colonial history and the cultural norms and values of the time.

Generally, then, it can be said that the *Hikayat* are useful resource materials for sociologists and anthropologists who are particularly concerned with unravelling early Malay ideology and patterns of cultural behaviour associated with Malay kingships or the Malay State. This study uses the *Sejarah Melayu* as the main text of reference and focuses on the *Rumi* version published by Shellabear in 1909.[7]

The Creation of Malay Dynasties

The emphasis in the *Hikayat* on royal genealogy reflected the political ethos of the raja and sultan in pre-colonial Malaya, to obtain legitimacy for 'royal' families who were mostly the earliest Malay pioneers and conquerors of the Peninsula and its neighbouring islands of Singapore (Singapura or Tumasik), Riau and Lingga. Significantly, these genealogies were usually traced to the Hindu states of Sri Vijaya (sixth to eleventh centuries AD) based at Palembang, Sumatra. Sri Vijaya was eventually absorbed by the Malay states of Melayu at Jambi in the thirteenth century (see Map II).

The Kedah Annals probably recorded some of the earliest events in Malaya's social history, concerned with the state of Kedah in the north-west of the Peninsula. It was said that the first raja of Kedah, Sri Mahawangsa, was descended from a Hindu royal family in India. Descriptions of the Melaka raja in the Malay Annals showed that the earliest genealogies could be traced back to the Hindu Chola invaders of India of the eleventh century, when the son of Raja Chulan, the Chola conqueror of India, ruled Palembang under the name of Trimurti Tribuna. One of his sons , Nila Utama, 'founded' Singapore and changed its name from *Tumasik* to *Singapura*, bestowing upon himself the title of *Batara Sri Tribuna*. The last but one king of Singapura was given the old Sri Vijayan title of *Sri Maharaja*, while the last was said to have become a Muslim and assumed the title of *'Raja Iskandar'*, after Alexander the Great. According to local mythical sources, Alexander the Great brought Islam to the East and was linked with the Sailendra dynasty of Sumatra. Thus, the Melaka rulers traced their descent from the Chola Kings of India, the Sailendra dynasty in Sumatra and Alexander the Great.

Permaisura (Parameswara), the founder of the Melaka Sultanate, was said to be the last ruler of Singapura (Singapore), who was defeated by Majapahit invaders in the late thirteenth century (1292). Winstedt (1935: 34) dismissed these early accounts of the rise of the Kingdom of Singapore in the Malay Annals as a 'hotch-potch of myths and traditions'. While it is difficult to verify or disprove many of these events described in the *Hikayat* and Malay Annals, it is nevertheless important to understand that anthropologically, the emphasis on creating fictitious royal genealogies and the importance of divinity, magic and court rituals have been integral features of Malay kingship. The formation of the Malay State was an extensive process of symbolic and ritual creativity designed to spruce up an otherwise unstratified social order with metaphors of hierarchies and opposition. Hinduism converted the bilaterality of the masses to a hierarchical political order. Animism and magic were no longer the monopoly of the masses but a powerful instrument to legitimize the separation of a

Map II: The Malay Archipelago and Melaka, 15th Century

few families from the rest of the populace. This new knowledge that the most powerful gods and spirits now supported a favoured few left the people to ponder about their relationship with the king.

In this study, the focus on the kingdom of Melaka is not to suggest that kingships in Malaya began with the Melaka dynasty. Records from the *Hikayat* and other written sources (Pires, 1967; Braddell, 1980; Wheatley, 1964) indicate that Malay 'States' have been known to exist in Pattani and Kedah, in the north, from as early as the sixth century. However, the processes of expansion of the present Malay states are directly linked to the early Melaka kingdom which gradually spread its influence over the other areas in the Peninsula (see Map II). For this reason, it is felt that Melaka may be a good source to locate the study in its historical context.

Melaka Before the Malays

What was Melaka before its discovery by the Palembang Malay refugee ruler of Singapura? Who were its inhabitants and what kind of a relationship did they establish with these new Malays who claimed it as a kingdom? Tome Pires in the Suma Oriental, writing after the conquest of Melaka by the Portuguese in 1511, suggests that the Celates (*Orang Seletar*) were the original inhabitants of Melaka.[8] He described them as following (1967: 233):

> . . . they are men who go out pillaging in their boats and fish, and are sometimes on land and sometimes at sea, of whom, there are a large number now in our time. They carry blow-pipes with their small arrows of black hellebore which, as they touch blood, kill, as they often did our Portuguese in the enterprise and destruction of the famous city of Malacca, which is very famous among the nations.

According to Pires, the refugee ruler's entourage of men consisted of Malays from Palembang and thirty *orang* Celates, who formed his navy. They settled in Melaka with their wives and children 'at the foot of the hill where the fortress is' (p.234). The presence of the Celates amongst the new arrivals implied that a congenial relationship could be established with the rest of the Celates who were already settled in the creeks and estuarine areas of Melaka. Indeed, Pires confirmed that they carried on providing food and protection to the new ruler whom they made king. Those who settled on land were rewarded with 'some gift of honour, on which petition the said Paramjcura made them mandarins' (p.235). Here, Pires concluded his findings on a very important note highlighting the argument of this chapter (1967: 235-236):

... Hence, it is that all the mandarins of Malacca are descended from these, and the Kings are descended through the female side, according to what is said in the country.The fishermen having been made mandarins by the hand of the said Paramjcura, always accompanied the said King, and as he advanced them in rank they too recognised the favour which have been granted to them. They accompanied the King zealously and served him with great faith and loyalty, their friendship (being) whole-hearted; and in the same way the King's love for them always corresponded to the true service and zeal of the said new mandarins; and they strove to please him, and their honour lasted right down to the coming of the Diogo Lopes de Sequeira to Malacca, when their fifth grandson was the *Laksamana* and the *Bemdara* who ordered the treachery to the said Diogo Lopes de Sequeira and he was afterwards beheaded by the King himself, who lost Malacca, for the justice of God never fails . . .

Certain factors about early Malay kingship now seemed clearer. Reconstructing the Malay State of Melaka in the fifteenth century, it appeared that the royal court comprised essentially Malays from Palembang who intermarried with the indigenous native population, the Celates, from which developed a class of noble men, the House of *Bendahara* (Pires' '*Bendahara*'). The *Orang Seletar* or Celates people, as Pires called them, were not a small band of sea-faring 'proto-Malays' as they have been reduced to by present administrators of Malayan *Orang Asli*. The term 'Celates' is derived from the Malay term '*Selat*' (Straits) and possibly referred to the larger indigenous population of 'island hoppers' who roamed the islands and coast from Singapore to Palembang. They numbered in the thousands and were equally well adapted to land and sea.

Significantly, they reappear in Andaya's works on the kingdom of Johor (1975 a, b, 1984). Andaya (1975: 44) described the terminological difficulties concerning these sea-faring populations who were loosely referred to as *Orang Laut* (literally 'The Sea People'). He stated that the term *Orang Laut* obscured realities of the group's ethnic origins. The most prestigious and powerful were associated with the larger islands (*Orang Suku Bentan*) from the island of Bentan, *Orang Suku Mepar* from Lingga, *Orang Suku Bulang* from Bulang and *Orang Suku Galang* from the Galang Islands. He also affirmed the relationship of these communities with the Melaka and Johor royal family, probably dating from the Sri Vijaya and Palembang Empire (seventh to eleventh centuries), re-established in the fourteenth century with the refugee prince of Palembang and the ' founding' of Melaka and in the sixteenth century, with the establishment of the kingdom of Johor. By the seventeenth century, the *Orang Laut* formed a vital component of the power structure of Johor (1975 a: 44). Andaya also suggested that it was the *Orang Suku Bentan* of the *Orang Laut* who preserved loyalties with the first ruler of Melaka.

Although Pires referred to their headquarters at Bemtam or Bintang (which could refer to Bentan) the Celates probably maintained different bases along the straits stretching from Singapore to the northwest of Melaka. It was unlikely that the *Orang Celates* referred to by Pires comprised only the *Orang Suku Bentan*. From his descriptions of the Celates accompanying the Palembang prince and those already settled at Melaka, they more likely constituted a wider group of people living along the estuarine areas of the Straits of Melaka and Johor who were specially adapted to the land and sea. In this sense, they may be differentiated from the *Orang Laut* who were completely adapted to the sea and made a living purely from fishing and piracy. The *Orang Laut*, as we know them, formerly lived and today continue to live beyond the mangroves and marsh swamps. They are ecologically well adapted to the open sea, unlike the *Orang Seletar* who are well adapted to both cultivation and fishing. Is it hard to envisage a group of sea-faring *Orang Laut* opening up land or cultivation, as Pires describes them, at Bentan, Muar, Bertam and Bretao in Melaka (1967: 233-238). Furthermore, the Celates had light, small boats adapted for estuarine living, in contrast to the larger, swifter boats of the *Orang Laut*.

It is quite likely that the contemporary separation of habitat and ecology of the *Orang Seletar* (living mainly in the rivers and estuarines of Johor and Singapore) from the rest of the *Orang Kuala* and *Laut* groups in Sumatra and the Riau-Lingga Islands, bear some evidence of the earlier days of Singapore and Melaka. Significantly, the Malay Annals described Permaisura's exodus from Singapore to Melaka — via the straits, into Muar — a typical route undertaken by Malays when the guides on whom they were dependent were *Orang Seletar* (the tenth story, '*Maka Raja Iskandar pun berlepas turun dari Seletar lalu ka-Muar*' ['then Raja Iskandar ventured down through the Straits into Muar']:59).

About a century after the Suma Orientalis, the *Malay Annals* appeared, under the authorship of the *bendahara* Tun Seri Lanang, a Johor descendent of Tun Mutahir, the last *bendahara* of Melaka. In it was recorded a much more vivid descriptive account of Melaka, named, said the author, after a Melaka tree near which was poised a startled mousedeer (*pelanduk*) which, furious at the invasion of his privacy by a dog of the refugee king, Raja Iskandar Shah, chased it into the sea. The raja decided to name his newly founded kingdom 'Melaka' after the formidable Melaka tree under which he had rested and witnessed the strange act of courage by a mousedeer. Later writers confirmed the location of Melaka geographically, commenting on its site at the narrowest part of the Straits which afforded easy landing access and on a hill suited for defence. Across the hill, a group of small islands offered a sheltered deep-water anchorage (Malacca Historical Society, 1936; Wheatley, 1964: 121-188). This strategic location partly explained its rapid rise from a home of sea-faring corsairs to the most prosperous trading port in Southeast Asia, in the fifteenth century.

Andaya's more recent account of the early history of the aquatic populations of Southeast Asia gives us some indication of the sociopolitical values of these people (1984: 44). The integration of the Celates people into the Malay court established them as Malay nobles overnight. According to Andaya, though the traditional view of historians was to see the Celates as eager to achieve upward social mobility and acculturation through the Palembang Malays, yet the Celates, like other *Orang Laut* groups (he mentioned the Duano of the Straits of Melaka), were excessively proud and thought of themselves as a superior race to the Malays. Incidentally, this was true of almost all aquatic indigenous populations of the Peninsula, from the *Orang Seletar* in Ulu Tiram, Johor, to *Orang Kuala* of Kuala Benut in Johor and the *Ma Betisek* of Carey Island in Kuala Langat, Selangor. A sense of cultural distinctiveness, political and religious autonomy and evidence of earlier historic origins on the Malay Peninsula served to reinforce this view (Ariffin Nopiah, 1979; Karim, 1981, Oyvind Sandbukt, personal communication, 1976). Hence, rather than argue that status and prestige were the ultimate reasons for aquatic indigenous populations entering into formal relationships with stranger-kings, Andaya suggested that it was economic considerations which motivated them to do so. He argued:

> In order to participate fully and most profitably in international trade, the aquatic populations realized the necessity of acquiring a lord on land who would be the visible symbol of authority in a particular port. But entering into such a relationship with a coastal ruler was by no means regarded as an act of submission, but rather as one of equality dictated by economic motives (1984: 45).

Thus, although the Celates entered the 'Malay fold through royal fiat', it was not so much derived from motives of prestige and rank but of trade, within the notion of calculated reciprocity and risk. The exotic mythical origins of Malay stranger-kings offered enough legitimacy for a state to be established but on the land, labour and effort of the Celates. Andaya's observations of the arrangement as a partnership of equality rather than a hierarchical feudal arrangement of ruler/subject has important implications for this study. Significantly, it is from this principle of equality through reciprocal needs and obligations that the *bendahara* and the women of his household derived their main source of knowledge of political rule. Hence, the emphasis on reciprocity and equality become a potential source of conflict with the king who also required obedience and servitude. Pires describes this relationship of conflict as inevitable since the king formally admitted his indebtedness to his Celates subjects through a public oath. Pires, records an important event before a crowd of Celates , of the king taking a public oath and promising them 'honour and assistance' for allowing him to be a king in Melaka (1967: 234). From this developed the first *adat* tradition of the Malay Court, the relationship of balanced reciprocity between ruler and subject — 'A just King is a King obeyed, a cruel King is a King defied'.

Clearly, it was the need to legitimize the ruling class that the first known king of Melaka, Raja Iskandar Shah established a court system characteristic of Hindu kingdoms in India at that time.[9] This system was eventually adopted by other kings in the Peninsula. The rulers were drawn from royal patrilineages (*keturunan diraja*), symbolically upheld by characteristics of divinity (*daulat*). Court etiquette and protocol (*adat-istiadat*), court language and poetry (*bahasa dalam*), royal colours and regalia (yellow), music (*nobat, rebana*) and a written constitution (*Kanun*) symbolically and ritually set the royal family and other courtesans apart from the Malay peasantry.

These symbols of social differentiation, of royalty aristocracy and commoner, were from time to time, conveyed to the common people by members of the Court through ritualistic procedures and ceremonies. The *penglipor lara*, story-tellers who conveyed a pedagogy of the feats and fame of the ruler and his courtesans, and the performance of the *wayang kulit* (shadow play) served to reinforce these differences while rendering an illusion of romanticism and grandeur to the activities of the royal court. Through ritual communication, the people were given a colourful education in royal history and culture amidst the 'nitty gritty' of village life.

The Hikayat and Women of the Court

The *Hikayat* indirectly provided useful information on the role of women within the court. The women who were highlighted in the Annals concerned with the Melaka dynasty, the *Sejarah Melayu*, came from the line of *bendahara*, men who became advisers and prime ministers to the raja. On the *bendahara* (*Bemdara*), Pires wrote:

> Where there is no aforesaid official, the *Bemdara* is the highest in the Kingdom. The *Bemdara* is a kind of chief-justice in all the King's revenue. He can order any person to be put to death, of whatever rank and condition, whether nobleman or foreigner, but first of all, he informs the King, and both decide the matter in consultation with the *Laksamana* and the *Tumunguo* (1967: 264).

These *bendahara* fathered the women *Seri Kandi* in history, a class of women with qualities of leadership which often surprised men, rendering them the status of warrior heroines. A woman *Seri Kandi* metaphorically evokes the spirit of *Seri Kandi*, the wife of *Arjuna* a brave and powerful mythical figure in Hindu mythology.[10] Significantly, the emphasis in the *Hikayat* on the activities of these women's fathers and their relationships to the king, elucidated Malay values of valour and honour where a class of titled commoners, through their women, sought to balance the spheres of political dominance upheld by the king. This theme transpired in all courtly episodes of the *Hikayat*. Significantly, the author of the *Malay Annals* who documented the genealogies of Melaka kings, also attempted to introduce the perspective of this class of titled commoners through oblique references of honour or *nama*.

As mentioned previously, the *Hikayat* as a formal media was the monopoly of the Malay rulers who developed and controlled the Malay literate tradition for the purpose of preserving genealogies and rendering credibility to the various kingdoms and statehoods which were created from time to time. In contrast, the Malay peasantry remained embedded in an oral tradition of folklore (*cerita-cerita dongeng*). These were not, until recently, taken up in classical Malay literature so that indigenous literary sources provided little material on the relationship between the activities of peasant women and wider historical processes concerned with the formation of kingships. Thus, another perceived separation was high-lighted between the royalty and aristocratic class and the peasantry. Royal and aristocratic families were projected as the main contributors to political and historical processes while peasant families were seen as part of an individually unidentifiable population with little collective thought and action. However, when the *Hikayat* dwelt on titled commoners, their marginal status within the higher political order was often revealed in contradictory idealism between royal allegiance and self-worth. An important theme was the dilemma between maintaining loyalties to the king and members of one's family, kinsmen, followers and friends. It was this apparent conflict and its resulting political consequences which con-tributed towards the turning points of events in Melaka's social history.

One of the most famous examples of these contradictory states was spelt out in *Hikayat Hang Tuah*, set in the reign of Sultan Mansur Shah, the successor of Raja Kassim in 1456 (*Malay Annals*, the Fourteenth Story, Shellabear, 1952: 104). It focussed on the choices of a warrior, Hang Tuah, between allegiance to the sultan and to his comrade, Hang Jebat. Though the *Hikayat* showed that allegiance to the sultan was an overriding consideration and that any other choice was inherently destructive, yet the ethos of the story, highlighting the blind loyalty of Tuah to the sultan, Jebat's revenge against the sultan for his best friend's honour, and the unspoken regret of Tuah for murdering his good friend who avenged his honour, expressed some of the underlying ideals of social justice and balance reciprocity during this period in history (see Parnickel (1960) for an interpretation of the conflict).

In the *Malay Annals* (the Tenth Story), a notable character highlighted in pre-Melaka history was Dang Anum, daughter of the *bendahari*, or State Treasurer, Sang Rajuna Tapa.[11] The latter was a native of the island of Singapore, unlike the raja (named as Raja Iskandar Shah) a refugee Prince Consort (with the title of *Permaisura/Parameswara*) from Palembang. As a native of the island, the *bendahari* was probably of the *Orang Seletar* (Celates) or *Orang Laut* community, the indigenous people of the islands south of the Peninsula. Significantly, Raja Iskandar Shah's entourage which fled to Muar and finally Melaka included the *Orang Celates/Seletar*, as shown earlier. That the *Orang Seletar* served Malay kings from as early as the Kingdom of Singapore in the fourteenth century is therefore a logical possibility.

Sang Rajuna Tapa being a very loyal servant of the raja, allowed Dang Anum to be taken into the palace as a concubine (secondary wife) of the raja, even though the event was not entirely to his wishes. Significantly, she was believed to have led a life of unhappiness and misery in the palace. Popular literature portrayed her as already betrothed to a Malay warrior (Malang) who had been selected by the raja to fight the Javanese. In the *Malay Annals*, it was recorded that the Javanese of the Majapahit Empire had launched an unsuccessful attack on the Malays of Singapore. It was in this period in Singapore's history that the story of Dang Anum is set. Though she had been made a concubine of the raja, Sang Rajuna Tapa's loyalty to the latter prevented him from doing anything that would harm her. Unfortunately, Dang Anum herself had earned the wrath and hostility of the other concubines through her beauty and because of her special position as the favourite concubine of the ruler. The raja's concubines, together with an official of the Court, Dato Biji Suram who was against the *bendahari* and his family, made it appear that Dang Anum had committed adultery (with Malang) in the palace. The couple were seen together by the raja. The enraged ruler ordered the execution of Dang Anum and her alleged lover.[13] This act of *fitnah* (malice) resulted in catastrophe, not only for the innocent victims of the plot, but for the Malay kingdom of Singapore.

Though the drama of this event was not described in any great length in the Tenth Story in the *Malay Annals*, and Dang Anum was not even named, nevertheless the brevity and understated nature of the descriptions does not diminish the historical importance of the story, of the gruelling consequences of despotism on both ruler and subject. It was stated in the *Malay Annals* that the *bendahari*'s response to his daughter's execution was complete anarchy. He left the palace gates, to open the outer gates of the city to let in the most dangerous enemy of the Malays, the Javanese from Majapahit. A bloody war resulted, ending in defeat at the hands of the Javanese and the collapse of the Malay kingdom of Singapore. For his treachery, he was 'turned to stone', but he was also responsible for dethroning a cruel ruler and destroying a kingship which did not respect values of honour and justice, ingrained in Malay subjects at the time. Hence, the *bendahari*'s decision was suggestively presented as an act of honour and valour of a subject against a tyrannical king.[14] It was also important that this form of tyranny and treachery was seen as the ultimate reason for the collapse of a thriving Malay Empire.

The *Malay Annals* suggest that the Malay Sultanate of Melaka developed as an alternative site to the Singapore kingdom after the victory of the Javanese. What had clearly been revealed in this episode was the relationship of conflict between the *bendahari* and the king, a conflict which had parallels to the *bendahara*/king relationship in Melaka later. In both relationships between ruler and subject, the source of the problems was the status of women identified with these powerful men of the court. The status of a concubine to a king was completely unacceptable — it expressed loss of family honour, reputation, and autonomy. On the other hand, while the expression of support and loyalty to the king meant dishonour to the *bendahari*'s family, the reverse was also true. Defending family honour implied disloyalty and treason to the king. Ultimately, it rested on the commoner's attempts to redefine the spheres of power relations between him and the king which were resolved by the overriding consideration for balanced reciprocity or failure to achieve it, in revenge. In this first incident, the decision of the ruler to take in the daughter of a courtly aristocrat and a commoner as a concubine ultimately led to the destruction of the Malay kingdom of Singapura and the sovereignty of the king.

Wilkinson (1935: 19) provided a vivid translation of this event in the *Malay Annals*. He described Dang Anum as the 'comely daughter' of Sang Rajuna Tapa 'whose charms had won the King's favour'. When she was impaled alive for a false accusation of infidelity to the king, Wilkinson attempted to reconstruct the mood of the day to explain Sang Rajuna Tapa's act of treachery. It appeared to be a combination of family loyalty, public humiliation, and revenge. He concluded that Sang Rajuna Tapa was embittered; 'if she had been guilty, well and good; but why shame us all on mere suspicion?' (p.19) It was for this gross injustice to his daughter and family that he opened the gates of Singapore to Javanese invaders from Majapahit. Significantly, Wilkinson's translation of events of history coincided with concurrent Malay interpretations of Dang Anum's misfortunes and the king's cruelty towards her.

Generally, the event records two modes of *adat* characteristic of Malay kingships; one of the rule of absolute loyalty of subject to king, derived from Indic symbols of divinity and sovereignty, and another of the rule of honour, of king to subject, derived from indigenous norms of interpersonal relationships within the Malay family and kinship order. The co-existence of both rules suggests the importance of preserving balances and compromises within hierarchies that are inherently incompatible in Malay society.

There is some discrepancy with regard to the date of the event which led to the destruction of the Malay kingdom at Singapore. According to Wilkinson, the date given in a Majapahit poem was AD 1361 while Chinese chronicles made it to be 1377, the date when Chinese envoys in Singapore were waylaid and killed by the Javanese.[15]

From the story of Dang Anum, the *Malay Annals* moved to further episodes in Melaka's history. Significantly from this period onwards, the daughters of the *bendahara* were involved as consorts, legally married to the royal patrilineage through the system of matrilateral filiation. Significantly, the foreign origin of rulers was a major factor in determining the need for legitimacy through local marriages with women from the *bendahara* household. Raja Iskandar Shah, the foreign prince from Palembang and Singapura, was said to have brought along with him a Malay wife. However, according to the *Malay Annals*, he contracted marriages with local women all along the way. This suggested a period of domestication through marriage before the royal entourage settled in Melaka. The *Malay Annals* is the main source available on the life of this first Prince Consort of Singapore who gave rise to the Melaka line of kings, beginning with Raja Iskandar Shah. However much of the events recorded during this period remained clouded in animistic logic and supernatural mystery.

In Shellabear's fifth edition (1952) of the *Malay Annals* recording the early period in Malay history (The Second Story), a reference was made to the marriage of a visiting king, Sang Si-Perba, to the daughter of a local Palembang chief or raja called Demang Lebar Daun. The story was located in Palembang and in all probability referred to an ancestor of the first *Permaisura* Iskandar Shah or 'Prince Consort' who settled in Singapore. It was in this context that the formal oath of allegiance to kings was formulated. Thus when Permaisura Raja Iskandar Shah laid the foundation to the Melaka Sultanate at the turn of the fifteenth century, he was probably already supported by mythologies of domestication, that is, the granting of legitimacy to 'stranger-kings' through marriages with important women of the local community (see Sahlins, 1981). The local population of Melaka at this time was sparse, as explained earlier, comprising a few Celates families making a living from fruit cultivation. Thus, at this early period, as explained by Pires and subsequently the *Malay Annals*, legitimacy for the kingship had to be sought through marriage to courtesans, obtained from the newly created House of *Bendahara* — the indigenous Celates, *Orang Seletar*, who served the Permaisura Raja Iskandar Shah who formed the Kingdom of Melaka.[16] By 1446, evidence of the king's marriage to the daughter of the *bendahara* was already recorded. Significantly, this coincided with a critical period in Melaka's history when a half-Tamil prince,

Raja Kassim, assumed the throne by murdering his half-sibling of fully Malay descent. The latter, Raja Ibrahim, had in fact already assumed the throne when he was killed, since he was preferred to his half-brother by virtue of his descent. Raja Kassim's conspiracy to murder Raja Ibrahim (d.1446) and his enthronement was probably only rectified and resolved when he married Tun Kudu (Twelfth Story, p. 71), the daughter of the *bendahara*. Significantly, this pattern of contracting marriages implied that male offsprings from such unions could be manipulated to become the *bendahara* and even future kings if the daughters of the *bendahara* utilized their role to the maximum. The wide powers of these women in fact were revealed in subsequent generations when the children of Tun Kudu and Tun Fatimah became the preferred choices of *bendahara* and king, respectively (see Figure 2.1).

The process of granting the *bendahara* a legitimate status within the ruling class may be said to have stabilized the position of the royal patrilineage within the populace. It demonstrated processes of symbolic mediation between commoner and king, and on another level, king and consort. The necessary alliance was subsequently upheld in other State Annals, notably the Perak Annals (*Salsilah Raja-Raja Perak*) by a different version of the same incident featuring Demang Lebar Daun and his encounter with Raja Singa. The Perak version of the story locates the marriage in Singapura instead of Palembang, and actually provides an explanation of marriage alliance principles between the *bendahara* and Malay raja. The event is narrated in the following way:

> The King of Singapura was Raja Singa who appeared from the sea. He met Demang Lebar Daun, a local Malay chief and married his daughter. Raja Singa and his Malay Consort ruled in Singapura and had two sons, the elder of whom became Raja and the younger *Bendahara*. An agreement was made that the male descendants of the *Bendahara* would not marry into the family of the Raja, and had to seek wives elsewhere. They were however, entitled to be addressed with respect. It was however, lawful for the Royal family to take wives from the family of the *Bendahara*, so that the descendants of the *Bendahara* could also be addressed as Raja.[17] (1972: 206).

Hence, based on the traditions of Melaka, Perak evolved similar *adat* rules concerning marriage alliances between the daughters of the *bendahara* and the sultan, although in this version of the myth, the younger son assumed the title of *bendahara*, a natural off-shoot of the expansion of Malay kingship and kinship within the court. However, the source of these marriages remain in the divine marriage of a visitor-king with the daughter of an aristocratic. In this way, the system of matrilateral filiation was ritually and symbolically legitimized. It also described the limits of spheres of control of aristocrat Malays (the *bendahara*) within the court, preventing

44

Figure 2.1 Marriage Alliances between the *Bendahara* and Royal Households

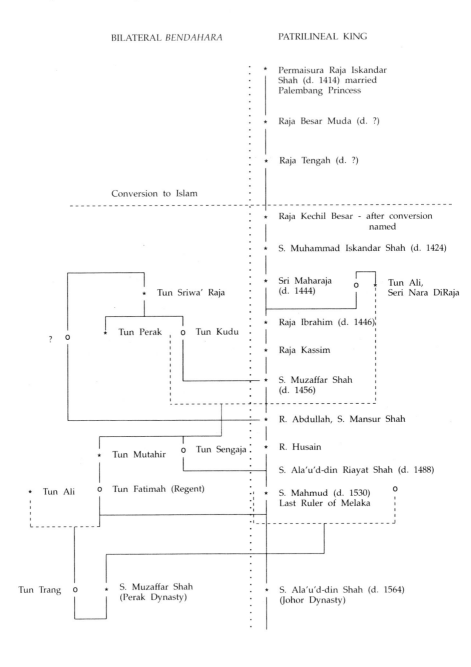

BILATERAL *BENDAHARA*   PATRILINEAL KING

* Permaisura Raja Iskandar
  Shah (d. 1414) married
  Palembang Princess

* Raja Besar Muda (d. ?)

* Raja Tengah (d. ?)

Conversion to Islam
- -

* Raja Kechil Besar - after conversion
  named

* S. Muhammad Iskandar Shah (d. 1424)

* Tun Sriwa' Raja   * Sri Maharaja   o   Tun Ali,
                             (d. 1444)   Seri Nara DiRaja

* Tun Perak   o Tun Kudu   * Raja Ibrahim (d. 1446)

? o   * Raja Kassim

                           * S. Muzaffar Shah
                             (d. 1456)

                           * R. Abdullah, S. Mansur Shah

* Tun Mutahir o Tun Sengaja   * R. Husain

                             S. Ala'u'd-din Riayat Shah (d. 1488)

* Tun Ali o Tun Fatimah (Regent)   * S. Mahmud (d. 1530)   o
                                      Last Ruler of Melaka

Tun Trang o * S. Muzaffar Shah   * S. Ala'u'd-din Shah (d. 1564)
                (Perak Dynasty)   (Johor Dynasty)

Source: Drawn by author from Shellabear's *Malay Annals*, 1954. (Rumi translation of Jawi, 1896)

their male descendants in a way from inheriting the throne, by transferring the line of inheritance from the royal patrilineage to the *bendahara* family.

The *bendahara*-raja conflict again surfaced through Tun Kudu, daughter of *Dato Bendahara* Seri Wak Raja, the Royal Treasurer and Premier to the court of Melaka during the reign of Raja Ibrahim, Sultan Abu Sahid Seri Parameswara Dewa Shah. As mentioned earlier, Raja Ibrahim was murdered by his cousin, Raja Kassim (1446) a young man of half-Tamil ancestry. The latter was assisted by some conspirators headed by his uncle, Tun Ali Seri Nara DiRaja. Raja Kassim was installed as the next ruler of Melaka under the name of Sultan Muzaffar Shah ibni Al-Marhum S. Muhammad Shah.

Tun Ali, anxious to obtain the position of *bendahara*, conspired in another act of treachery to eliminate *bendahara* Seri Wak Raja from the royal court. The *bendahara* was later poisoned and Tun Ali was installed as *bendahara*. Determined to avenge her father's death, Tun Kudu agreed to become the consort of Raja Kassim (who it is said, was captivated by her beauty) although she had already agreed to marry Tun Pateh, a warrior of the Melaka court. She soon discovered that Tun Ali was responsible for her father's death and revealed this to the ruler who immediately expelled his uncle from the court. Tun Perak, the younger brother of Tun Kudu, was recalled from his post in Kelang as Governor to take over his rightful position as *bendahara* (see Figure 2.1). Unfortunately, Tun Ali refused to leave and threatened to destroy the State of Melaka unless the sultan gave him Tun Kudu as his bride. This was a grave insult to the sultan, who was reluctant to give in to his uncle's wishes until he was persuaded to do so by Tun Kudu, who knew that Tun Ali was capable of destroying Melaka. Tun Kudu married Tun Ali to ensure continuing peace for Melaka during the reign of Raja Kassim. Her sacrifices to forego her love for Tun Pateh to marry the sultan, to install her younger brother as the rightful heir to the position of *bendahara*, and finally to marry Tun Ali to ensure peace for Melaka, made her the kind of heroine which was popularly upheld in Malay versions of *Seri Kandi*. She has been described in literature (Hamdan: 1967) as *bunga bangsa* ('the flower of the people') and *tiang negara* ('pillar of country').

Again here, the spheres of control of power in the court were 'woman-centred'. Women determined the limits of power of the king in both real and symbolic terms and the *bendahara*, the trends of politics of the state.[18]

In *A History of Malaya* (1935: 46), Winstedt wrote, 'Diplomacy made Muzaffar Shah marry Tun Kudu, a daughter of the dead Sriwa Raja, a Malay lady destined to play a great part in politics.' Confirming evidence in the *Malay Annals*, he attributed the rise of Tun Perak, the famous *bendahara* of Melaka who brought Melaka to its heights of glory during the reign of Muzaffar Shah (d.1456), to his sister, Tun Kudu. He stated:

Perhaps it was her influence that brought to Court her brother , Tun Perak; as *Penghulu* of Klang, a hero of Proto-Malay tradition, winner of campaigns against Siam, Pahang, Pasai, the brain of Melaka's imperialist policy in Malaya and Sumatra for more than three reigns (1935: 46).

Tun Kudu also monitored Melaka politics for several generations through her second marriage to Sri Nara DiRaja, the raja's (her first husband) uncle of Tamil ancestry. Two of her three children by this marriage, Tun Mutahir (*bendahara* till 1510) and Tun Sengaja (wife of Sultan Ala'u'd-din (d.1488), controlled the trend of politics in the Melaka Sultanate to its final invasion by the Portuguese in 1511 (see Figure 2.1).

The events narrated in the story of Tun Kudu were almost parallel to those recorded for Tun Fatimah, another colourful figure in the Melaka *Hikayat* set in the period prior to the fall of Melaka in 1511. Tun Fatimah, the daughter of *bendahara* Seri Maharaja Tun Mutahir, the son of Tun Kudu by her marriage to Seri Nara DiRaja, was a skilled warrior trained in combat and martial arts. Being beautiful as well as accomplished, she attracted the attention of Sultan Mahmud who wanted her as his consort. However, Tun Mutahir was eager and anxious to test his powers over the king and did so by marrying Tun Fatimah off to an unknown warrior, Tun Ali. He was one of the many who assisted Tun Fatimah's elder brother, Tun Hassan Temenggung, in driving out the first group of Portuguese traders from the Port of Melaka in 1509. Tun Fatimah herself took part in this battle by disguising herself as a male warrior. This deliberate breach of diplomacy forced the ruler to seek revenge by entertaining a conspiracy against the *bendahara* and using this as a suitable event to curb the powers of the *bendahara* permanently.

It so happened that a misunderstanding between two traders, Nina Sura Dewana and *Syahbandar* Raja Mudeliar, could not be resolved without the intervention of the *bendahara*. Nina Sura Dewana attempted to bribe the *bendahara* with gold and this came to the attention of *Syahbandar* Raja Mudeliar who complained to *laksamana* Khoja Hassan that the *bendahara* had accepted gold from Nina Sura Dewana. The *laksamana* reported to the sultan that the *bendahara* was trying to overthrow him since he had accumulated enough gold to set up a golden throne (*takhta emas*). The sultan deliberately chose to believe this version of the feud by ordering the death of the *bendahara*, his heirs and members of the household, sparing only Tun Fatimah. He subsequently forced her to be his bride. Doubtless, he married a much embittered woman who sought to reinstate her family's honour by convincing the king to eliminate the *laksamana* Khoja Hassan, the *Syahbandar*, and his go-between, Ketil.[19]

In 1511, the Portuguese returned with Alfonso d'Alburquerque's fleet to avenge the loss of their men and the destruction of their ships during the battle of 1509 when Diego Lopez de Sequeira and his men were defeated. Melaka, considerably weakened by internal strife and a weak sultan, was defeated and Sultan Mahmud had to flee for his life. He took Tun Fatimah with him to Batu Hampar but was besieged by the Portuguese and had to flee to Paguh. He was again besieged at Paguh, then Bentan and Kopak; finally, in desperation, he fled to Kampar in Sumatra (see Map II). Tun Fatimah, who was said to have controlled the reins of the throne in the absence of her father and family, died soon afterwards of fever and grief, for the final disintegration of the Melaka kingdom she had helped to rule.

The *Hikayat* depicted Tun Fatimah to be a high spirited warrior in contrast to the portrayal of the sultan, as a weak, scandalous and incompetent king. Again, her love and pride for Melaka was highlighted to clearly demonstrate her spirit of sacrifice in defending Melaka against her enemies, in particular the Portuguese, despite her contempt for the king and her misery over the violent death her family suffered under his rule. The Malay writer, H. Hamdan (1977), called her *Semangat Melaka* (the 'Spirit of Melaka'), to signify her capacity to place national interests before personal sentiments. Her death at Kampar acted as a landmark for the final collapse of the Melaka Sultanate.

Though the Melaka kingdom flourished for less than a century, the pattern of marriage alliances between the family of the *bendahara* and the raja was clearly formulated at each stage of succession to the throne. Of those marriages which were clearly verified by history, Tun Kudu probably assisted in crystallizing the powers of the *bendahara* even more, by contracting marriages with both the sultan and his father's brother. This enabled her brother, Tun Perak, as the new *bendahara*, to dominate Melaka's politics for three generations of kings. The marriage of his second cousin to Sultan Mansur Shah and that of his niece, Tun Sengaja, to the next king, Sultan Ala'u'd-din Riayat Shah, further confirmed his position. The next *bendahara*, Tun Mutahir, was believed to have been killed because of his inability to maintain the delicate balance of power between adviser and ruler, but his daughter's marriage to the young Sultan Mahmud ensured the continuity of the rule of matrilateral filiation within the court. Significantly, the two parallel lines of control, exercised by the king and *bendahara*, maintained a system of checks and balances. It implied that either side could, at any point, attempt to extend its sphere of influence over the other, to the extent of assuming total control over the kingdom. Such forms of political extremism were symbolically controlled by the relationships of wife-giver and wife-receiver, maintained by the *bendahara* and the king respectively (Figure 2.2).

The *bendahara* in the position of wife-giver symbolically if not formally assumed a higher hierarchical position than the king, for his ability to

FIGURE 2.2   Pattern of Alliances between the *Bendahara* and the King

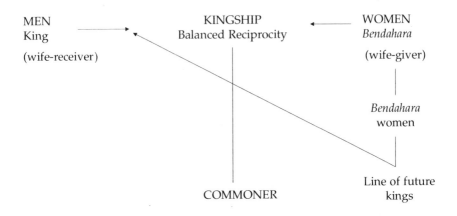

provide women and to withdraw them if necessary placed the king in a relationship of dependence and humility. Thus, in reality, the relationships were based on ideal notions of reciprocity, ritually upheld by marriages rules which were politically advantageous to both parties. The important point to consider was that the spirit of diplomatic alliance was constantly threatened by the opposing alternative — the strategy of non-co-operation through the withdrawal of women. Other checks were introduced into the system. The taboo on revolt or rebellion against the king (*Pantang orang Melayu derhaka kepada Raja*) that a Malay could not commit treason against his king was counter-checked by the oath a king had to swear to, not to be despotic or tyrannical to his subjects (*Pantang raja belot* or *raja adil raja disembah, raja ta' adil, raja dicanggah*).

In general, although the states of dissonance between the king and the *bendahara,* and between the king and his subjects, were often increased by values of personal and family honour and political ambition and revenge, it was clear that a king who practised despotism and injustice was seen to have broken the code of oath with his subjects.[20]

The 'fencing' politics of Melaka between the king and *bendahara* had interesting consequences in other Malay states which carried on the Melaka dynasty. Tun Fatimah's son, Ala'u'd-din, became the first Sultan of Johor at Sungei Telor, near Kota Tinggi. Hence, the *bendahara* line through female descendants shaped the new Malay throne at Johor. The Melaka line ended in 1699 almost two centuries later with the death of Sultan Mahmud of Johor since he died without issue and the next sultan was established directly from a new line of *bendahara*, Sri Maharaja Abdu'l-Jalil, a local

Malay family from the area. Tun Fatimah married her daughter, Tun Trang (by her first marriage to Tun Ali) to Raja Muzaffar Shah, the son of Sultan Mahmud (of Melaka) by his previous marriage to a Kelantanese. With Tun Trang as his consort, Raja Muzaffar Shah became the first Sultan of Perak. The Sultans of Pahang and Selangor were also directly descended from the Melaka line of kings. It seemed as if finally the indigenization process of Malay kings was expressed in a check-mate, with the triumph of the *bendahara* family over Malay kings. This also expressed the symbolic inversion of the hierarchy between the king and subjects, royalty and commoner, men and women. As the centres of power relations between commoners and royalty, women managed to dominate the trends of indigenization of political rule. While patriliny was the principle which provided kings with ritual legitimacy, it was guarded by rules which were more bilateral in form, giving opportunities for women to play a major role in state politics. Malay *adat-istiadat* relating to the state suggested that while patriliny made 'strangers' into kings, it was bilaterality which determined their longevity.

Within the Indonesian region, systems of wife-exchange were usually circulatory where wife-givers were regarded to be hierarchically superior to wife-receivers. The Batak *hula*, refer to their wife-takers (the *boru* group) as their perpetual slaves while in Minangkabau tradition, the bako group (wife-takers) were obviously subservient to the *ana' pisang* (wife-givers). De Jong (1952: 63-65) attributes this to the circulative connubial system which is characteristic of the area. The wife-giver — wife-taker relationship between the House of *bendahara* and the king, however, cannot be said to be another classical example of this circulative connubial system. The king married the daughter of the *bendahara* and a royalty and commoner alliance was established. The *bendahara*, however, within the order of the Court was hierarchically subservient to the king, but in reality, this hierarchical distinction was underplayed since the marriage system gave him considerable power to determine the future of line of kings. He also became the father-in-law of the king. His grandson or granddaughter from his daughter's marriage to the king, could very well become the next ruler, if the king had no sons from a previous marriage. This indeed materialized towards the decline of the Melaka Sultanate during the rule of Tun Fatimah.[21] Hence what would normally be a hierarchical relationship of king and prime minister/vizier became charged with a variety of kinship commitments and divided loyalties which produced permanent states of dissonance between the two households.

In the next generation, the young crown prince again sought a wife from the *bendahara*'s household, usually a cousin, assuming that the *bendahara* was still in command and had not yet been replaced by his son. According to Melaka *adat-istiadat*, however, the House of *bendahara* could not obtain their women from the royal household but from other families of the commoner class. The relationship was obviously hierarchical all the way — royalty marries commoner-aristocrat, commoner-aristocrat marries commoner and commoner marries commoner. Hence, although the pattern of wife-giver — wife-receiver relationship within the court did, at face value, suggest that the king maintained his supremacy over the prime minister and vizier, yet his position as son-in-law and that of the prince-regent as grandson to the *bendahara* set off new possibilities for dominance, in the opposite direction. The *bendahara* controlled both processes of kingship and kinship, by giving his daughters or nieces to the royal family. Furthermore, in the event of illness or death, consorts became heads of state. Thus, the *bendahara*'s position as a wife-giver gave him a superior advantage.

Why, one may ask, would a king place himself in such an impossible position? Possibly, it is as mentioned earlier, that Malay kings already viewed their position to be disadvantageous from the start, recognizing the importance of alliance and legitimacy from the native populace. Bowen (1983: 164), pursuing the theory of alliance along the line of Dumont (1968) and Levi-Strauss (1969), suggests that the alliance was asymmetrical from the first, since the early Melaka kings only gained legitimacy through marriages with local women from the peasantry. Indeed, alliance rather than descent, and domestication rather than conquest, are the key principles to Malay kingship. Doubtless, as members of royal households grew, the classical European alliance patterns of royal marriages developed amongst the different Malay states but in early Melaka history, marriage arrangements between the *bendahara*'s daughters and the king was more common. Often, even when the Melaka kings contracted polygamous marriages, this was not done to the exclusion of a marriage with a woman from the *bendahara* household. One needs only to consider the position of Tun Fatimah, who was a secondary wife but eventually became a consort and, through her own influence, ensured that her son would be the first ruler of Johor and her daughter, the first consort of the Perak line. Thus the future rulers of the emerging states of Malaya were offshoots of the *bendahara* line.

If this perspective is plausible, then it would be possible to say that Malay kingships were formed through patriliny but ordered through bilaterality. This helped to preserve some basic elements of homogeneity in Malay society which currently transpires in folk *adat*. On the level of the State, this was achieved by making women the power centres of the court, where stranger-kings sought legitimacy through ritual marriages with women of the commoner class. As the commoners married into royal households, their descendants became part of the aristocrat ruling class. Malay chiefs oscillating between the peasantry and the ruling class utilized patrilineal and matrilateral principles of behaviour when it came to the acquisition and distribution of titles and women respectively.

Modes of organization that developed within the populace preserved bilaterality, which became an essential feature of Malay *adat*. Amongst the peasantry, hierarchical distinctions of class and gender were underplayed in preference to a traditional ranking system based on pioneer status, social rank, informal leadership or charisma and eldership. It will be shown later how, in the evolution of a Malay village, leadership amongst the peasantry highlighted hierarchical difference based on genealogy, descent, and control over labour and land. However, although hierarchical distinctions were clearly upheld between the ruling class and the peasantry on the macro-level and within both of these categories on the micro, yet rules of action and interaction were uniformly ordered by *adat* principles which were more complementary or egalitarian in form. This will be demonstrated in greater detail in the following discussion on the peasant polity. It covers the period in Malay history from the decline of the Malay kingship in Melaka to the rise of other Malay Sultanates in the peninsula, including the period of British intervention in the eighteenth and nineteenth centuries. The discussion is more concerned with the macro relationships between kings, chiefs, and subjects, following the crystallization of these social hierarchies in Malay society. On this level of analysis, the roles of women in kingship formation, earlier described, were symbolically parallel to the roles of the peasantry in state formation. They both represent or symbolize relationships which have come to be accepted as essential within prescribed codes of reciprocity in *adat-istiadat*.

Conclusion

When the Portuguese captured Melaka in 1511, the Malay raja managed to maintain his hold over Johor at the extreme southern region of the Malay Peninsula (see Map II). The present twelve states of the Peninsula were created with the development of independent sultanates or, in the case of Negeri Sembilan, a chieftaincy. The southern sultanates including Perak were directly descended from the original Melaka patrilineage or created by petty Bugis chiefs who gradually claimed control over coastal and riverine areas and established themselves as 'rulers'.

The occupation of Melaka by the Portuguese accelerated wars with the Bugis mercenaries and weakened the position of the Portuguese in Melaka. Eventually, in 1641, the Portuguese lost Melaka to the Dutch, but the Dutch administration of Melaka was equally short lived and in 1795, gave way to British control over Melaka and the rest of the Peninsula. The trading interests which the British maintained in the Peninsula necessitated greater centralization of their powers, with the result that they eventually extended their rule from the three lucrative port centres of Melaka, Penang and Singapore, thence called the Straits Settlements, to the other states in the Peninsula. This was achieved by rendering military aid to the rulers and petty chiefs against invading marauders, pirates and mercenaries from the Archipelago, particularly the Moluccas, who threatened the status quo of the existing rulers of the various states.

The discussion of the early Malay state of Melaka in the fifteenth and sixteenth centuries showed how processes of matrilateral filiation ensured the inclusion of local populations into the kingship structure. The resulting hierarchies of king and subject, commoner and royalty eventually suggest a process of development of the culture itself and the development of Malay rules of *adat-istiadat* in sociopolitical relations. This will be developed further in the next chapter. Generally, though numerous sociopolitical hierarchies were created over history, they were controlled by norms of reciprocity and mutual co-operation on different levels of interaction. Conclusively, reciprocity and bilaterality were the rules of *adat* produced in history.

These processes bear certain structural similarities to the phenomenon described by Sahlins (1981: 126-127) of the 'domestication "of Hawaian and Fijian" Stranger-Kings', when native women from chiefly families are made to wed visitors to the islands, converting them ritually and symbolically to the status of kings and gods, a phenomenon reinforced by pre-existing mythologies. This, according to Sahlins, makes women the power centres of the society and determine the way in which indigenous structures create and direct the processes of social history in Polynesia.

Earlier, Josselin de Jong (1952: 96), writing on Minangkabau kings in Sumatra suggested that although they were of Javanese-Hindu origin, it seemed obvious that they came with 'a ready-made technique for integration into the existing system'. In this sense, the application of standard conquest/domination theory analysis seems incorrect. In Sumatra, the imposition of patrineal kingship structures upon a system of matriliny was neatly upheld by mythologies, similar to that of the Malays but with more anthropomorphic features of 'domestication' — stranger-kings married local creatures (tiger, cat, dog), their female offspring then marrying aboriginal men and eventually becoming the ancestors of the present day tribe or *luha*.

The above discussion of Malay kingship attempts to explain the emergence of fundamental rules and values of *adat* in social and political relations. Relationships of hierarchy were ordered according to bilateral or ego-centralized values rendering formal distinctions of inequality less significant in ordinary life. On the macro-level, relationships of hierarchy between the king and countrymen, king and kinsmen, king and consort, men and chief, and men and women rested on values of personal and family honour, reciprocity and independence, mutual trust and consideration, blurring the ritual formality of hierarchical distinctions which were created and publicly upheld. The king could only uphold a conical power structure symbolically since the people strove to operationalize it in a more egalitarian way. In the same way as women became the mediatories in power relations between the king and the *bendahara*, so did Malay chiefs perform the task of mediating hierarchies created between kings and commoners. The pattern is repeated in numerous other Southeast Asian societies (de Jong, 1952; Leach, 1970; Siegel, 1969) exhibiting the kind of phenomenon argued by Winzeler (1976) to be expressive of state processes which were 'incomplete'.[22] This 'incompletion', however, can be more meaningfully expressed in another way, that the leaders of Malay states assumed limited proportions of strength or power over their subjects on account of the way in which cultural processes through *adat* were vitally linked to the formation of state histories.

Notes

1. As explained in Chapter 1 terms like 'power', 'power relations' and 'political relations' are used in a general sense to express formal and informal nexus of decision-making with personal autonomy. In processes of state formation, the 'power' of women vis-a-vis men is seen in the light of their ability to exercise these formal and informal nexus of decision-making in political leadership.

2. 'Traditional' is here used as a general temporal reference point, to describe the prevailing systems before colonial rule.

3. Understatements and disguised ideas expressed through symbolic or metaphorical language is a characteristic of Malay classical literature as seen in the *pantun*, *sya'er* and other forms of writing.

4. Wilkinson (1935, b: 31) writes of the *bendahara* family, 'The *Bendahara* held the position of Prime Minister and Premier Noble of the State . . . Though not of the blood-royal in Malacca, he was far the greatest figure in the State, leading the army when he wished to serve in war and sitting as the highest Court of Justice when he wished to try a case. He was Viceroy, King's Deputy, Grand Vizier'.

5. It is for this reason that historians relied extensively on Chinese chronicles written by Chinese or European travellers to the East such as I-tsing (671), Marco Polo (1292), Wang Ta-yuan (1349), Admiral Cheng Ho (1409) and Ma-Huan (1425-32), a Chinese Muslim interpreter to Admiral Cheng Ho in the East in 1413. Muslim Arab writers were widely quoted; the formation of Kidah or Kedah, Ibn Khordadzbeh (844-8) and for Melaka, Ibn Batuta in 1345. See Winstedt (20-24) and Wheatley (1964, 122-125). The formation of the oldest Malay Kingdom in Malaya Langkasuka (Land of Asoka), said to be located in Kedah, at the foothills of Gunung Jerai in the Merbuk Valley, as early as the sixth century, was confirmed by numerous Chinese and Arab travellers (I-tsing, Lang-ya-Sieu, Ibn Khordadzbeh) who visited

this region from the seventh to the tenth century A.D. Archaeological evidence was also another valuable source of information on Malay early history, and the changing influences of ideology from Hinduism to Islam.

6. Apparently, Sultan Muzaffar Shah of the Perak dynasty (d. 1756) awarded him the title 'Raja Kecik Besar'. Sultan Iskandar Shah was so impressed by Raja Chulan's ability to compose poetry (*sya'er*) and verse that he commissioned Raja Chulan to write the history of Perak during his reign (1756-1770). The popularity and fame of the author caused much misgivings, finally culminating in his death at the hands of a jealous husband. The *kris* which killed him, known as *tiga lok*, has since then been banned from use by the royal court. He was awarded the name 'Marhum Pulau Juar' after his death.

7. Shellabear's first translation of the original text was published in 1896. Subsequently, two other editions were published by the same author in 1898 and 1909 respectively. In 1948, this original version was used officially in Malay schools as a standard text. The Ministry of Education subsequently published another version which made further changes in spelling and punctuation, in accordance with new developments in translation from *Jawi* to *Rumi*.

8. Pires wrote several letters in Melaka between December 1513 and January 1515 stating that his accounts of pre-Portuguese Melaka were based on research, while serving as an apothecary to the King of Portugal. The Suma Oriental was a report sent to King Manuel, probably in discharge of a commission. Pires was executed in 1524 in Canton after being taken prisoner by the Chinese, on his voyage out of Melaka, as ambassador to the King of China. His daughter, Ines de Keiria, confirmed that Pires and his men were mistaken for spies (xiix).

9. This was confirmed by the *Sejarah Melayu*, which described Raja Iskandar Shah as a non-Muslim from Palembang who ruled Melaka for 30 years. It was only the next generation of Melaka kings, from Raja Iskandar Shah, i.e. Raja Kecil Besar, who converted to Islam under the name of Sultan Muhammad Shah (Shellabear, 1952: 62). The following dignitaries comprised the early Malay royal courts in Melaka. Below the ruler (raja, later called sultan) was the *Paduka Raja*, a kind of Viceroy, second to the king. Next was the *bendahara* who held the position of Treasurer and Prime Minister, followed by the Temenggong or Minister of War. The *laksamana* was Naval Commander followed by the *Dato Seri Biji DiRaja*, who was Captain of the Guard. Court attendants were under the orders of the *penghulu bendahara* or Chief Treasury Officer. See Wilkinson (1935 b: 30-33) for a vivid description of old Melaka court symbols and ritual, derived and translated from the *Malay Annals*.

10. The Seri Kandi are also popularly featured in Malay historical romances (*romanza sejarah*), the opera or *bangsawan* and the theatre (*panggung drama*).

11. This woman remains unnamed in the *Sejarah Melayu*. Recent operatic performances of this epic through the *bangsawan theatre* names her a Dang Anum, a character which has since then appeared in several literary works, the most popular of which is A. Aziz's book, *Dang Anum*, the date of the publication of which is unknown. In the *Sejarah Melayu*, this epic is set in the pre-Islamic period of the history of Malaya. References are made to gods and deities which are Hindu, such as Sang Dewata Mulia Raja, to refer to the Sun God which reigned supreme in pre-Islamic Malay culture. Shellabear, however, argues that this population was

already converted to Islam, from their place of origin at Pasai, Sumatra, in the early thirteenth century.

12. Much confusion over the name of this first ruler of Melaka results from the use of the title *Permaisura* (written as *Parameswara, Paramicura, Permicura,* and *Permicuri* in Portuguese sources and *Pa-li-su-la* and *Pai-li-mi-su-la* in Chinese sources, showing various influences of accents on the Sanskrit origin *Permaisura*. Pires (1967) however, mentions the equivalence, noting that *Permaisuri* was the title of the wife of the Prince Consort.

13. The Malay writer, A. Aziz, expanded on the misery of the *bendahari* and his family by suggesting that on the day of the execution, Dang Anum's mother threw herself at the mercy of the raja. However, he did not relent and she was subsequently (though accidentally) slain in public. Apparently, the raja merely wanted Dang Anum to recognize his powers by making a public proclamation of her guilt and a plea for mercy. When she refused to proclaim her guilt and instead accused the king of being a despotic tyrant, with an irrational wild taste in women and a sense of cruelty which breached his own loyalty to his subjects, the furious raja ordered her to be speared (*sula*) to death.

14. The bravery of Dang Anum in facing a torturous death and her candour in condemning the actions of the raja encouraged the Malay writer A. Aziz, to write:'*Apabila ia dipermalukan dan dibunoh, terbunohlah nama Singapura sa-bagai negeri yang patut dihormati*' (undated: 113). Literally, it suggests that her humiliation and death brought on the demise of Singapore and its good name as a state that was honoured and respected.

15. Munshi Abdullah, the scholarly Tamil Muslim who became Stamford Raffles's personal assistant and interpreter, noted a stone inscription in Javanese Kawi, deliberately broken by Mr. George Coleman the chief architect to the Colony. A piece which was preserved was noted to contain a Majapahit Kawi script, older than AD 1361. Munshi Abdullah reported evidence of old fruit trees, sandstone blocks and a terraced royal tomb and Javanese gold jewellery found on Fort Canning Hill indicating that the palace was located on this strategic site. See Wilkinson (1935: 20-21) for a detailed description of old Singapore under the Malays. The gates to the city were merely made of bamboo and wood and were believed to have been destroyed during the war.

16. Pires explains the Melaka *adat-istiadat* of the king's son taking over the throne once the king became a grandfather (1944: 265). If so, reviewing the wanderings and exploits of 'Permaisura' from Singapore to Muar and finally to Melaka, many years had passed by (from 1361 or 1377 in Singapore) before the throne of Melaka was formed and it would be logical to suppose that Raja Iskandar Shah was a son of 'Permaisura' and not the original Prince Consort as sometimes assumed. Before Sultan Muhammad Shah, the *Malay Annals* traces two generations of kings after the first Prince Consort Permaisura Iskandar Shah, Raja Besar Muda and Raja Tengah, but these have not been substantiated, at least not by British writers of Melaka history.

17. This has been translated by Winstedt and Wilkinson in 'The History of Perak', MBRAS reprint No.3, p.206.

18. In the *Malay Annals* (as highlighted in more recent accounts of the story of Tun Kudu) are regular references made to the 'Constitution' or *Perlembagaan* of the

Malay state, which described the moral relationship and unwritten oath made between the raja and his subjects. The most important *ikrar-kata* or oath relates to the taboo of treason by subjects against the raja and the taboo against the raja ruling with injustice and cruelty (*Pantang Melayu Derhaka dan Pantang Raja belot and Raja adil, Raja disembah, Raja tak Adil, Raja dicanggah*). This moral code constantly appears in the *Hikayat* and literature based on the *Hikayat* to show the balanced, harmonious nature of the relationship expected between the raja and his subjects. The *Seri Kandi* are usually highlighted in events showing imbalances originating from poor judgement, jealousy, arrogance and incompetence on the part of the raja against his subjects and the collapse of each reign spearmarks the catastrophic nature of events which follow when such an oath to the *rakyat* is not adhered to.

19. It is significant that the *Malay Annals,* believed to be written by a descendent of Tun Mutahir, Tun Seri Lanang (son of Tun Ahmad Paduka Raja) focusses almost entirely on relationships of the *bendahara* family with the royal patrilineage. The political ethos of the *Malay Annals* clearly reflects anarchial sentiments, not only between the *bendahara* and the royal family, but also between the Tamils and the Malays of the royal court; the latter might have felt that they were the rightful heirs to all important titles and positions. These Tamils in Malay history were constantly referred to as *orang asing* ('the other people') and *Keturunan Kling* (of 'Kling', i.e. Tamil [derogatory] origin).

20. This code was maintained in the other Malay sultanates which emerged and may be summarized in a statement by Hughes. He wrote:

'. . . there often lacked the correct degree of obedience between the Princes and their subjects. For this reason, 20 years before the King of Gior himself was murdered by his vassals, either he was lacking in understanding and reason or his government had degenerated into tyranny . . .' (1935: 122).

21. In the thirty-third story of the *Sejarah Melayu,* Tun Fatimah was said to have aborted her pregnancy before Sultan Mahmud was aware of it. Extremely distressed, he begged her not to abort her next pregnancy promising that if it was a son, he would make him the next ruler of Melaka. She, however, bore him two daughters, Raja Puteh and Raja Khadijah. It is possible to see her act as conniving and an expression of revenge and hostility against the ruler, who killed her father, husband and brother, agreeing to have his children only if she could ensure that her son took over the throne of Melaka. Her wishes, however, were never realized as Melaka soon afterwards fell to the Portuguese.

22. Siegel's work which has not been highlighted here comments on the inconsistencies in the relationships between the king and certain classes of subjects like the *ulubalang* and *ulama* and notes the resulting contradictions in the superiority but 'powerlessness' of the rulers.

3

Adat as Ideology and Practice

Ikutlah resmi padi;
makin berisi makin menunduk
Follow the way of the padi stalk;
the more it fills, the more it bends

— *Malay proverb*

Introduction

This chapter provides useful background information on the development of Malay social relations in the late nineteenth and early twentieth century. It attempts to describe the tensions between hierarchy and equality in Malay interpretations of power. On the level of ideology and practice, many of these tensions are contained within the interpretive mode of *adat* which recognizes rules of social differentiation while simultaneously underplaying them through ideas of reciprocity and autonomy. The underdevelopment of these rules of differentiation provides the peasantry and women with opportunities for performing reciprocal and autonomous relationships with the elite and men, respectively. The system of operationalizing complementary relationships in non-hierarchical terms gives way to a bilaterality in power politics and gender. Theoretically Islam may introduce further tensions in this bilateral mode with its emphasis on formal ideology and female exclusion but since these differences are brought to the attention of the Malays through *adat* rather than in spite of, its mode of defining power and gender is more democratic than autocratic.

The complementarity of *adat* and Islam is evident in the way Islam was adopted as a formal political ideology within the pre-colonial Malay state. Fundamental institutions of *adat* which guided folk day-to-day relationships were superimposed by new rules of protocol and behaviour ordered by Islam. Islam enhanced the strength of pre-existing political structures with more worldly preferences to authority, legitimacy, and justice. In a sense, Islam provided the Malays with an additional ideological framework to understand and operationalize power and authority.[1] It also gave the Malays new symbolic notions of cultural advancement and intellectualism, rendering additional venues for those in positions of power to advance their influence within the population. Because Islam did not rule out *adat* and merely utilized the pre-existing system of social relations to gain legitimacy, women's political and socioeconomic roles were not significantly affected by the advancement of Islam except possibly in matters of inheritance and Islamic leadership, where women were excluded from formal and informal decision-making processes.

Adat and Islam in Early Malay History

Islam has been associated with earlier movements of Malays from Sumatra to the Peninsula, before the formation of the Sultanate of Melaka in the fifteenth century. As early as 1281, the Muslim state of Jambi had employed Muslim envoys to China (Wheatley, 1964: 98-99). Ten years later (1291), Marco Polo noted that the people of Perlak in Sumatra had already converted to Islam (1967: 338). In 1297, the ruler of Samudra embraced Islam, an event narrated in the *Sejarah Melayu* in the Seventh, Eighth and Nineth stories. According to the *Sejarah Melayu*, the Islamization of northeastern Sumatra began with Samudra, then Pasai and Perlak, that is from north to south (Map II). If this is so and considering that the Malay state of Jambi was already Islamized by 1281, the Islamization process of Malays in eastern Sumatra must have proceeded very rapidly in the last two decades of the thirteenth century. Braddell (1980: 507), quoting from the *Pasai Annals*, places the death of the first Muslim ruler of Pasai at 1297 (according to his gravestone which was brought from Cambay, a port of Gujerat).

The quarrel between the ruler of Pasai and his brother subsequently led to the latter being banished to Manjung (the Dindings District of Perak). This explains population movements and kinship affiliation between northern Sumatra and Perak as early as the thirteenth century, before the formation of the Sultanate of Melaka. The political domination of Acheh later revitalized these links. More recently, much of Braddell's earlier hypothesis of Muslim linkages between the Muslim state of Jambi and Perak have been substantiated by the discovery in Bruas, Perak of the 'Batu Bersurat', a stone with Qur'anic verses engraved on it (*New Straits Times*, 17 September 1986). Sources claim that the inscriptions date to the tenth century, suggesting that Bruas was an ancient Islamic kingdom established prior to the Hindu kingdom of Ganga Negara in the same area in the twelfth century. It is more likely, however, that the kingdom was formed after the Ganga Negara, in the thirteenth century, to coincide with the coming of Islam to the Northern Archipelago. While the Manjung (the Dindings) History Research Enthusiasts Association believes that Bruas was the site of an ancient Islamic state, dating more than two centuries before the discovery of Melaka, Muzium Negara curators feel that existing evidence is insufficient and that no stone should be left unturned to confirm this finding in history. The *Batu Bersurat* found in Terengganu, dated 1203, suggests that early Islamic influences in the eastern states of the Peninsula were more likely to have come from different sources, most probably Muslim envoys from China who also found their way to Melaka in the fifteenth century (as mentioned in a previous endnote Chapter 2).

Significantly, the *Hikayat* and *Annals* describe the coming of Islam to Sumatra and the Malay Peninsula through mystifying circumstances, in the form of prophetic dreams and revelations experiences by Malay sultans, as if to suggest that the spread of the religion was from the ruler to his people, rather than a grassroots movement. Yet, historical sources suggest that the Sufi mystics who brought Islam to Southeast Asia did so unobtrusively and quietly, usually through interpersonal interaction with the peasantry. The *Hikayat* probably attempted to justify the formal legitimizing of Islam by locating its sources in heads of states rather than the people.

Despite the early origins of Islam in the Peninsula in Bruas, Perak, Islamic laws were probably given some form of legal status and institutionalized only after the formation of the Melaka Sultanate. Sometime between 1414 and 1424, the *Malay Annals* suggest one of the early kings of Melaka, Raja Kecil Besar embraced Islam through a prophetic dream and subsequently formalized Islam as a courtly religion.[2] His conversion to Islam was symbolically expressed in his acquisition of a Muslim name, Muhammad Iskandar Shah, the title 'Sultan', and the instatement of his descent from Alexander the Great who was mythically Islamized in his 'wanderings' in Sumatra. By the reign of Sultan Mansur Shah in Melaka, men and women of the court were already acquainted with Islamic writers like Amir Hamzah and Muhammad Hanafiah and the mystic of Sufism. The life styles of the sultans were similar to those of the wealthy from the Muslim world, and poetry, music and slavery became part of the vogue of court life of the day. It appeared that the attraction to Islam was at this period, esoteric, and at the most, provided some additional procedures for legitimacy of the sultanate. Hence, the *Hikayat,* narrating courtly events after the coming of Islam to the Peninsula, used sacred verses from the Qur'an as openings and endings of epical stories as if to convey their sanctification by Allah. The philosophy and morality of Islam was not a significant feature of the *Hikayat*, which continued to be dominated by Hindu mysticism and anthropomorphisms.[3] Indeed, the *adat-istiadat Di-Raja* or ritual regalia derived from Indic notions of hierarchy and protocol was progressively intensified in Malay courts as Islam began to be incorporated into formal laws. In this way, Islam merely provided a fresh dressing to an unchanging life style.

Writers on pre-colonial Malay history do not seem to be in complete agreement on the importance of Islam in Malay political life. Gullick (1965: 134) suggested that Islam was not significantly integrated as a state religion since Muslim judges and registrars (*kathi, kadi*) were not a feature of the early Malay states, nor was Islamic law adopted as an effective legal doctrine in the administrative machinery. Milner (1980), however, said that authoritative figures in Islam, like the *kadi*, were mentioned in the *Malay Annals* and that the *Undang-Undang Melaka* compiled in this early period of Malay history included many 'Islamic elements', particularly in matters relating to matrimony and commerce.

The *Undang-Undang Melaka*, a set of legal digests of customs and rules which have been transmitted from generations and codified as customary social legal practices of the Malays, was the first formal attempt at the institutionalization of *adat* and Islam in Malay social organization. Significantly, though the word *adat* is derived from the Arab *'ada'*, meaning custom and tradition, it is clear that these sets of rules were referred by this Arabic term, only after the coming of Islam to the Malay Peninsula. An examination of the laws, however, showed that Islamic institutions or doctrines of law were not fully integrated into the Malay political and administrative system and could at best function as an alternative mode of reference and decision-making to specific matters which were not clearly or fully formulated in *adat*. However, as shown earlier, the conversion of the Melaka raja to Islam suggested that the religion had strong political and intellectual appeal to rulers who could now assert their authority in a new symbolic form by developing a mode of life similar to that of Muslim leaders elsewhere, and gracing the Court with an aura of cultural respectability and literary wisdom which was uncommon to many.

The processes of integration of Islamic law with *adat* was significantly revealed in subsequent compilations of Legal Digests from the fifteenth century to the period of British colonization in the nineteenth century (Hooker, 1970: 51-56). The period in which these digests were written and compiled coincided with the expansion and development of Malay states in the Peninsula and was possibly an attempt on the part of the sultans and members of their court to clarify the status of Malay kingship in relation to local customs and tradition.[4] These digests were simply variations along a theme of provisions and penalties that did not attempt to discriminate against women in any significant way other than ordering certain conditions of marriage and divorce according to Shafie Islam in a flexible form. Most provisions and penalties were based on *adat*. Hooker (1970: 56) noted that most of the text contained non-Islamic penalties for offences against public law or customary practice.

Hooker writing on *adat* law in Indonesia, explained these compromises in legislation in the following way:

> in the version of Islam introduced, there was a lack of the excessive legalism characteristic of Middle Eastern Islam, and the dominant missionary role was taken by Sufi mystics who were prepared to allow some accommodation between orthodoxy and indigenous religious beliefs (1978: 91).

This observation has been noted elsewhere. Peacock (1973) suggested that in the fourteenth century, Sufi orders could only venture into Southeast Asia via the ships of Muslim traders, so that clearly the association of Islam with trade, and trade with Islamic conversion was a fundamental characteristic of Southeast Asian Islam. For Malay elites (merchants, businessmen, members of the royal court and rulers) Islam was associated with wealth, progress, and power. The economic motive of conversion preceded any intellectual or ideological consideration. As explained by Reid (1984: 24), despite the popularity and prevalence of animism 'the spirits of the ancestors, the trees and the mountains did not travel easily'. Eventually, Islam and the Malay language became the manifest symbols of successful economics, a 'social system' for traders. For the masses, the way of Sufi mystics suited the 'heart and imagination' of Southeast Asian animists, with their ardent love for trance, dance, song and other ecstatic experiences. Peacock wrote:

> Sufis rejected the ossified dry, and torturously complex legal systems of the medieval Muslim scholastics . . . .. The simplicity of early Islam may have suited the tribal Arabs, but the Indonesians, like the Persians, the Chinese and the Indians, partook of a civilization already possessing complex cosmologies and ecstatic mysticism. Especially since the Sufis proved willing to syncretize their own teachings with the native ones, and also because the Sufi teachers boasted personal charisma and the power, to do magic and to heal, the Indonesians were receptive to their teachings (1973: 24).

The rapid Islamization of Southeast Asian trading ports was clearly associated with the rise of Muslim trade in the thirteenth and fourteenth centuries, when these centres became the seats of pioneer Malay governments seeking to consolidate military and economic power. That Melaka was eventually more successful than others could be a direct result of its ability within a short space of time to amass political and military control over eastern Sumatra and the Archipelago, which drew the interest and commitment of traders throughout the world. Indeed, at the height of Melaka's glory, Pires (1967: 263) recorded that it had four municipal *Syahbandar* (representatives of Mercantile Shipping and Trade) and one for every foreign trading group: one for the Gujeratis, the most important trading community; one for the Bengalis, Pegus and Pase (Parsi); one for the Javanese, Moluccans, Banda, Palembang; and one for the Chinese.. Every trader reported to the *Syahbandar* of his nation when he disembarked with cargo and merchandise. The volume of trade was so massive that it required official representation by country. However, contact with Muslim merchants at ports was not a sufficient explanation for Malay Islamization, for the sociocultural and psychological factors remain unexplained — 'reconciliation between long-held assumptions about the shape of the world and the control features of the new doctrine' (Reid, 1984: 15). The formalization of Islam in the Malay state had to tread carefully on this soft ground and it was for this reason that fundamental institutions of *adat* remained the main feature of Malay social life even when state laws later attempted to incorporate Islam more seriously.

Adat Perpatih and *Adat Temenggung*

In the Peninsula, from as early as the fifteenth century, *adat* law began to be differentiated by two guiding systems of administration known as *adat perpatih* and *adat temenggung*. While *adat perpatih* was based on a elaborate code of written law, derived from the Minangkabau principle of exogamous matriliny where women maintained control over rights of succession to land and other forms of immovable property, *adat temenggung* was more closely associated with existing rules of social organization of the Malay-speaking communities in Palembang, Sumatra. The latter set of *adat* was patrilineally structured in their provisions for Malay kingship, but in all other matters significantly bilateral, in principle and content. To date, Malay customary land law, which is an important component of Malay *adat*, gives recognition to the right of occupation and cultivation of land, regardless of gender or other kinship principles of ordering relationships according to age, seniority, or marital status. This right is regarded as transmissible from one generation to another and forms the basis of private land ownership and rules of land inheritance which precedes Islamic or *Syariah* law. In land inheritance, *adat temenggung* provides equal opportunities for men and women to control and inherit land, as long as the individual is actively involved in cultivation and economic production. The law also provides for property inheritance for social reasons and sentiments and is commonly utilized within the kinship and family order, particularly between mother and daughter, to ensure that land and other forms of immovable property can be given, in love and affection over other formal rules of inheritance based on principles of consanguinity and affinity.

The Minangkabau *adat perpatih* system has been studied and analysed extensively by both colonial and modern scholars of Malay culture even though it encompasses only the southwestern region of the state of Negeri Sembilan. However, people like Lister (1890), Parr and MaCray (1910), Caldecott (1912), Tylor (1929), Blagden (1930), and de Jong (1952), writing on the matrilineal system in Negeri Sembilan constantly stressed that it was only *pusaka* land (inherited; family land) which was usually kept in the *perut* (family) through the female line but that even so, within the *suku* or clan, considerable power was given to the mother's brother in the final distribution of *pusaka* land to the next generation of women. Today, with the rapid decline in the wandering *merantau* spirit of Minangkabau men (for example, due to unavailability of land elsewhere, stabilization of village life), *harta sepencarian* or property acquired during marriage is more often owned by men than women. Furthermore, Islamic law allows men to accumulate land more rapidly than women. In the context of land succession, the matrilineal system does not appear to protect the rights of women as effectively as before.

Tylor (1937: 3, 9), writing on *adat*, suggested that the Palembang *adat* land code in the Peninsula was very much influenced by *adat perpatih*, accounting for the fact that *tanah pusaka* or family land in areas outside Negeri Sembilan very often passed from mother to daughter rather than mother to sons and daughters. This argument has been questioned by Josselin de Jong (1952) who commented that it was difficult to ascertain whether *adat perpatih* preceded *adat temenggung* in the Peninsula, or indeed, if *adat temenggung* was introduced earlier and subsequently became influenced by Minangkabau principles of social organization. He (1952: 31-32) stated that 'the laws of the two contrasted territories had totally different histories, and we do not think it is justified to consider the *adat temenggung* (in its Peninsula sense), the *adat* of the Malays who were already settled in the Peninsula, and who did not come there via Sumatra, a 'decayed form of *adat perpatih*, the *adat* of the Minangkabau population which immigrated in Negeri Sembilan at a comparatively recent date'.[5] Part of the problem arose probably because writers like Tylor, Wilkinson, and Winstedt claimed that Minangkabau immigration into Negeri Sembilan had occurred as early as the fifteenth century, during the formation of the Sultanate of Melaka. If this was so, considering the location of Melaka next to Negeri Sembilan, and the early origins of *adat temenggung* in the former, it would be difficult to separate the spheres of influence of the two systems of *adat*, in place and in time. This diffusion of boundaries between *adat temenggung* and *adat perpatih* in early Melaka probably explained the coincidence of kingship patriliny, matrilateral filiation, and kinship bi-laterality in the development of the Malay social system in the fifteenth century.

As mentioned, the subsequent attempt to compile Legal Digests or *undang-undang* by the various states coincided with a concern that Islam should be integrated more closely into Malay social life although this process did not in any way lead to the displacement of *adat*. It was only in the regulation of rules of marriages and divorce that Islamic Shafie Law was effectively operationalized. In matters of land inheritance and proper-ty, the emphasis appeared to be on preserving customary Malay procedures of utilization, distribution and division, with Islamic law providing a source of formal consultation when conflicts arose amongst benefactors of the deceased. Generally, conformity to the formal ritual necessities of the religion seemed to be the policy of the day, where requirements of praying, food taboos, fasting and performances of the Haj were observed, while other social activities proceeded normally as before. Belief in supernatural entities, sorcery and witchcraft, for example, was an essential feature of Malay life, despite regular attempts made by the *ulama* and other religious specialists to prohibit activities relating to these beliefs (Skeat, 1900; Winstedt, 1929).

Significantly, it was only in the 1970s that animistic community rituals such as *lancang-kuning* (the sending off of spirits to distant lands), *pemuja pantai* (the 'worshipping' of spirits of the sea) and *semangat padi* (the 'rice souls' ritual) were gradually prohibited by the various states, subject to pressure from local religious authorities. Animistic beliefs, however, remained firmly retrenched in the Malays. On the personal level, animistic practices continued to be performed as before. Evidently Islam did not succeed in curbing animistic beliefs and rituals in most aspects of daily life. The appeal of Islam continued to be relevant in the public' sphere of activity while *adat* was essentially internalized in socialization as modes of social conduct deemed appropriate and necessary. The intuitive inter-nalizing of *adat* in social behaviour and socialization in fact contributed to Islam's prominence in the more formal public dimensions of social life.

The Language of *Adat* and Islam

Adat *as Metaphor*

Much of the Malay *adat* is metaphorically expressed in proverbial sayings (*peribahasa*), verse and quatrains (*pantun*) which transfer imageries of natural phenomena into cultural wisdoms and idealisms. The messages may denote sentiments for the village or nation, kinship, parental guidance, romantic love or passion, but cloaked in oblique references and ideas about social relationships and emotions, generally called *sindiran*, they are subtly provocative without being directly authoritive or offensive. The saying *Hujan mas di negeri orang, Hujan batu di negeri sendiri* ('Rains of gold in other countries, Rains of stone in one's own') does not in fact encourage a person to quit his land and seek his fortune elsewhere, but to tolerate hardships in his own country to preserve origins and maintain a sense of belonging. Again, the metaphor, *Ular bisa menyusor akar* ('The venomous snake glides over roots') does not refer to a situation of imminent danger, but a disguised reproach that a person with power or rank would not stand to lose much if he were to make himself amiable and approachable to the ordinary man.

Many of these sayings appear to encourage equality, humility, generosity and consideration for one's fellow men, particularly in situations where clear hierarchies and differences are discerned, as between ruler and subject, chiefs and followers. Thus, the proverbs *Setinggi-tinggi tupai melompat, akhirnya jatuh jua ke tanah* ('No matter how high the squirrel hops, it would in the end fall to the ground') and *Seperti resmi padi, makin berisi, makin tunduk* ('Like the habit of the padi stalk, the heavier it is filled with grain, the more it bends') express fundamental equalitarian values in Malay society. Others encourage self-reliance, initiative and wit. Some examples are *Malu bertanya, sesat jalan* ('Shy to ask, you will lose your way') and *Pikul beban raja di kepala; jangan lupa bungkus di tangan* ('When you carry the King's burden on your head, do not forget the bundle in your arm').

A Malay who attempts to check or correct another openly without 'sparing his words' as it were, would invariably be considered brutish or vulgar, expressed in statements like *tidak tahu adat* ('does not understand customs and traditions'), *tajam mulut* ('a mouth with a razor edge') and in extremely negative situations, *kurang ajar* ('without education and refinement'). Generally, much of *adat* is expressed in metaphorical concepts and idiomatic sayings into which the Malays are intuitively tuned. It is perhaps for this reason that quatrains are popular, for the media of poetry, music and song it utilizes converts normally difficult and tense interpersonal situations into tolerable encounters which are then more easily handled on the personal level. The following *pantun* expresses the disguised passions of a tormented lover;

Berapa tinggi pucuk pisang
Tinggi lagi asap api
Berapa tinggi gunung melintang
Tinggi lagi harap hati

However high grow the shoots of plaintain
Higher still goes the smoke of fire
However high stands the mountain summit
Higher still the hope in my heart

The sentiments revealed are expressive of Malay notions of courtship which are coveted rather than open, provocative rather than revealing, and cautious rather than reckless. It calls for a statement of decisiveness without being forward to the extreme and the reaction is similarly studied and hesitant less spontaneity be mistaken for wantonness. Consider the next quatrain:

Kalau jumpa jarum patah
Bawa disimpan di dalam peti
Kalau kata-kata saya salah
Harap jangan disimpan di dalam hati

If a broken needle is found
Keep it in a safe chest
If I have uttered words too harsh
Do not keep it in your heart

It is these subtle revelations of morality, values and sentiments that made earlier British writers on Malay culture, like Winstedt, Swettenham and Wilkinson, rave about the refinements of *adat* and refer to its metaphoric translations as the 'odes and sonnets' of the East.

Minangkabau Malays, who are guided by *adat perpatih*, based on matriliny, have an extensive media of free verse which reveals most of the fundamental ideas of relationships within such a system. These are ritually recalled during marriage and other ceremonial events and are spontaneously recited by male and female elders when explanations of the nature of consanguinal and affinal relationships have to be made. The following verse (originally translated by Sir Andrew Caldwell, Resident of Negeri Sembilan) is representative of the free style adopted by the Minangkabaus to explain spouse relationships;

When we receive a man as a bridegroom
If he is strong, he shall be our champion.
If a fool, he will be ordered about
To invite guests distant and collect guests near;
Clever and we'll invite his counsel;
Learned and we'll ask his prayers;
Rich and we'll use his gold;
If lame, he shall rear chicken,

If blind, he shall pound the mortar,
If deaf, he shall fire the salutes,
When you enter a byre, low;
When you enter a goat's pen, bleat;
When you tread the soil of a country and live beneath its sky;
Follow the customs of that country . . .

Again, the media of expression encourages conformity without offence and renders informal acceptability to fundamental values and norms which are preserved by the society.

A Malay when asked to define *adat* will usually reply that everything is *adat*, indicating the superficiality of the question. Indeed, to be 'a Malay' is to have *adat*. It encompasses the total system of values, norms and mores which govern Malay life or which contribute to the essence of Malay culture. It also refers to the code of morality which encompasses Malay social relations particularly that pertaining to the family, kinship and village community. The Malay proverb *Biar mati anak, jangan mati adat* ('Better a child perish, rather than our custom die'), denotes the overriding importance attached to the continuity of *adat* principles in Malay society.

Islam in Ritual Language

The Islamization of the Malays has resulted in many different kinds of standard conventional statements (derived from Arabic) being regarded as important in Malay ritual language. These greetings or messages in fact have been universally adopted by most Muslim communities, to a greater or lesser extent, and have in many cases superseded similar words and expressions in the local languages and dialects. Amongst the Malays, greetings like *As-salam 'alaikum warahmatullah hi wabarakatuh* (God be with you), *Insya'allah* (God willing) and *Syukur Al-ham dulillah* (Praise be to God) are commonly used in both formal and informal gatherings or meetings, on a group or personal level, and have come to be regarded as 'cultural' or polite ways of social interaction. The frequent or over usage of these terms in public speaking may be regarded as affectations of language and style but in a ritual situation, such as 'the seeking out of a bride' (*menengok*), proposal for marriage (*meminang*) or wedding (*akad nikah*), these expressions become an integral aspect of the esoterisms of Malay ritual language. One may rave about the beauty of a maiden through Malay poetic language or verse (*peribahasa*) but it is also equally acceptable to do so through Arabic expressions and semantics that convey notions or ideas of different kinds of social relationships and how they should work. This implies that to understand Malay morality or ideology, one would need to have a proper understanding of Malay imagery or metaphorical language from Sanskrit, Persian or Arabic sources.

Often, values of *adat* are equated with Islamic notions of social behaviour, and when this happens, *adat* expressions are incorporated into Islamic social philosophy to emphasize some of its finer points. To illustrate, the notion in Islam that the mother and child relationship is extremely important for spiritual and mental development is elucidated by the saying in *adat*, *syurga itu di tapak kaki ibu* ('heaven lies at the sole of the feet of the mother'). This expression is now often used to reiterate some ideas in Islam on the importance of motherhood and of children's loyalty to their parents.

In the context of rituals of sorcery, love and magic, healing and curing, derived from Indic and animistic ideas of the cosmology or of man's relationship with the cosmic verses from the Qur'an are often added on to charms and spells, usually as opening or closing statements. Consider the following spell for 'capturing' a person's soul:

Bismillahi 'al-rahmani'I-rahimi
Nur Mani nama engkau
Panca Awal nama aku
Kabul berkat aku memakai do'a
Kundang Maya Cinta Berahi,
Bercinta 'kau kepada aku,
Berahi 'kau kepada aku,
Gila 'kau kepada aku,
Gila siang, gila malam,
Gila tujuh kali sehari,
Gila tujuh kali semalam,
Pulang lah ke rumah engkau,
Pulang lah ke istana engkau,
Dengan berkat la-ilaha-illa-'llah Muhammad 'a Rasul Allah.'

In the name of God, the Merciful and Compassionate
Your name is Nur Mani
Si Panca Awal is my name
These prayers will be granted,
I wear the charm
Of the passionate Love, Kundang Maya
You will love me
You will be mad for me
Madness in the day, madness in the night
Mad, seven times a day
Mad, seven times a night
Return to your home
Return to your palace

*Granted with the blessings of the one God, Allah, and
Muhammad, the messenger of God.*

Significantly, the inclusion of Qur'anic verses in animistic charms and spells provides shamans and healers with continued legitimacy to practise their professions. It also extends their acceptability amongst a clientele that is conscious of differences between animistic ideas and the monotheism of Islam. However, the fact that Islam did not displace animistic forms of healing and curing but rather contributed to their value and credibility is evidence of the denuded impact it had on pre-existing ideologies. It became first and foremost a symbol of legitimacy and authority for state formation and formal leadership. Its attack on animism succeeded only on the level of public activity when witchcraft and sorcery so openly defied Islamic religious teachings. Even so, witchcraft, sorcery and shamanism continued to thrive in villages and towns and resurfaced whenever the need arose (Karim, 1990). Islamic idealisms on the supremacy of God, creation of man and the universe had no practical appeal to the Malays, yet its esoteric quality enabled it to penetrate the existing ritual sphere without changing much of the original form.

Malay Social Relations in *Adat* and Islam

Development of the Village and Social Groupings

In the Peninsula, Malay villages were customarily formed by pioneers who cleared land in a particular area and eventually established propriety rights over the cleared land. A pioneer could maintain customary rights over land, as long as it was cleared and utilized for rice cultivation (*bendang, sawah*), mixed cropping (*ladang*) or fruit cultivation (*dusun*), but once it was left unattended and became secondary forest (*belukar*), any other family could have access to the land. It was important for these pioneering families to consolidate labour to maintain food production over the long term and indirectly to preserve customary land rights over a certain territory. During this early stage in the formation of a village, it was important for pioneers to obtain the assistance of others to open up the land, and it became a regular practice for earlier Malay settlers to draw upon families from their own place of origin within the Peninsula (Gullick, 1984:3).

According to Gullick (1984), these pioneers could attract further settlers only if they could show some financial or economic reward. A village headman with entrepreneurial spirit had to attract men and women with money or cash advancements. Alternatively, he had to attract a Malay entrepreneur to do this burdensome task by loaning him money. Gullick provides a description of the task of opening a Malay village:

The first three years was the period of their greatest need. Unless you have seen it the sheer desolation of small areas of land recently cleared by manual labour is difficult to visualize. The land, uneven, undrained, strewn with half-burnt trunks and large branches of felled trees. Here and there a rickety shanty of palm thatch and poles. The settlers arrived penniless and they would not garner their first crops until the end of the season — like the Pilgrim Fathers at their first Thanksgiving in Massachusetts (1984: 3).

The more recently settled immigrants of the Peninsula from neighbouring Indonesian islands would draw upon kinsmen from their village of origin in Indonesia. A cluster of homesteads, comprising a few nuclear families who were consanguinally or affinally linked to one another, formed the foundation of a new Malay village, with the first pioneer as the village headman (*penghulu, ketua*).[6]

As the population grew, a village founder could extend his jurisdiction over a wider territory and could eventually establish himself as an *Orang Besar* or territorial chief, enabling each cluster of families to appoint a *ketua or* headman. Expansion of village boundaries eventually led to segmentation of the core kinship unit. The optimum size of the village depended on the availability of land and physical accessibility to river transportation or road. Hence the villages were kept small, not exceeding fifty households or so (Map III). The average village comprised twenty households or more and a populace averaging around a hundred (Maxwell, 1884).

Though small, nucleated settlements were often characteristic of Malay villages which were newly established, dispersed settlements, adopting a linear pattern along the coast or riverine areas were not uncommon. Hill (1977: 135) stated that dispersed settlements were found in Melaka and Negeri Sembilan in the late nineteenth century, and would have been the characteristic of the settlement patterns along valleys and rivers in other parts of the Peninsula. However, he concluded, that dispersed settlements often assumed the form of nucleated villages at some stage in their development; 'The pattern of dwellings dispersed over flat land, with a thickening of settlement into a hamlet or village here and there . . .' (p 135). Nucleation of settlements within a confined riverine area., usually the mouth of a river or spread along natural transportation lines, continue to be two characteristic settlement patterns of the Malays today.[7]

It is significant that the pioneering family (*keluarga asal*), to which belonged either a *ketua/penghulu* or a *Orang Besar*, was usually in a position to utilize to its advantage institutions like forced labour, slavery or debt-bondage particularly with respect to the more recent settlers who were dependent on its services and patronage.[8] However, this, as explained earlier, clearly depended on the extent to which they recognized and maintained the system of moral reciprocity which so strongly ordered *adat* relations between the headman/chief and the rest of the villagers. Events

Map III: Development of Malay Villages and Domestic Groupings

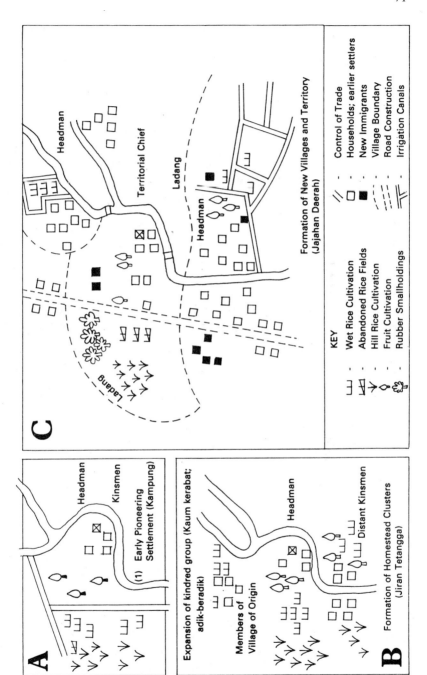

A

Headman

Kinsmen

(1) Early Pioneering Settlement (Kampung)

B

Expansion of kindred group (Kaum kerabat; adik-beradik)

Members of Village of Origin

Headman

Distant Kinsmen

Formation of Homestead Clusters (Jiran Tetangga)

C

Headman

Territorial Chief

Ladang

Headman

Ladang

Formation of New Villages and Territory (Jajahan Daerah)

KEY

	Wet Rice Cultivation
	Abandoned Rice Fields
	Hill Rice Cultivation
	Fruit Cultivation
	Rubber Smallholdings

	Control of Trade
	Households; earlier settlers
	New Immigrants
	Village Boundary
	Road Construction
	Irrigation Canals

during this period in Malay colonial history revealed that Malay families freely left villages to settle elsewhere when they considered the oppression from the village headman or chief to be no longer tolerable.

Development of Malay Villages and Domestic Groupings

Likewise, there was also a high rate of abscondence of slaves or debt-bonders from landed families who made undue demands on their labour. The impact of these institutions of slavery and debt-bondage on the Malay family and kinship structure has been the subject of much discussion in recent works on Malay history, but most of these works focussed on Perak, which achieved stability in settlement pattern and cultivation only in the late nineteenth century. Feuds between chiefs over tin rights, debt-bondsmen and slaves were fanned by the British who eventually succeeded in controlling the administration of the state in 1877. Accounts of feudal class elements in the Malay family and kinship system in Perak are contradictory to *adat* rules of family and kinship organization but this could have been a specific feature of late nineteenth-century Perak society, necessitating some caution in generalization. Even so, a review of some of these new arguments is necessary, considering its relevance to this study.

Slavery, Debt-bondage and the Control over Labour

Recent publications of Malay cultural history have given importance to class analysis where interpretations of inequality and social differentiation have been based on the principles of ordering labour within the kinship and family order.[9] Sullivan (1982), in his study of nineteenth century Perak, discussed the relationship between debt-slavery (*hamba hutang*) and Malay social organization. He wrote that even in the late nineteenth century, Malay families were not autonomous as had been assumed because of the rampant practice of slavery (*hamba abdi*) and debt-slavery (*hamba hutang*). The former involved minority groups of *Orang Asli* (Malayan Aborigines), Bataks, Banjarese, and other Indonesians captured during wars, raids and feats of piracy and consequently sold or auctioned off to local *Orang Besar* and raja. On the other hand, the majority of the debt-slaves or *hamba hutang* were Malays who in one way or another found themselves in positions of debt-bondage to a chief or an influential local personality.

It is undeniable that in the nineteenth-century Malaya, it was a standard practice for the *Orang Besar* to draw upon the labour of men and women who were directly indebted to him for land, food, protection and shelter. These usually comprised families who cleared land (which had been claimed by the *Orang Besar* as part of his territory) for agricultural production and in return offered their labour to show their indebtedness.[10]

The *Orang Besar* also indirectly accumulated labour from those who had been 'mortgaged' or sold to him by other *Orang Besar* to settle debts of war.[11] Quite often, the *Orang Besar* would take women from these households as his secondary wives or concubines (*gundik*) or personal servants (*orang pesuruh rumah*) with the men acting as warriors (*hulubalang*), informants or spies (*tali barut*).

In other circumstances, however, men attempted to escape a tyrannical chief who constantly subjected them to forced labour (*kerah*) by throwing themselves at the mercy of another chief, noted for his benevolence and righteous behaviour.[12] Such a chief drew upon the services of these men and their family members by engaging them as warriors or domestic help. However, the arrangement was usually based on an ordered system of moral relations in which both parties had to demonstrate values of mutual gratitude (*budi bahasa*), loyalty (*kejujuran*), righteousness (*keadilan*), mutual consideration (*timbang rasa*) and a sense of compromise (*tolak ansur*). The power of an *Orang Besar* was invariably determined by his command over labour so that it was important for him to maintain these relationships with his debt-slaves in a form which was most socially acceptable. This delicate balance of power and control between the chief and his followers, based on compromise, mutual consideration and the need to reciprocate a good deed, has indeed been underplayed by Sullivan in his analysis of social relations in nineteenth-century Perak.

Accordingly, Sullivan suggested that in the nineteenth century, taking Perak as an example, state formation was in a process of transition from kin-based to class-based power relations for the providence of debt slavery enabled powerful individuals, exemplified in the *Orang Besar* and the raja to control the most dominant mode of production, which was then labour. He argued (p.xx) that 'the establishment of wide quasi-kin groups based on debt-slavery should be conceived of as a social class, for this was the most important institution which led to the development of social hierarchies within the Malay political order'.

What exactly was the form and modus operandi of these quasi-kin groups which were supposed to exist in the nineteenth century? An examination of these processes of social formation of kinship groupings in the nineteenth century shows radical differences between the household or *kelamin* structure of aristocrat and royal families and those of the peasantry. The households of chiefs comprised 'compound families' since they were usually polygamous (Bird, 1967: 327; Hamdan 1967: 5). They included the wife or wives of the chief and their children, families of domestic servants (*pesuruh rumah*), personal maids and companions of the wives of the chief and their daughters (*dayang*), personal companions or mother surrogate to the daughters (*Mak Inang*), household guards, warriors or soldiers (*hulubalang*) and, occasionally, some bought slaves (*hamba abdi*).

Other *kelamin* who were in debt-bondage to the chief did not form part of this household but maintained their own homesteads in the neighbourhood. Thus, households of the *Orang Besar* were disproportionately large in comparison to the regular Malay household and comprised normally about one-tenth of the total population of the village. The majority of Malay households remained autonomous nuclear family units.

A review of some of these earlier descriptions of the social organization of the Malays derived from sources of Malay cultural history, such as the *Malay Annals* and other literary narrations of social biographies of Malay warriors, heros and heroines, confirm that the extended household structure comprising a core family unit, close kinsmen and servants was obvious from the formation of the Melaka Kingdom in the fifteenth century. Descriptions of the family organization of the *bendahara*, adviser to the raja or sultan, point to the same pattern of quasi-kinship grouping. The family of *Dato Bendahara* Seri Wak Raja, adviser to Sultan Abu Sahid (Raja Ibrahim) of Melaka and father of Tun Kudu, included amongst others, also adoptive kinsmen and orphans who had lost their parents in wars (*Malay Annals*). It was also regular for affines, male and female, to accompany their spouses so that such families were normally extended and compound, comprising at least three generations. Till the late nineteenth century, this form of family grouping was a stable kinship and family unit which thrived through the labour of men and women from poorer families or poorer kinsmen.[13]

The important question to raise here is whether the system of creating quasi-kin groupings implied that the earlier Malay family was not an autonomous social unit with its own rules of organization. Indeed, Sullivan (1982) mentioned that the Malay family extended into a system of enslavement where men were converted to labourers and women to prostitutes. He concluded (p.69) that 'debt-slavery was an important institution determining the economy of the Malay states until the late nineteenth century when the British abolished the system and debt-slaves were converted to peasant free-holders, tenant farmers and free wage labourers'.

Sullivan's speculations on the politics of social relations in nineteenth-century Perak is an attempt not only to elucidate the underlying structural instabilities in the Malay social system, but also to reconceptualize indigenous institutions of dependence in terms of modern Western concepts/ideas of class and political ideology. While this exercise may be warranted in the light of trends of rethinking of the cultural histories of pre-colonial states in the Third World, it is apparent that some of his basic assumptions about Malay kinship and household unit contains inherent conceptual fallacies. First the household structures of elite families have to be differentiated from the ordinary. The majority of the Malay families were not absorbed into the households of the rich and powerful, even in the nineteenth century Perak. Gullick (1984) observed the calculated entrepreneurial spirit of the Malays — they could work for money or they could run. Secondly, the *adat* system of kinship grouping based on ego-centred kindred expressed rules of complementarity and interdependency, bound by notions of *budi-jasa* (mutual indebtedness and obligations), *tolong-menolong* (mutual help) and *tukar-menukar* (reciprocal exchange). Just as individuals were bound by these rules of social organization in an interpersonal way, so were members of a household intertwined by these moral values. In an elitist household, various forms of indebtedness and reciprocity ordered relationships amongst unequals. The relationships between an *Orang Besar* and members of his household, his kinsmen and his bondsmen were also bound by these same principles of moral reciprocity so that even when tyranny or despotism was shown, it could not last long. The *Orang Besar* without popular support from kinsmen and bondsmen rarely managed to retain their positions of power, making them vulnerable to attacks from others who harboured ambitions to take over their privileged position in the village.

Thirdly, Sullivan provides a very rigid, immobile image of Malay cultural history in the nineteenth century. His argument that the social system of enslavement through quasi-kinship groupings did not provide channels for alternative forms of decision and behaviour is factually inaccurate for records show population mobility between states and between villages to escape wars, *kerah* and debt-slavery (Bird, 1967: 149). The followers of a fallen chief were encouraged to flee, to escape harassment from unknown marauders and simultaneously to establish allegiance with other *Orang Besar* or men of wealth and influence. In the early period of the nineteenth century in Perak, it was reported that the Sultan of Perak complained that 80 per cent of his people had fled to another chief.[14] Khoo (1972), Innes (1974), writing about debt-slavery in Selangor and Perak, described how chiefs constantly lost their debt-slaves and made appeals to the British Residents to retrieve them.

The wars between Perak chiefs in the latter half of the century in connection with the development of mining considerably weakened their ability to sustain their following and villagers fled into other territories to ally themselves with new leaders. Sir Hugh Low, as the British Resident of Perak in 1877, finally attempted to curb the power of the *Orang Besar* by abolishing 'slavery' — reducing their power to control, organize and amass labour.

It was frequently recorded that escape (*cabut*), running amok (Malay *amuk, mengamuk*) or establishing new allegiances were customary alternatives for the Malay to avoid political oppression of harassment.[15] Gullicks's work on the indigenous political systems of Peninsular Malaya may be currently questioned in the light of the static structural-functional approach utilized, but even so, he did admit more mobility and flexibility in Malay grassroots politics than Sullivan. Though he adopted a holistic mode of analysis which portrayed greater internal social stability than that assumed in this period of political turmoil, he appeared to show greater sensitivity and understanding of Malay social and political values. To quote Gullick:

> A chief had to hold and if possible to increase the population of his district. . . . It was by no means inevitable that the population of his district would remain or increase. If he oppressed them unduly or failed to protect them against marauders, the people would flee away and settle elsewhere . . . In some societies, land is scarce or has a special value so that a ruler who can allot land may be sure of attracting and holding subjects by that means. Where land is not a scarce commodity however, and this was the case in the Malay states, political power, even though it is exercised in respect to defined territorial areas, is based on control of people (1965: 113).

This statement has been upheld by other writers on Malay rural life in the nineteenth century. Isabella Bird in 1879 commented that nucleated villages were rare. Settlements were loosely scattered with small clusters of households surrounding the homes of pioneers of the area. These pioneers were usually the local *Orang Besar* or *Orang Kaya* of a particular area. However, as Maxwell (1884) stated, territories were not mapped by formal boundaries of ownership. Proprietor rights over land was created by the clearing of land followed by continuous occupation. Thus, although control over labour was crucial for pioneering individuals to extend political power, it did not necessarily imply that they had absolute control over manpower even with institutions like debt-slavery and corvee operating actively. These institutions contributed to population mobility, dispersed settlements, *ad hoc* utilization of land and agricultural production. The nucleation of settlements, following the formalization of state, district and village boundaries through charting and the issuing of land titles, accelerated the sedentarization of the Malay populations and gradually transferred the emphasis from labour to land. This probably had the effect of solidifying kinship groups, in the sense that kinsmen and affines became an important basis for labour recruitment and exchange within the confinements of the domestic group.

Fourthly, it is also apparent from early historical records documented by British European historians and writers that clear semantic distinctions between the institutions of slavery and debt-slavery were not always made. The term 'slavery' was used by British officials in Malaya in the nineteenth century as a standard given reference to include all men and women who were providing regular services to the *Orang Besar* and raja. These men and women were not 'owned' like 'cattles and elephants' and maintained their own homesteads. They also handled and carried weapons and were not very responsive to demands for forced labour. Some writers, like Innes, referred to the majority of Malay commoners as 'savages', which she found to be synonymous to 'slaves'. In the same light, she named the children of such women as 'slave children' and the servants of such households (*orang pesuruh rumah*) as 'slave girls'. It is in the context of such references that writers like Innes found it hard to resolve seeming contradictions between the status and behaviour of such men and women who generally adopted a free and open manner. The followers of Tunku Dia Udin, the son-in-law of the Sultan of Selangor, she complained (1974: 177) did not behave as attendants or as slaves for 'they did not do a stroke of work and were occupied with covering themselves with krises and other weapons and lie about in the shade of the house, or swagger down to the bazaar'. It was probably in the light of such references that Sullivan (p. 69) reported that 'three-quarters of the population of Perak were in debt-slavery in the late nineteenth century'.[16]

Accounts of debt-slavery by other authors reveal the same loose application of the term to include all those who were part of the royal or chiefly household and who were not kinsmen or affines of the raja or chief. Bird (1967: 325) referred to all men, women, children and infants who form the entourage of raja and chiefs as 'slave', 'slave-women', and 'slave-children'. Hence, it is extremely difficult to discern between 'slaves' in the more conventional sense and 'debt-bondsmen' or 'servants'. The rate of population mobility appears to be extremely high in this period and is possibly attributed to wars and/or debt-slavery. Thus, it may be possible to say that the kind of permanence said to exist in the control over labour (both forced labour and debt-bondage), supporters or followers has been significantly overemphasized by writers on Malayan history. Bird noted that Melaka in 1883 had a population of 67,000 Malays but that this number was continuously increasing from the influx of refugees or fugitives from neighbouring states. Aminuddin Baki (1983) mentioned the differences between slavery in the American colonies and in Malaya by noting that approximately half of the slaves in Perak in 1879 were bondsmen (1,380 of which 652 were women). He wrote (p. 23) in the eyes of the Malay public, debt-slaves were still free men (*orang mardahika*) who could 'transfer his allegiance to another master provided the new one would pay the amount owed to the previous owner'. Swettenham (1942: 52-53) said that despite the prevalence of debt-slavery in Perak, a man or woman would not submit to hard labour without resentment. In men, this very often surfaced in amok.

The proportion of slaves or debt-slaves in the free population varied from state to state, and records clearly showed Perak to have the highest number of bonded men and women, this group being hardly discerned in Melaka. Winstedt (1969: 73) noted in his personal records that in 1874 in Perak, one person in every sixteen was a slave or bondsman making the percentage to be 6.25. In a census conducted in 1879 by Hugh Low, Resident of Perak, a total of 47,359 was enumerated for the free native Malay population. The number of slaves was returned at 1,670, of whom 775 were males and 895 females. Slave-debtors amounted to 1,380, with 728 males and 652 females. In all, of a total population of 50,409, 3,050 (6.05 per cent) were bonded or enslaved, a percentage significantly different from that accounted by Sullivan in the state at the same period. Nevertheless, Hugh Low admitted the number of slaves or debt-bonders to be marginally higher since returns were not made by the 'Regent of Perak and one or two chiefs'. His general comment on slavery is worth noting:

> I cannot undertake to say what may have been the practice in former times, as to the treatment in Perak, of this class of persons, but no case of cruelty or any great hardship has been brought to my notice since I came into the country. By far, the larger number of the slave debtors live with their families apart and often at great distances from their masters, enjoying all the fruits of their labour, rendering occasional assistance to them when called upon to do so, which, in the majority of cases, is of rare occurrence (1878: ii).

Generally, it appears that despite the prevalence of institutions of debt-bondage and slavery, the Malay family was able to maintain a degree of autonomy and independence in the affairs of their daily lives. The notion of 'quasi-kinship groups' as dominating the social order in Perak in the nineteenth century stems from obscure generalizations (both in terms of statistics and terminological interpretations) made of the situation of slavery and debt-bondage in the state. Furthermore, the situation in Perak was not representative of the conditions in the other states in Malaya, so that it is even more inaccurate to apply the general argument of slavery upon the rest of the Malay population.

The Moral Polity

What, then, was the nature of the relationship between the Malay peasantry and local chiefs, and how did this code of behaviour reflect rules of Malay *adat*? Generally, the indigenous political system was derived from basic principles of morality which defined all forms of relationship contained in *adat*. In leader and follower relationships, this may be defined through the 'moral polity' — the system of determining behaviour which is regarded to be socially acceptable within a period of time, between leaders and followers (and ultimately, the king and his subjects), either according to a written doctrine or informal unwritten principles of conduct. It expresses salient rules of social conduct in power relations which provide acceptable patterns and expressions of leadership. When this notion of moral conduct is applied at a higher level of analysis, it expresses the balance of relationships between the king and his subjects.

Adat Values in Relationships between Chiefs or Petty Chiefs and Their Followers

The Malay chief who controlled the sphere of political relations within the Malay peasantry, may have had the powers legitimized by the raja or sultan but his powers were ultimately defined by the villagers, who could choose to either support or reject him, depending on his own treatment of them. Thus, his powers were operationalized by certain codes of acceptability, defined by the peasant polity. The raja, on the other hand, did not have to be dependent on codes of conduct developed by the peasant polity. He could create elaborate symbolic rituals of hierarchy, separation and distance that gave an image of a centralized state system which was acceptable to the chiefs because they could, at this level, be included in it. However, the raja's notion of centralized power, extended through the sultanate, reached the peasantry only in a symbolic (or a number of symbolic) ritualistic ways. People at the grassroots were generally unconcerned with symbolic social hierarchies since these did not affect social conduct and political behaviour in interpersonal terms.

The notion of the ruling class as omnipotent and generally unconcerned (Chandra Muzaffar, 1979; Shaharuddin Maaruf, 1984) is true only in the sense that the kingship system created highly ritualistic barriers of separation of power. Yet, they still had to use their chiefs and ambassadors to win over the people. They had to remain popular and approachable to retain their position. Whatever the interests and motives of the chiefs, the fact remained that the people did not offer loyalty through fear, blind subservience and humility (Gullick, 1984). Leaders had to earn it and the *adat* of moral relations amongst unequals formed the basis of this politics. There were many contenders and potential rival contenders from which to choose, to transfer gratitude and indebtednes. Consider Wilkinson's perceptive observation of the emerging Malay state in the nineteenth century:

> In theory the Sultan was omnipotent; in practice, he knew the limitations of his power. For his authority and even more for his own safety, he was

dependent on the forebearance of his people and the loyalty of his chiefs
. . . In any case, history made it quite clear to every Malay prince that he
could not afford to be too unpopular. Still less could the great vassal chiefs
be indifferent to the feelings of their own followers. Having to hold their
own against the jealousies of their neighbours and the exactions of their
suzerains, the chiefs dared not allow their districts to become impoverished,
depopulated or disaffected (1971: 36).

Indeed, the sense of powerlessness of Malay rulers over their subjects
and the system of identifying leadership by persons rather than office
appears to be typical of a number of Southeast Asian political systems as
shown in Siegel's study of politics in Acheh (1969) and Kiefer's study of
Tausug politics in southern Philippines (1972). Kiefer (p.109) explains the
sultan's limited powers in the notion of the 'segmentary state' where a
centralized government exists, with 'peripherals points over which the
centre has little control'. Hence, in the Tausug state, power was more fully
concentrated at the bottom of the system where it was ordered through
the reciprocity of *buddi* or *budi*. This is a typical feature of Southeast Asian
bilaterality in politics and social relations, where the ordering of relationships among unequals is constantly guided by principles of moral reciprocity which balances needs and services between leaders and followers.

Although Malay chiefs frequently attempted to ally with royal patrilineages, it was in reality necessary for commoners to compete with one
another to demonstrate the right personal qualities of leadership. Titles
like *Orang Besar* ('big man'), *Orang Kaya* ('rich man') and *pendekar* (warrior)
were granted by the sultan to individuals after they had established
considerable power through a display of wealth, popularity, bravery or
skill in the martial arts, mystical or magical feats, etc. (Shaharuddin Maaruf,
1984; Razha Rashid, 1990). Personal qualities such as generosity, benevolence, charismatic appeal, cunning and oratory appeal brought a person
mass popularity and fame, and provided the basis for informal leadership
which could be given formal acknowledgement by a sultan concerned
with maintaining close linkages with the peasantry. On a lower level, petty
chiefs in the form of village headmen had to demonstrate the same qualities
of leadership (Razha Rashid, 1990). The term for these chiefs, *penghulu* or
ketua kampung, literally he who leads or 'heads', expressed a fairly simplistic
notion of a popular leader with a following.

It was also vital for an *Orang Besar* or a *penghulu* to gather his kinsmen,
affines and friends as loyal supporters by granting personal favours or
budi which bound them into further ties of obligation (*berjasa*). The *berbudi
berjasa* system of extending favours and obligations created a kind of moral
reciprocity which was ultimately the most effective base for popular
leadership within Malay society. Indeed, it maintains itself even in the

modern political party system when politicians grant favours and titles to supporters, often on a personal basis, for their loyalty and support during an electoral campaign or party election. The *berbudi berjasa* system of moral relations continues to transcend all forms of interpersonal interaction amongst the Malays in village or urban life. Other traditional values, such as a sense of sensitivity and consideration for the problems of the peasantry (*timbang rasa*) and a sense of justice or righteousness for those who had been wronged (*keadilan*) were also crucial for maintaining the leader and follower relationship. Other than being a good fighter or strategist, such a leader had to exhibit personal qualities that expressed gentle patronage and a strong code of personal ethics. For this reason, at the grassroots, the leader and follower of a political unit was limited in size, encompassing individuals who were in contact with the leader personally and who were bound in the web of social relationships maintained by the leaders and his close associates (Razha Rashid, 1990). Despite the existence of a kingship system which emphasized centralized power and formal political hierarchies, the only kind of politics which was operationally possible was one which utilized some of these egalitarian rules.

Generally, the 'centralized state system' was only a political concept recognized by members of the aristocracy and the colonial administrators who were concerned with imposing common rules over the population. The population conceptualized the sultanate as a court rather than *a system of government* while the sultan believed that his system of government determined the political affairs of the peasantry.[17] Hierarchy was the formal code of separation but symmetry the practical rule of inclusion. As mentioned earlier, the constant display of pomp and alacrity through theatrical entertainment techniques gave the king the symbolic value of a 'cultural maker'. He was a supreme head with a remarkable genealogy. He was a mystical leader with divine and profane qualities. Ritual symbols exaggerated differences of prestige and power. However, despite these codes of separation, the people worked more easily with those with whom they were familiar and with those who were approachable. This political relationship implies that it is erroneous to assume that the king and subject as components of a state had a sense of 'social cohesion' as perceived by Gullick (1965), or that the ruler and subject relationship was one 'of the most intimate nature' as described by Milner (1982). A structure was created when increasing alienation from the state rendered it greater stability. The people were mainly involved in political events which immediately concerned them. This gave the appearance of support and approval for an autocratic order. In reality, the state system was ideologically separated and isolated from the indigenous leader and his followers. The only common social denominator between the ruler and his subjects were chieftains who utilized both the state system and the local moral polity to their advantage to maintain their 'status quo'.

Generally it appeared that Malay chiefs were mediators between spheres of power defined by the peasant and kingship order. They sought to be included within the class of rulers by accepting prestigious titles and 'letters of authority' (*surat kuasa*) from the kings while simultaneously accepting the informal codes of popular leadership upheld by the peasantry. The prevailing political order was based on ideologically opposing notions of power-egalitarian and personalized and conversely, hierarchical and ritualized. Both forms were capable of co-existing as long as the codes of moral conduct between leader and follower or king and subject were not confused for each other. To reflect, the principle of symbolic mediation between egocentric and patrilineal modes of ordering power relationships had parallel similarities with the *bendahara* and king relationship in the fifteenth century Melaka.

British support for the sultans gave them patronage and eventually control over the Peninsula. Under British rule, the state boundaries were formally institutionalized into kingships or sultanates while the Straits Settlements became governorships directly administered by the colonial office in India. British rule in the Peninsula also formalized district (*daerah*) boundaries within the states. Districts were further subdivided into sub-districts (*mukim*) which comprised a conglomeration of villages but the boundaries of these villages and hence the *mukim* were not clearly defined since village chiefs (*penghulu*) were constantly trying to extend their authority beyond the physical limits of settlements over which they had control.[18] This gave rise to considerable discrepancies between physical village boundaries and the limits of human settlement and utilization of land within an area. Towards the end of the nineteenth century, the British increased their development of the infrastructure of the Peninsula to exploit Malaya's natural resources more effectively and simultaneously directed their efforts at issuing land titles to British entrepreneurs. As a consequence, district and sub-district boundaries were officially surveyed and mapped and it became increasingly difficult for village chiefs to stake their claims over labour, land and natural resources beyond the physical boundaries of their own villages. In this way, British colonization in Malaya established limits on the political strategies of Malay village chiefs.

The process of concretization of formal kingships and states under British domination, in a sense, was passed unnoticed by the more recent Bugis and Rhio pioneers who roamed the countryside in bands, staking their claims over existing settlements and resources. Generally, the leaders of these bands challenged the authority of the earlier pioneers of the area who had established links with local rulers. Their authority was embodied in the *surat kuasa* granted by the ruler that they had absolute powers to rule the territory as they so wished, provided they collected taxes and paid homage to him (Gullick, 1958). However, since the powers of the existing chiefs were dependent on the strength of their following, in reality anyone who could amass enough support from the villagers could gain favour and formal recognition as a *penghulu* and, eventually, a chief. This implied that the ultimate legitimization of his authority depended firstly on popular support. Rulers were obliged to accept the power base that evolved through popular support, by handing out these 'letters of authority', which served to legitimize power in symbolic rather than in physical terms, to whoever established control over a certain territory at a particular time. Consequently, factions regularly developed in the village between loyalists and dissidents of established chieftaincy.

Dissidents regularly allied themselves to other influential men when they felt that they could obtain more benefits in material or social terms from a new leader or when the chief they supported developed despotic ways which contravened the acceptable codes of behaviour between leader and follower. Despotism was mainly resented when followers themselves were subject to corvee or forced labour (*kerah*), debt-slavery (*hamba hutang*), and concubinage (*mengambil gundik*).[19] Various options were open to individuals and families who suffered directly or indirectly from these practices. They could flee or run amok for instance but these forms of action were personally and socially disruptive and hence resorted to only when other alternatives were not available. A common practice was therefore to switch allegiance to other influential men in the village or ally with other settlers who were anxious to overthrow the existing chieftaincy. Social banditry in Kedah is explained against these background factors (Cheah Boon Keng, 1981: 98-130). The anarchial character of many villagers surfacing in political intrigues and rivalry and competition demonstrate the competitive egocentred pattern of political relations within the peasantry.

Women, the Family and the Household as a Unit of Production

The general inability of headmen or chiefs to extend forms of administrative and social control over the majority of the villagers was attributed to the decentralized or non-integrated form of agricultural production, which was dependent on the minimal mode of division of labour practised by nuclear family-type households. Malay households which practised wet rice-cultivation would clear the fields, irrigate, broadcast and transplant independently, without any form of collective decision-making on the most appropriate time, method and unit of labour required for optimal results.

When co-operation in labour was practised, it was based on a system of labour-exchange or labour redistribution (*berderau*) amongst households from the same homestead cluster (*jiran setangga*). These were often kinsmen who attempted to cultivate their fields simultaneously to enjoy the benefits of labour-exchange over specific seasons relating to irrigation, transplanting and harvesting.

The contribution of women to rice cultivation, horticulture and mixed cropping depended very much on the size of the family and household unit one was able to maintain: the larger the household, the easier it was for a woman to divide her time and attention between domestic and economic matters. A woman's labour contributions in agriculture would have been greater if she had more children to whom to assign various domestic tasks in the household. Hill (1977: 82) stated that larger family units encouraged larger holdings since '. . . a holding worked by young adults would more quickly reach its maximum productive capacity, soon resulting in a further search for land'. The size of holdings were also equated to the status of the family and it followed that a woman's status was reflected in her ability to amass land with the labour inputs from her immediate family and, to some extent, her kinsmen. Significantly, figures of ownership of rice farmlands in northern Malaya, particularly in Seberang Prai (Province Wellesley) between 1829 to 1833, showed women to have the largest median size 3.8 orlong, relative to a median of 3.0 orlong for the Malay *rakyat* in general (Hill, 1977: 82). However, as noted by Hill, female landlordism did not emerge in any significant way in Seberang Prai. Landlordism was prevalent amongst traditional and new elites, comprising the categories of *Haji, Shaik, Penghulu* and *Orang Besar* (S. Husin Ali , 1975; see also Scott, 1985b: 13-22). These men, on account of capital, political influence and entrepreneurship, could amass enough land to create a system of tenancy for new immigrants. Malay women, on the other hand, were rather occupied with rice cultivation and other forms of horticulture which did not really give them much opportunity to accumulate land.

The *ad hoc* form of organization of wet rice-cultivation made certain measures like irrigation, water control, pest control, clearing and burning, impossible to organize, creating a fair amount of intra-village conflict, competition and rivalry. Other forms of cultivation such as dry or hill-rice cultivation (*padi huma, padi bukit*), fruit and root crops like cassava, yam, sweet potatoes were carried out singly by the women of a particular family, without much assistance from other kinsmen or neighbours. When these plots were some distance away from the homestead, in the fringed foothill areas (*ladang*) of the village, help was obtained from the men of the household and again did not involve the other members of the village (Hill, 1977).

Generally, the small units which were cultivated with wet or dry rice cultivation, averaging around one or two orlong per household for both forms of cultivation, made it easier for the members of a family to leave the village when the taxes levied on rice cultivation were considered to be too high or when the headman or chief made excessive demands in kinds over labour or food supplies of the household. Abandoning a plot of land did not entail much hardship, mainly because land rights were not yet procured and immovable property, as such, did not impose constraints on residence. A family would take along with them items regarded to be valuable such as jewellery, clothes, knives, cooking utensils and pandanus mats and attempt to settle in another village where the headman was reputed to be a fair leader, in terms of possessing qualities relating to righteousness, generosity and a sense of fair play. The gradual introduction of land titles and delineation of village and state boundaries in the early decades of the twentieth century, introduced greater permanence in residence and consolidation of land rights and ownership.

Pioneering Status, Birth Rights and Residence

Against this background of events, in the late nineteenth century Malay villages evolved to a greater or lesser extent, a structure of social ranking based on birth rights, length of residence, descent and economic wealth which became integral rules of relationship in Malay *adat*. These were the determinants of social acceptability and status, differentiating individuals and family groups from one another in an elaborate system of relationships based on equality and hierarchy. Patterns of establishing communication and interaction amongst equals and unequals were elaborated in symbolic language, and in joking behaviour. Avoidance behaviour marked strained relations between kinsmen or patron and clients occasionally surfacing in accusations of witchcraft and sorcery.

The author's own research into the remote histories of three villages in the Seberang Perai and Kedah border at Kulim revealed that in politics, pioneering families attempted to maintain their privileged position by establishing a system of patrilineal descent through inheritance of headmanship titles. However, these rights were not formally institutionalized. The position of such families was usurped by others when they became more influential and wealthy with time. Included in this category of rural elites were the *Syed, Shaikh, Haji* and schoolteachers who continue to represent the core of rural Malay landlords. The introduction of the system of appointed headmen by the British Government eventually reduced the power of these pioneering families considerably.[20]

Wherever traditional Malay villages exist, this core group of settlers can be found. The existence of this core group of villagers implies that later settlers, including spouses of local residents from other villages, are ranked as outsiders. This status of exclusion occurs for at least a generation, before their children born within the village can claim to be original residents of the village. Terms such as *orang kita* ('our people') and *orang asal* ('the original people') continue to distinguish pioneering families and those born within the village (adults and children) from newly settled immigrants. The latter are commonly referred to as *orang asing* ('different people'; 'others') or *orang dagang* ('outside traders'). Wilder (1982: 33-34) observed similar distinctions in his village of study in Pahang. Often, these terms express not only lower status, reflecting a varying degree of social acceptability, but also a derogatory image of homelessness, destitution or vagrancy. The term *dagang merempat* refers to 'outsiders' who are homeless and choose to be squatters in another village. Occasionally, the term *orang bangsat* is also used to refer to 'outsiders' as 'desperate destitutes'. Significantly only the children of such immigrants may be accepted as 'proper' villagers so that birth-rights are often used as an important criterion for acceptability.

The relationship between rank and social acceptability, determined by pioneering status, birth-rights and length of residency, may also be applied to recent immigrants who have considerable wealth and fortune. While their wealth may be acknowledged by a term of reference as *Orang Kaya Hamid* (the wealthy man Hamid), this may nevertheless be qualified with another reference to his 'outsider' status such as *dia bukan orang sini* (he is not from here) or *dia orang luar* (he is an outsider). Such qualifications may make it difficult for a family to gain complete social acceptability for the first generation even if they display a fair amount of amicability and generosity towards the rest of the villagers. Their children, both male and female, however, may be in a good position to establish high social ranking, through wealth, competition for positions within the Village Committee or political parties or other religious or secular positions obtained through professional training (such as *imam masjid/surau, ustaz/ustazah, bomoh, or bidan*). In many of the other villages today, villagers may have resided for a considerable length of time — even for ten to thirty years but are nevertheless considered as *orang luar*. As long as the residents of a village can differentiate between early settlers or those who are village-born and more recent immigrants, the ranking system persists, creating permanent boundaries of inclusion and exclusion in village membership.

It can be seen that the development of Malay *adat* in relation to land and labour is closely allied to processes of village formation and expansion and the conversion of the Malay household as a viable economic unit in agriculture. In economic matters, women's contributions to labour productivity are not very different from men and in many cases, their farming activities and responsibilities surpass that of the men (Ong, 1987). Thus, *adat* land law provides equally for both women and men and the inclusion of the Islamic principle of *pakat* (from *muafakat*) or consensual decision-making in *adat* law allows personal preferences and sentiments to influence decisions relating to land and property (Banks, 1983: 83). Men and women can be equally favoured depending on the individual circumstances of the case. Thus, *adat* law by incorporating the Islamic principle of *pakat* or *muafakat* became the preferred mode of inheritance and sub-division of property. Islamic inheritance law was interpreted in accordance with *adat* rather than against it.[21] The preference for *adat* continues in most Malay states today as borne out in a research study on the implementation of Syariah Family Law in Malaysia (Jamilah Karim Khan, 1989). This issue will be discussed in greater detail in another chapter, but it is important to note here that Malay indigenous values of ownership are derived from the practical *adat* rationale of providing formal recognition to women's extensive contributions to economic production. Tylor (1937: 54) mentions a local *adat* law in Ulu Perak which actually spells this out in *harta syarikat, sama-sama kerja, sama sepencari* (together they worked and together they acquired property). The share of property received by a woman depended on whether she had actually worked on the land.

The integration of Islamic fundamentals in Malay village life is oriented around the formal recognition given to religious specialists and leaders and their jurisdiction over places of worship (*masjid, surau, madrasah*). Significantly, *adat* law recognizes the importance of the *imam* as a central authoritative figure in the village and as a principal figure in public decision-making but does not dismiss the importance of other non-religious figures such as the village medicine-man or shaman (*bomoh*) or traditional midwife (*bidan*) who may indulge in practices contradictory to Islam. The formal recognition of the *imam* and *kadi*, as mentioned earlier, can be traced back to early Malay history so that it is not surprising that religious leaders have become incorporated into the core authority structure of villages. Their role in religious socialization, in settling informal disputes and in conducting matrimony provides them with wider powers than what is officially prescribed and may enable them to challenge other formal and informal leaders, like the village head or the shaman. However, the very fact that Malay villages or districts are not administered according to Islamic law suggests that social controls through Islamic law are not easily achieved, except informally under the auspices of religious parties like PAS (*Parti Islam SeMalaysia*) or fundamentalist associations. Alternatively, charisma or public oration may sway public opinion or enhance acceptance of Islam. Significantly, the popularity of religious classes (*mengaji Qur'an*) and religious activities like *nasyid* (Ar. *nasid*) of hymns in praise of the Prophet, *kenduri doa selamat* (thanksgiving) of *kenduri aruah* (memorial service for the dead) depends on the encouragement given by religious specialists to others to fulfil certain basic religious responsibilities and to extend the spirit of generosity, participation and co-operation through religion.

Malay villages today are officially administered by the *Jawatan Keselamatan dan Kemajuan Kampung* (Village Security and Development Committee) which normally comprise respected elders, men and women elected by the villagers, but the headmanship (*ketua kampung*) has to be approved by the government. A *penghulu* (*penggawa* in Kelantan) who presides over a sub-district (*mukim*) is an official government administrator. The British, while giving greater recognition to male leadership, did not, however, exclude women from the Committee and a number of two was generally agreed upon. This followed some of the traditional laws of the Malay states, at least theoretically. In the Ninety-Nine laws of Perak (Rigby, 1970: 61), it is said that the officers who should be in charge of a *mukim* (district) should include the local judge (*hakim*), the *imam*, the *penghulu* (who is responsible for the maintenance of a mosque), the *pembaca* or reader, the *muazzin* (caller of prayer), the *pawang* (medicine man) and the *bidan* (midwife). The midwife is described as 'queen in the house where a childbirth is in progress'. Thus, professional specialization or experience was the suggested criterion rather than gender. However, despite the emphasis on professionalism, social acceptability was often based on origins and length of residence and authority bestowed by the existing government did not necessarily imply formal acceptance.

Notes

1. The ordering of society according to Islamic principles and *adat* is sometimes expressed in notions of embracing Malay culture or ethnicity instead of 'embracing Islam' for Muslim converts (*masuk Melayu*), or expressions like *adat Islam* (Islamic customary practices, instead of *adat Melayu*).

2. In the eleventh story of the *Sejarah Melayu* (Shellabear, 1952), this event took place after the death of Raja Tengah, the son of Raja Besar Muda. Raja Kecil Besar had a dream in which he saw the face of Allah. Allah said to him, 'Repeat the *Kalimah syahadat'* (There is no God but Allah and Muhammad is the Prophet). Allah then said to him, 'Your name is Sultan Muhammad. Tomorrow at *asar* (the third prayer), a ship will arrive from Jeddah. A man will descend and pray on the beach of Melaka and you are to follow him.' He agreed and the image of Allah vanished. The next day, he woke up with a shock, uttering the *Kalimah syahadat* repeatedly and frightened everyone. The Queen Consort called the *bendahara* for help. After being told of his dream, the *Bendahara* Seri Wak Raja said that if the ship arrived as told to him by Allah, then the event is true and he had not been shaken by evil spirits (*iblis*). The ship actually arrived at *asar* and the *Ulamah* Saiyid Abdul Aziz knelt on the beach of Melaka and prayed. From that day onwards, the king and the rest of his courtly officials converted to Islam (61-63).

3. Liaw Yock Fang (1975), a specialist on Classical Malay Literature, categorizes the *Hikayat* according to three main epical periods:

1) The India and Hindu Epical Period — seventh to fourteenth centuries, including the influences from Java and Thailand.

2) The Transitional Period between Hinduism and Islam — fourteenth to fifteenth centuries.

3) The Period of Islamic Literature — fifteenth to twentieth centuries.

4. The most important of these relate to the following:

1) The *Undang-Undang Kerajaan* (State Law), translated by Kempe and Winstedt in 1948.

2) The Minangkabau Digests, translated by Winstedt in 1953 and Josselin de Jong in 1954.

3) The Kedah Digest, translated by Winstedt in 1928.

4) The Malacca Digest, translated by Winstedt and Josselin de Jong (1959) and Winstedt and Kempe (1952).

5) The Ninety-Nine Laws of Perak, translated by Rigby (1908).

While the *Undang-Undang Kerajaan*, the Kedah Digest and the Ninety-Nine Laws of Perak were based on *adat temenggung*, the Minangkabau Digest was based on *adat perpatih*. The Malacca Digest contained features of both *adat perpatih* and *temenggung* since it covered areas of the Naning district which were populated by Minangkabau Malays. Melaka *adat* in this region has come to be referred to as *adat Naning*.

5. Part of Josselin de Jong's concern with the relationship between *adat perpatih* and *adat temenggung* in the Peninsula stems from the fact that the two are clearly regarded to be descriptions of social systems with separate sources of origins from Sumatra. He states that this is contrary to Minangkabau traditions in Sumatra, where *adat perpatih* and *adat temenggung* are mythically and operationally inter-linked. Two great leaders in the dawn of Minangkabau history were half-siblings, Kjai Katumanggungan and Parapatih, who appear in many different versions of the same myth of origin. However, the same theme of incest with a half-sibling (female) is given, necessitating the complete separation of the tribe into two divisions, Koto-Piliang and Bodi Tjaniago, ordered according to strict rules of exogamy. However, the former became associated with Katumanggungan principles of organization which supported the kingship system and hence was more patrilineal while the latter was more closely associated with Parapatih, upholding matrilineal principles of organization. The emergence of the phratry system, according to Josselin de Jong, is fundamental to Minangkabau organization and while some clans may lean on one form of organization, more than the other, the dualism in social organization is contained in all, expressed in the Minangkabau saying, '*Datue' Katumanggungan punjo Karadjoan, Datue' Parapatih punjo pajueng*' (Katumanggungan possesses the kingship and Parapatih the seal of Sovereignty {i.e. the royal umbrella; *pajueng*}). Thus, the oppositions of *temenggung* and *perpatih* express further symbolic oppositions of male and female, king and subjects, form and formation processes. On this symbolic level of meaning, *temenggung* and *perpatih* in the Peninsula should be seen to be more complementary rather than dissimilar. *Perpatih* is to the Minangkabau what bilaterality is to the Malays, supportive of kingship, yet bestowing leadership upon the people, providing men with titles, yet making women the keeper of the title or the means through which they were awarded.

6. *Penghulu*, literally 'the one who leads; and *ketua*, 'the one who heads' or 'the one who leads'.

7. Linear settlements developed extensively with the development of major transportation lines, particularly roads and railways. These encompassed not only Malay but also Chinese and Indian settlements. The linear settlements described in colonial history by Logan (1887: 48) and D'Almeida (1876: 375) seem to represent Malay villages in a very early stage of development along plains and riverine areas, before the influx of new migrants into the region.

8. This will be discussed more fully in a later section of the chapter.

9. The term 'family' here refers to nuclear or extended types which characterized the Malay household. In this period of history, chieftain families generally contained extended households with bondsmen, secondary wives, and members of their kindred normally living in.

10. This practice differs from *kerah* or corvee labour which can be imposed upon anyone within the jurisdiction of the *Orang Besar*. In fact, *kerah* was more often used as a source of labour to clear jungle and pioneering land which was then 'offered' to various families to utilize. This placed the families under an obligation of *berhutang budi* (indebtedness) which was often resolved through debt-slavery, over an indefinite number of years.

11. See Bird (1883), Appendixes B and C, concerning letters of correspondence between Sir Hugh Low, Resident of Perak, and Sir Frank Swettenham, Resident of Selangor, written between 1875 to 1882. Hugh Low explained the form of slavery and debt-bondage which was practised in the nineteenth century Perak.

12. Gullick (1958: 104-108) discusses this in some detail.

13. See Hamdan, (1967: 5). Another, European source was Innes (1974). Bird (1967) also freely commented on the large entourage of kinsmen and servants (including debt-slaves) who accompanied the sultan, his consort or son everywhere and who remained an integral part of the household of these royal or chiefly families.

14. Khoo (1972) describes that at some length.

15. 'Amok' is here taken to mean the procedure of suicide- homicide occasionally resorted to by Malays and, indeed, many other Southeast Asian communities, to resolve a state which is perceived to be unresolvable. In the traditional Malay states, it was more common for people to overcome political or social harassment through escape (*cabut*) and to establish links with other influential men as an attempt to seek revenge, rather than to resort to amok which is self-destructive. Running amok because of political and social oppression has been described previously by English writers (Clifford, 1908; Newbold, 1839; Shaw, 1972) but it also appears in Malay *Hikayat*, folk legends and social customs. The amok of Hang Jebat in *Hikayat Hang Tuah* (Hang Kasturi in Shellabear's *Malay Annals*) is perhaps the most widely quoted example of amok in the history of the Melaka Sultanate in the fifteenth century. See Wilkinson's remarks on this amok against the sultan in 'The Melaka Sultanate' (1935), based on the *Malay Annals*. Hughes (1935: 135) commented on the danger of antagonizing the Malays and their chiefs. 'The Governor has been warned that these chiefs had all the appearance of 'Amoucos' (possessed of the same determination as the Roman Decimvirs who sacrificed their lives but at the cost of the deaths of many of their enemies).

16. It is for this reason that the term 'debt-bondage' appears to be a more suitable word that 'debt-slavery'. It has less connotations relating to permanent

enslavement, or intergenerational subservience or oppression by a chief or raja. See the author's commentary on the Sullivan-Milner debate (1985a, 3[1]: 163-168).

17.   This does not fully exemplify the concept of the 'theatre state' in precolonial Bali (Geertz, 1980), which describes the ritual force of Balinese Court life in dominating and controlling the social order of Balinese society. However, some of the 'public dramatization' of social inequality and status pride (Geertz, 1980: 13) was enacted through rituals.

18.   All leaders had their *tali barut* (literally, a long waist cloth), a term of reference for men assigned the special task of spying on the activities of rural chiefs.

19.   The term 'feudal' has been avoided in this study because it does not appear to be completely applicable to the Malay pre-colonial situation. A landlord/tenancy system did not exist as in medieval Europe. There were, however, certain salient features of feudalism in terms of vast ownership of land by sultans, forced labour, debt-labour, debt-marriage, slavery, collection of land taxes by chiefs (for themselves) and the sultans even in situations of acute poverty, and the possibility of tyranny whenever a chief or sultan decided upon it.

20.   Informally, old traditions die hard and these families continue to compete in modern spheres of leadership, including political parties, youth associations and clubs, at the village and regional levels.

21.   Hooker (1970: 102) suggests that the traditional legal system in Melaka probably set the basis for the recognition of *adat* as the proper system of allocating land and property in the Malay states. Evidence from the early 1920s shows *pakat* to be the standard principle utilized, in which case equal shares were awarded to male and female. In all cases of dispute, however, government authorities used Islamic law as the binding authority, showing its formal institutionalization with land authorities (Blagden, 1930: 307). In Jasin, Melaka, a non-matrilineal (*perpatih*) area, this principle of land distribution of estates of the deceased is consistently linked with the term *adat temenggung*.

4

Party Politics, Voluntary
Movements and the Formal
Construction of Power

Dayung sama di tangan, perahu sama di air
The oars are both in our hands, the boats both at sea
— *Malay proverb*

Introduction

Malay women's political consciousness has been directly linked to the nationalist movement towards political independence. It was not founded through an emerging gender consciousness on the subjugation of women under Muslim law. Indeed the Muslim world under colonial rule developed a political consciousness through Islam and women were able to participate directly in nationalist political struggles because Islam had become a weapon for the weak, rather than a weapon for men. However, the politicization of women through Islamic rhetoric, which was political and anti-West, evoked a concern for personal and social advancement, a concern that was sometimes articulated against Islamic rules of gender differentiation and segregation, and other times ignored these differences completely to utilize family, affinity and kinship as a launching pad for public and political office. Non-formal education through Islam and formal education through a Western curriculum were both equally successful in evoking a spirit of independence and autonomy. History decided which was the more successful strategy of the time.

Islamic Education as the Basis of Malay
Female Literacy

Prior to the introduction of English-medium secular schools in the Peninsula in the late nineteenth century, Malay men and women went through residential Qur'anic education (*mangaji pondok*) or a more casual form of religious instruction conducted by religious instructors (*ustaz, ustazah*) or the local *imam*.[1] More specialized skills relating to pottery, weaving, wood-carving, metal craft, health care and medicine were attained from family apprenticeships and most of these, with the exception of wood-carving, belonged to the exclusive domain of women, or were shared with equal interest by men. Generally, in the late nineteenth century, Malay education was 'diffused, informal and undifferentiated' (Loh, 1975: 12). In religious instruction, women had as much access to this system of informal learning as men. Indeed, mothers placed a high premium on their daughters completing Qur'anic religious instruction (*khatam*) for this usually marked the age of entry into marriage, or at least the recognition of eligibility. Women who went through the more formal *pondok* system of learning under a renowned *guru* could eventually become religious instructors (*guru* Qur'an) and have a career for themselves in Islam, in the same way as men.

British education policy in the Straits Settlements (Penang, Melaka and Singapore) in the 1860s affected educational development in the Malay states. In line with the thinking that traditional Malay education should not be disrupted by English education, Malay medium secular schools were set up in the Straits Settlements, but these schools only took off in Melaka. In Penang and Province Wellesley , most of these schools closed due to poor enrollment.

The Malays were generally suspicious of new educational institutions set up by the British, seeing these to be part and parcel of an attempt to gradually convert them to Christianity. In the 1870s, the British decided to introduce Qur'anic lessons in these schools in an attempt to boost their enrollment. However, the rule was that parents, and not the state should pay the 'Hadjee' or 'Khatib' (terms used by the British for religious teachers). In other words, no official recognition was given to Islamic religious instruction in secular schools. Gradually, this system was introduced in the Malay states. By 1895, a little more than 5,000 were registered in government Malay schools; the figure had risen to 8,000 at the turn of the century (1901), a ratio of 1:3 against the school-age Malay population of 6:12 (Loh, 1975: 14). Malay parents, however, still hesitated to send their daughters to these schools so that the enrollment was predominantly male. This reflected trends of thinking about the usefulness of religious education to women; they could be retained at home under the protective wing of their mothers, would be less susceptible to unforeseen influences from strange men, could make a modest career in religious education (secular Malay education was not a means to upward economic mobility), and finally would be more desirable as wives if they were to remain 'traditional', which means conforming to pre-existing institutions of socialization and learning.

This traditional value orientation towards education was also prevalent in the other dominant ethnic groups, Prior to 1900, Chinese women were a rare sight in the Peninsula. Chinese male immigrants had to either import them from China or marry local women to establish a family life (Ward, 1980: 133-134). By 1900, with the disintegration of the Ch'ing Dynasty, Chinese women were freer to emigrate and began to accompany their male counterparts to countries in Southeast Asia. By the 1940s, the growth of Chinese families was significant enough to create a demand for Chinese education. Again, the demand for Chinese education rather than English reflected the value orientation of the Chinese, the need to preserve social values and sentiment and to preserve some kind of ethnic identity through language. However, Chinese education remained for the most hierarchical and anti-egalitarian, in relation to class, eldership and gender. As explained by Loh (1975: 35) in Chinese society men were 'perceived as superior to women, elders to juniors and the literate to the illiterate'. Nevertheless, the Chinese were very aware of the importance of formal education, and began enrolling women in Chinese schools. It has been argued that the strength of the Chinese value system upheld by Chinese women within the family and school increased the anti-Chinese sentiment in Southeast Asia, particularly in Malaya and Thailand (Ward 1980: 134).

In British Malaya, this sentiment coincided with the rise of Malay nationalism. With increasing class hierarchies developing amongst the Chinese in the Peninsula, the more wealthy began to break this trend of vernacular education by sending their sons and daughters to Hong Kong, Europe, England and the United States. The middle class in urban centres began to patronize English medium schools which eventually provided a new alternative education for Chinese women. Indians from the middle and upper class in urban centres began to enrol in English medium schools while workers and labourers in the rural areas and in estates maintained the vernacular. The movement of Malays into towns did lead to the enrollment of a smaller number of Malay girls in English-medium schools but the size was insignificant. In Penang and Singapore, however, the urban Muslim population, comprising Gujeratis, Arabs, Pakistanis and Southern Tamils, was more enthusiastic in enrolling their daughters in English medium schools, including convents run by various Catholic and Anglican orders.[2] These minorities were usually more cosmopolitan and European in their orientation and attitudes. The value orientations of these

English-educated women emulated those of their parents, that 'British was best', that colonialism brought new venues for progress and development and that the Malays were rather backward not to recognize this. Indeed, with their parents firmly entrenched in the Malayan Civil Service, British professional schemes or British companies, most of these young women and men only interacted with Malays as hired domestic help (drivers, servants or gardeners) and therefore formed a rather derogatory picture of the Malay-educated young boy or girl who had never heard of Enid Blyton nor taken any piano or ballet lessons.

Obviously here, class rather than religion was the determining factor for acceptance of Western education. The rural Malays, for the most impoverished and hostile to foreign intruders, deliberately avoided symbols of European colonialism and, along with it, English education. In contrast, urban Malay and non-Malay Muslim families, with their closer social and economic association with those in power, emulated the British way of life. Firmly entrenched in this mode of socialization was the accepted truth that mobility could be achieved only through English education. Hence families did not hesitate to send their sons and daughters to English medium schools. Professionalism and economic specialization was an important value orientation and this did not allow for any kind of discrimination in gender. These regional (rural and urban) and class discrepancies in the acceptance of Western education was probably most strongly maintained by members of the Malay royalty. The British set up a special public school to nurture English upper-class values in the children of the royalty, to groom them in the style of leadership of British aristocrats in the East. The Malay College at Kuala Kangsar was established in 1905 for Malay royalties and aristocrats. Elsewhere, class hierarchies permeated the schooling system where special English elite schools began to cater for children whose parents were already entrenched in the elite structure of colonial society. Amongst these elite schools were the Victoria Institution in Kuala Lumpur and the Central School in Perak established in the 1880s. Not surprisingly, the seeds of political discontent developed from the vernacular, for the Malays from rural religious-type schools and the Chinese, Chinese medium schools which were urban-based.

Ironically for Malay women, participation in the political process began with religious education in Islam, rather than in spite of. It was here that Malay women were infused with ideas of nationalism from scholarly religious experts. Furthermore, besides developing reading and writing skills, experience in public oration and debate built up a fair amount of self-esteem and confidence in a world of men. In a sense, in the pre-independence period before the 1950s, Islamic education initially accommodated to the *adat* tradition of the Malays, being essentially secular, political and pragmatic with an inbuilt anti-Western and anti-colonial ideology. Rather than confine Malay women to domesticity, it provided them with a professional and political platform to participate directly in the nationalist movement of the 1930s and 1940s.

Women, Nationalism and Politics

The first reports of Malay women's active interest and participation in regional or national-level politics was in the 1930s when a group of young Malay women were sent to be educated in Padang Panjang, Sumatra, in a school named Diniah Puteri (Karim, 1983). The Diniah Puteri Secondary School attracted young Malay women from rural elite families in the Peninsula, particularly the class of *ulama* who believed that existing local provisions for education for women in Christian English medium schools were highly unsuitable for their daughters since Christian morals were included in the educational curriculum.[3] The reaction against Christian missionary education was probably much more strongly felt for women than men, since Western education was also associated with Western morals which were believed to intervene with Malay values of propriety derived from Islam and *adat*. Women had to be protected from these modern Western trends since they would stand to lose more from these changes than men, in terms of reputation and marriage. For the majority of Malay parents, the question of choice of education did not arise; economic constraints did not allow them to educate their daughters and sons beyond primary schooling or the sixth grade. Others were more willing to see their daughters through local Malay-medium or Arabic secondary education partly because of the lower expenses incurred and partly because they believed that a conservative approach to education was necessary.

The choice of the Arabic school, Diniah Puteri, at Padang Panjang was not only due to its close physical proximity to Malaya but also because of its reputation for preserving a radical Islamic tradition of teaching, where the majority of the teachers were local Indonesian scholars, highly nationalistic and anti-colonial in their teaching and sentiments. In accordance with the Islamic tradition of education, the students here learnt techniques of public oration and political debate and effectively used their knowledge of Islamic law (*fiqh*) and philosophy (*falsafah*) to develop a political consciousness which rejected Western systems of administration and power over Muslim nations. Significantly, the majority of the Indonesian students here were children of political detainees (*anak-anak buangan politik*) and Indonesian nationalists fighting against Dutch rule. Feelings of nationalism and patriotism were deeply implanted in the minds of these young women and remained after they returned to their villages in Malaya.[4]

Among the rural women who were deeply affected by these more revolutionary educational experiences in Indonesia were Datuk Aishah Ghani, Datin Sakinah Junid and Samsiah Fakeh, who together in 1945 laid the foundations for the first women's movement in Malaya called AWAS or *Angkatan Wanita Sedar* (The Movement of Conscious Women) (Datuk Aishah Ghani, personal communication, 1982). This movement formed the woman's wing of the Malayan National Party of *Parti Kebangsaan Melayu Malaya (PKMM)*. Although the core of its leadership was formed by these politically radical women, the other members of AWAS comprised Malay women who were trained schoolteachers or religious instructors, the core of the rural gentry. This movement obtained warm support and encouragement from members of the Malayan National Party formed in October 1945 by radical Malay intellectuals such as Dr Burhanuddin al-Helmi, Musa Ahmad, Haji Moh, Abdullah C. D., Ahmad Boestamam and Salleh Ahmad.

In 1947, a Malay woman, Cik Zahara bt Noor Mohamed formed the Malay Women's Welfare Association of Singapore (MWWA). The Association was concerned with improving the position of Malay women which was threatened by practices of forced marriages and easy divorce. Dancz (1981: 201) lists the objectives of MWWA;

1. To reduce the sufferings of widows, orphans and destitutes.
2. To promote the cultural, social, moral, physical and spiritual progress of women.
3. To create moral courage, common sense and independence among Malay women.
4. To provide equality for Malay women, similar to women of other communities.
5. To be able to advice menfolk on matters of common interest.

Several Muslim organizations opposed the association's activities, in particular their participation in a public procession to celebrate the royal wedding of 1947, between Princess Elizabeth and Prince Phillip (Dancz, 1981: 201). Such opposition undermined the success of the association considerably. However, despite the image of 'radicalism' projected, the MWWA highlighted many intrinsic social values upheld by Malay women through *adat*. The need to be independent and autonomous and to be given social recognition were not radical feminist concepts introduced from the West. It merely expressed the perpetual line of tension between *adat* and male interpretations of gender in Islam. Women were indeed already publicly visible in 1945. What they had not done before this, was to demonstrate their visibility through a public platform. The MWWA and AWAS did not gain massive support not because they evoked female radicalism or gender consciousness but because they were not sponsored by political male and female elites who determined the form of political resistance against colonialism. This will become clearer in the following discussion on the rise of Malay women's power through the *Kaum Ibu*.

From 1945 to 1948, a number of political parties were banned by the British government in Malaya for their radical anti-British manifesto and for collaborating with the Malayan Communist Party (MCP). The MCP who drew their support largely from Malayan Chinese women (*Asia Week*, 9 February 1990: 36) was formed at the end of 1930 and conducted an aggressive campaign against the British authorities. Amongst the political parties or political organizations which were banned were AWAS, MCP, PKMM, API (Angkatan Pemuda Insaf) the Malayan Democratic Union and AMCJA (All Malaya Council of Joint Action or Majlis Tindakan Bersama Seluruh Tanah Melayu).[5] With the collapse of AWAS, the women went their own separate ways. Aishah Ghani later became a member of the woman's division of UMNO, the Kaum Ibu, in 1950. Sakinah Junid joined the Pan Malayan Islamic Party (PMIP) formed in 1954, after her marriage to the chairman of the party, Datuk Muhammad Asri Muda and became the President of the *Dewan Muslimat* or Women's section (Datuk Aishah Ghani, personal communication, 1982). Samsiah Fakeh went underground and became a member of the Malayan Communist Party Army in Pahang, a branch of the tenth Regiment of the Malayan National Liberation League (MNLL). She was instrumental in directing the political interests of many Malay nationalists including Ahmad Boestamam (whom she married), Wahi Anwar, Abdullah C. D. and Rashid Maidin, all of whom were exposed to Islamic teachings in Indonesia and who became the most revolutionary Malay patriots of the time. A recent report confirmed her second marriage to Ibrahim Mohammed, the head of the Jakarta-based Malayan National Liberation League (MNLL), in the late 1960s. She is now believed to be living in China with her son Kamaruddin Ibrahim (*New Straits Times*, 10 August 1987).[6]

The Indonesian political experience derived from Islamic education was equally strong in other women's movements which began in Malaya. In 1944, Khatijah Sidek, a Minangkabau Sumatran woman married to a Malay, formed the Woman's Military Voluntary Corps or the *Badan Sukarela Tentera Wanita*, known more commonly as *Puteri Kesatria*. Later, she started a movement called the *Taman Didikan Puteri Kesatria* concerned mainly with training children to join the army as well as to develop technical skills and expertise as teachers and informal community leaders. Although she began these movements in Sumatra, she became more involved with the activities of the radical Malay intellectuals mentioned earlier, particularly Dr Bur-hanuddin al-Helmi who was propagating the notion of Melayu Raya in response to the Indonesian Raya movement which aimed to see the Malays and Indonesians united as a militant cohesive force against British and Dutch rule respectively.

Her attempt to set up a branch of the *Taman Didikan Puteri Kesatria* in Singapore was a cover to excite stronger nationalist sentiments in Malay women. Her marriage to a Malay and imprisonment by the British in Singapore between 1948 and 1950 intensified her determination to establish a woman's movement in Malaya. However, the Kaum Ibu (in UMNO [or UMNO Baru]), (see *New Straits Times*, 14 February 1988) was the only legitimate venue for Malay women to voice their political sentiments and her Indonesian Minangkabau origin and reputation as an aggressive fighter alienated her from the other women in the organization. The Kaum Ibu chairman of the United Malay National Organisation then, Ibu Zain was unwilling to accept her in the organization. Finally, in April 1953, she was accepted as a member in the Kaum Ibu and immediately pursued her efforts to elevate the status of the Kaum Ibu in UMNO by asking for greater female representation in the UMNO General Assembly and more female candidates for the proposed general elections in 1955. She was bypassed for Puan Halimahton as a proposed party candidate because she was still regarded as an outsider who was Malayan only by virtue of marriage.

In an interview before her death in 1981 (*Nadi Insan*), she claimed that UMNO treated her badly because she was an embarrassment to the party, having a police record as a former political detainee in Singapore. She was, she said, 'like an old Qur'an (Qur'an *buruk*) ready to be thrown away after much use'. Increasing disagreements with members of the Kaum Ibu and Tunku Abdul Rahman, the Chairman of UMNO and first Prime Minister of Malaya in 1957, led to her final expulsion from the party in August 1956 (Manderson, 1980). That same year, she joined the PMIP, then under the leadership of Dr Burhanuddin al-Helmi and Ustaz Zulkifli Mohd. Together they swept to victory in the 1959 general elections and won the states of Kelantan and Terengganu. However, she left the party when it developed a provincial 'state' character under the leadership of Datuk Asri, but continued her social activities to improve the socioeconomic status of Muslim women in Malaysia through the Muslim Voluntary Organization, PERKIM, at Johor.

Fighting colonialism through Islam was almost a universal characteristic of the Muslim world but the role of women in these national movements has been much underplayed. In Algeria, women fought the French through religion and secularism either resisting unveiling to frustrate the French (in Fanon's 1967) terms, 'the unseen sees the colonizers and there is no reciprocity', or carry weapons to join the war. The woman nationalist,

Jamilah Buhrayd, said that 'heroism was a national duty, assigned to all Algerians' (Waddy, 1980: 175). In Egypt and Lebanon, Madame Hoda Sha'araway and Miss Ibtihoy Qaddurah co-ordinated a conference in the early 1940s which culminated in the formation of the All-Arab Federation of Women and this united action of Arab women played a vital part in the creation of the League of Arab States in 1945. In Muslim India in the late 1930s, active participation in the nationalist movement came with Western education and unveiling, under the leadership of Fatimah Jinnah and Begum Shaista Ikramullah, but the rhetorics of rallying public support was still traditional and Islamic (Waddy, 1980: 163). The social idealisms of these women inspired the formation of the All Pakistan Women's Association (APWA) in 1949 under the leadership of the wife of the first Prime Minister, Liagat Ali Khan. The development of revolutionary ideologies through Islam, with or without a degree of Western secularism, promoted women's political action and power in the Muslim world. In the course of history, Islam has been associated with both militant feminism and domestication. Hence, it is important to recognize the contrasting contributions of Islam to women's formal constructions of power in history, rather than to adopt the more simple homogeneous perspective of domestication. Bearing in mind the contrasting *adat* traditions in Muslim Southeast Asia and West Asia, the association of Islam with women's political power in West Asia suggest the temporary subjugation of *adat*. In Malaysia and Indonesia, Islam and women's political power merged more closely with *adat*.

Secular Education and the Development of Female Leadership in Political Parties

The political influences that guided the activities of the early informal women leaders in the Peninsular Malaysia were aligned with the spirit of Malay *Seri Kandi* in Malaya's early history; the difference between the two groups lie in the fact that the latterday leaders were commoners rather than members of the Malay aristocracy. Islamic education gave them the impetus to develop strong anti-colonial sentiments and to fight the British. They worked independently from men and were committed to political ideals to the extreme.

In contrast, the formal female leaders who laid the foundations to the Kaum Ibu organization within the UMNO were mostly wives of existing leaders of UMNO who were encouraged to take an active interest in the affairs of the party mainly to enhance the political careers of their husbands. Also, they did not have experiences beyond what was obtained within the party and did not go through the hazardous path of challenging the colonial government through revolutionary movements. The earlier group of AWAS women nationalists opposed the sultanate system as a legitimate basis of authority in the state. The early Kaum Ibu women, however, did not; nor did they have any direct connection with the militant activities of the Indonesian nationalists who were fighting the Dutch. The kind of female leadership that was considered acceptable in the Kaum Ibu was one based on a congenial system of co-operation and harmony, not only with their male counterparts within the UMNO but also with the British authorities in Malaya. The women were from conventional middle-class or upper middle-class backgrounds; some of them were already members of voluntary British associations like the Women's Institute. They were in the main, content with assisting their husbands in their careers by campaigning in villages and towns and holding charity events and bazaars to collect funds for their party.

When the Kaum Ibu was later expanded to include more female participation from the grassroots, the women became more interested in developing their own leadership potential and strength rather than being mere appendages of their husbands and this new tide of feeling culminated in the Pergerakan Kaum Ibu UMNO in 1949, when Kaum Ibu became the women's branch of the UMNO party. Everywhere Kaum Ibu branches attracted those who were already formally educated in Malay or Arabic, or professionally trained as primary or secondary school teachers. Aishah Ghani became known as the first 'grassroots' leader within the Kaum Ibu. Although she was not part of the elitist circle of wives of Malay politicians who took to politics through their husband's influence, she took up journalism and this, combined with her experience in AWAS and PKMM, gave her a considerable advantage over the other women.

The wives of civil servants, who were often urban-based, were attracted to the more multi-ethnic cosmopolitan Western organizations, such as the Women's Institute, the Red Cross and St. Johns Ambulance, and developed a free voluntary spirit that was not politically-oriented in any way. Indeed, they were disassociated from political activities, having husbands who were loyal to the colonial government and rather adverse to formal or grassroots political movements of any kind. These women formed the backbone of leadership of voluntary welfare movements and differences in priorities and interests eventually drew them away from their counterparts.[7] It can be said that voluntary organizations attracted women who were urban-based and Western-educated and who could socialize with the wives of British expatriates freely without prejudice, while the Kaum Ibu attracted rural Malay women who were not necessarily English-educated, but were concerned to see Malaya being ruled by Malays rather than English administrators. It is possibly for this reason that Malay women remain a minority group amongst voluntary social workers in the country.

Thus, since the politicization process of Malay women occurred at an early stage of the political development of the nation, they were channelled into political organizations much earlier and more extensively than women from the Chinese and Indian communities in Malaya.

While the majority of the members of the Kaum Ibu were rural women, the organization's leadership at the national, state and district levels became dominated by women who were already professionally trained in teaching, broadcasting, or journalism. Significantly, Tan Sri Fatimah Hashim's appointment to the UMNO Supreme Council in 1959 was closely associated with her husband's successful political career in UMNO and legal career as Deputy Public Prosecutor in Ipoh, and later as Attorney-General.[8] Her husband's close associate, Tunku Abdul Rahman, saw her leadership potential in the Kaum Ibu and appointed her as the Kaum Ibu representative in the Supreme Council (Fatimah Hashim, personal communication, 1982). Although she was part of the 'elite circle' within the Kaum Ibu, she realized the need for grassroot interlinkages and participation and made a tremendous impact on rural women in and out of Johor. The transference of the Kaum Ibu leadership from Tan Sri Fatimah Hashim to Datin Paduka Aishah Ghani in 1972 demonstrated a significant change in the formal female leadership pattern within the Kaum Ibu for Aishah Ghani's post was elected, not appointed, and she had massive support from the ordinary members.[9]

Reviewing Malay women's leadership development in processual terms, it is possible to say that although women's direct participation in and contribution to national-level politics emerged rather late in Malaysian history, it is not so much a consequence of cultural constraints but rather a result of developments in Malaysia's political history itself, that the ideas of nationalism and nation-building were only conceptualized in the early 1940s when surrounding Southeast Asian communities, particularly the Achinese in Indonesia, fortified Islam as a political tool against the Dutch. The spirit of nationalism which used Islam to develop internal resistance against colonial aggressors was similar to other nationalist movements in West Asia. Malay women were involved in the campaign for independence almost as soon as the men were fighting to bring about independence to Malaya. Clearly, the conceptualization of nation-building was accelerated by other independence movements around the region, and it may be said that if young Malay women were not already given opportunities by their parents to be formally educated in Malay and Islam, their participation in national-level politics would have been much later in the mid 1950s when political parties would certainly have needed to utilize women as campaigners.

At the state and district levels, active leaders of Wanita UMNO were either local Malay medium schoolteachers or religious teachers (*ustazah*) from primary and secondary schools.[10] Younger women who were active in village-level politics, through KEMAS, the Community Development Programme of the Ministry of Agriculture or informal community work, had the benefit of Malay secondary education but most were not professionally trained. Significantly, the professions that interested them were teaching, community work and social welfare. There was a clear relationship between their choice of careers and those of their fathers or close male and female kin of the older generation. Generally, these girls who opted for community work and local political activities through youth and women's organizations had parents who were already active in community politics and who held formal positions in the local village Development and Security Committee (Jawatan Kuasa Keselamatan dan Kemajuan Kampung) and political parties (UMNO rather than PAS). The careers of their parents or close kinsmen had moulded their interests, activities and professional development. These girls also considered factory work and farming to be derogatory occupations for women but would not hesitate to take on a clerical white-collar job if the opportunity arose. Generally, it appeared that at all levels of the political hierarchy in the country, women who participated in politics with the determination and motivation to be leaders had or were working towards professional careers which provided them with formal training and skills in organization and leadership. The preference was definitely towards professions in the field of education or a small business venture which could exploit a skill or ability which they already had (tailoring, handicrafts, shopkeeping, food manufacturing or processing).

Almost surely the data indicates a class bias in the formation of female leadership in rural Malay society. The opportunities for women to be professionally trained or to hold a job other than farming and home-based manufacturing depend on the socioeconomic standing of their families. Only those with economic means manage to explore and expand their interests and talents in the desired direction. These women may be given the necessary financial backing and encouragement to continue with their education, to repeat government examinations when they fail or do not perform as well as they would like to, or to pursue a course or training programme in the town or city. A primary or secondary schoolteacher, nurse or clerk enjoys a high social status and most families from the higher income groups in the villages and towns attempt to perpetuate their higher social standing by encouraging their children, including their daughters, to pursue such professions, or even enter local and foreign universities. Opportunities for university education exist as long as the girls possess the required entry qualifications but the ability to obtain these qualifications is not entirely based on intellectual achievement or motivation but the freedom to study without distraction and interruption over the long term. Thus, women from the less advantageous families only achieve high educational success when they are given the opportunity to leave their homes and enter residential institutions where financial assistance is available.

Generally, interviews with highly successful Malay women politicians and community leaders reveal that the socialization experiences of these women deviated from the customary expectations of young Malay women. During the pre-school and school-going period, they were given as much freedom as their male siblings to indulge in playful activities and escapades and to interact with boys from the same age group. Many of them happily claimed to have been ring-leaders and 'tomboys', dreaded by parents, but extremely popular with members of their peer group. Their extrovert personalities from childhood surfaced in school through participation in school committees, voluntary associations, sports and debating societies. Academic performance was not necessarily outstanding but participation in extra-curricular activities surpassed other members of their peer group. For those who progressed to higher academic institutions, these activities were merely intensified and expanded upon and many became active in student union activities, college committees, students' co-operatives and voluntary welfare work. In later stages of their career, encouragement from their family members, spouse and friends influenced their free participation in politics and community activities.

Interviews with married women politicians at the state and district level revealed that they received much encouragement from colleagues, parents and siblings. However, all married women politicians admitted that they could not actively participate as leaders of organizations and associations if their spouses were against their pursuits and preferred them to be conventional Malay housewives. They maintained that without permission and encouragement from their spouses, they would probably have had to terminate their political careers or community welfare work. They also believed that if their husbands had similar political interests, they would find it difficult to maintain harmonious relationships within the family and household.

Generally, although it was not unusual for these women to be married to men who were more passive or who were so well entrenched in their own professions that they were not threatened by their wives' careers, difficulties inevitably arose within the household. The major constraining influence was the inability of some husbands and children to cope with the long, irregular and unpredictable hours which these women spent on political and other community activities. Some admitted that their children were openly resentful that they were away from home most of the time, a problem partially overcome by the deliberate inclusion of their children in some of their activities. Familiarity with their mothers' associates and sociopolitical activities made it easier for the youngsters to accept the unusual position their mothers were in. In rural areas, women frequently took their little children along with them for meetings and functions, for fear of neglecting them.

Women leaders have a formidable task maintaining a balance between their sociopolitical and domestic activities and not many manage to achieve success in this sphere. The risk of a broken marriage, polygyny, poor school performance of their children, or delinquency were fears which they said they had to grapple with daily. These fears and anxieties were anticipated by a number of women who were interested in pursuing political careers but feared the repercussions on their husbands and children. Generally, the average Malay woman who was already politically or socially active did not usually give up her interests for her family. She merely resorted to managing her household in a more efficient manner like cooking the evening meal before leaving the house or hiring a very efficient maid. Respondents felt that their professions gave them the skill and ability to manage and maintain their households efficiently but life situations show this to be more ideal than real. Skilful management of the household ultimately meant transferring responsibilities to other members of the household or hired help and this was not always a satisfactory solution to all concerned.

The kind of motivation and interest displayed by these women for a public political career reflected certain *adat* traditions that were not unusual in Malay society. The majority of formal and informal leaders who had worked their way upwards through determination, self-motivation and resilience to criticism displayed a high sense of work ethics or commitment to work. Social confidence from a successful marriage, enhanced by a passive spouse, made them dominant partners in marriage, representing a special group on one end of the continuum of role complementarity and function. Husbands were often passive listeners rather than speakers and not generally adverse to domestication. Doubtless, not every one of the women had qualities that could be categorically viewed as 'charismatic'. What they had was a sense of purpose, commitment to long term targets, personal ambition and a desire for power. Having achieved some degree of independence from domestic responsibilities, these women sought a much more public life through party officiation. In a sense, it may be argued that in politics, class factors enabled *adat* principles to work more efficiently. Personal autonomy and extension of marriage into public life was more feasible when domestic functions were taken over by hired help or when spouses brought in enough income to support the household.

However, some of the older women politicians despair that the spirit of nationalism and dedication to political ideals has been lost. An UMNO veteran admitted that current leaders differed from the *Seri Kandi* of the past, like 'the earth and the sky' (*seperti langit dengan bumi*) or 'night and day' (*malam dan siang*). Today, without the same radical spirit of nationalism to shake away the colonial past, leaders depend on their personal abilities and experience to evoke support and commitment. Some of the older women politicians interviewed complained of the lack of direction, commitment and dedication of the younger members of the Kaum Wanita, be they leaders or supporters, claiming that the *'semangat perjuangan'* ('spirit of revolution'), whether ideological or concrete, concerning real social issues of national interest, was absent in most of them. They alleged that women were now hungry for personal power and status. As a result, the quality of membership and leadership has become 'diluted' or 'weak' (*'sudah cair'*) because more and more women were joining the party for personal gain rather than for ideological reasons. Under such circumstances, it was hard to detect sincerity, commitment and dedication in the members. Factions and alliances were not based on objective assessment of the calibre of leaders but on material gains and personal motives, weakening the ideological goals of the party itself.

The 'diluting' effect of membership in the Wanita UMNO, stated some of the earlier leaders could be arrested only if a 'spirit of revolution' or pervasive national ideology was developed to encourage women and men to bury their differences and unite consistently in the long term. Significantly, no one argued that party politics and public activity was a personal strategy against domesticity. The general consensus was that domesticity was not necessarily more important than political activity. Husbands and children were important, but it was also important for women to enjoy some of the new venues of self-expression and freedom offered in politics and community life.

In the decades after Independence, Malay women leaders had already established themselves as national politicians in their own right long before urban Western-educated Chinese and Indian women asserted their political rights. Of the three major ethnic groups in Peninsular Malaysia, Malay progress in establishing a women's movement within the political party system was indeed the fastest and most successful. The Kaum Ibu developed its own independent executive structure within the party under the name of Wanita UMNO in 1972, long before Chinese or Indian women in their respective political parties were able to do so.[11] In the national elections, Wanita UMNO had also fielded in more women candidates than any other party within the Barisan or the Opposition. In the August 1986 general election, Wanita UMNO fielded in 23 nominees, 15 for State seats and 8 for Parliamentary seats. In contrast, Wanita MCA fielded in only 4, and Gerakan Rakyat Malaysia (a Chinese-dominated party in the Barisan) one state seat. Significantly, all but one of the Wanita UMNO candidates won with substantial majorities against their male opponents in PAS. All the women contested in predominantly rural areas. One of the five non-Malay (Chinese) candidates in Barisan lost her seat to the Democratic Action Party (DAP) in Lahat, Perak. The Malayan Indian Congress (MIC) did not nominate any woman politician for State or Parliamentary seats. All in all, women candidates fared well, winning 24 of the 29 seats contested. Wanita UMNO's Datin Paduka Hajah Zaleha Ismail obtained a record majority of 31,472 votes in the parliamentary constituency of Selayang, Selangor (*The Star*, 6 August 1986). She also obtained a record majority of 31,142 for the 1990 General Elections. In the last General Elections in October 1990, Wanita UMNO fielded 22 candidates. 16 (6.5 per cent) for State seats and 6 (6.9 per cent) for Parliament seats. The splinter group from UMNO, Semangat 46 fielded 5 women candidates out of its total of 61 Parliament candidates (8.2 per cent) and 2 among its total of 152 State candidates (1.3 per cent). MCA increased its number of women Parliamentry' candidates to 4 (12.5 per cent) while MIC for the first time in history allowed one woman, Valli Muthusamy, to stand for the State seat at Prai, Penang (Gender Statistics in Malaysia, 1990). In total, opposition parties fielded less women candidates than the Barisan Nasional. PAS, following its previous tradition, did not allow women members to contest the elections.

In Wanita UMNO, the new nominees to the political scene comprised a mixture of professionals and housewives sharing the common experience of long term membership in UMNO. Although these women stood on the safe ticket of UMNO, it is apparent that backing from fellow members in Wanita UMNO and from the 53 per cent female electorate were important factors contributing to their political success.

Participation in Voluntary Organizations

When women leaders from political organizations are compared to voluntary community workers or voluntary social welfare workers, significant differences are discerned in the values of these two categories of leaders. Women who chose to engage in voluntary social work are normally politically neutral or, even if they did choose to join a political organization, remain back-benches in the political arena, rendering support, assistance and guidance whenever it was needed. They normally have a deep sense of commitment and responsibility to the voluntary organization and although personal differences often arise, these are seldom allowed to develop into long term factions or feuds. There are also less opportunities for fame, wealth or power through social work. Some become attracted to voluntary welfare or social work, mainly because they are housewives from middle- and upper-class families who have surplus time on their hands. While they are not inclined politically, they are also eager to utilize their time more effectively and the main venue for such women seem to be in voluntary social work. Most are urban-based and spend a considerable amount of their own money in travelling, contributions and donations. Such women develop into highly dedicated social workers. They have skills similar to those of women politicians in rallying mass support, public-speaking and debating, but they do not have the same access to the mass media.

Maintaining appropriate social connections and social networks with other women of the same socioeconomic background are also important, not so much to uphold or expand on existing power structures but to gain greater recognition and respect for the organization or agency they represent.

It is significant that younger members show great reverence and support for their leaders who have devoted many more years to the agency or organization. The idea of challenging seniority and eldership is not as obvious as in political parties. In some organizations like the Women's Institute or the National Council for Women's Organizations, some of these leaders have consistently and regularly held leadership positions for over a decade. Long-serving members normally tend to be elected as leaders and are seldom displaced by the younger members, no matter how much more educated and dynamic the latter are. Most of these leaders, in the later years of their life, surrender their posts to the younger members but are always given the honorific role of adviser to the organization. The leadership patterns in these organizations may be said to be more stable and predictable than those in political organizations but their very stability reduce competitiveness and as such do not encourage new dynamic leaders to emerge.

Government Inputs and Strategies for Female Leadership

In the government's efforts to improve grassroots participation in the community development and politics, women have become a major target group for political mobilization, particularly in rural areas. Here, the main strategy for encouraging women's active participation in community or national issues is to provide new formal institutions for collective action. These institutions also form the lowest hierarchical level of information dissemination in the country. Some of these institutions are controlled by Ministries which channel relevant public information and social services through a hierarchy of government personnel.

Kemajuan Masyarakat (KEMAS) administered by the Ministry of

Agriculture, provides a multitude of social services and facilities which theoretically aim at improving the socioeconomic livelihood of poorer women in rural areas. Its close association with the activities of the Wanita UMNO, however, also makes it an appendage of the most powerful women's organization in the country. Membership within these two organizations usually overlap so that KEMAS channels the same ideology and politics as Wanita UMNO. Since the political and socioeconomic interests of both organizations are so closely intertwined, the ideal goals of KEMAS to uplift the social position and economic livelihood of women are not always achieved. Women who are politically neutral or opposed to the goals and interests of Wanita UMNO are reluctant to participate in the activities of the organization, either from personal conviction or because of opposition from family or kinsmen who are aligned to other political parties. Because these political differences often arise, a fair percentage of women in 'opposition' areas do not participate in the activities of KEMAS (Hutheesing, 1981; Lochhead, 1984).

The kind of activities or programmes that are organized through KEMAS reinforce rather than restructure the traditional patterns of socioeconomic activity performed by rural women. Although these programmes cannot assist the ordinary woman in developing her full potential in public life, the administrative personnel of KEMAS (*penyelia*) often use it as a launching pad for a political career in Wanita UMNO. The participants of KEMAS programmes, however, merely gain new domestic skills which have the cumulative effect of increasing their consumption of material goods and demands for home gadgets and equipment beyond that which they can afford. Generally, little training is provided in the field of social or community management. Courses on leadership development are seldom organized and even if they are, do not involve the ordinary or poorer village women from non-elite families who have leadership potential or who may want to develop themselves as community leaders.

Hutheesing in evaluating KEMAS Family Development Programmes, writes:

> Programmes as shaped by *KEMAS* cater to a thin layer of educated young women and touch the *grass tops* rather than the grassroots. They fulfil the needs of the young female who because of her education has largely become unproductive rather than developing or increasing production (1981: 18).

Another women's organization which has penetrated a considerable number of villages in Kedah is Karyaneka, a subsidiary agency within KEMAS. Theoretically, its objectives of developing a collective forum of artisans is concerned with improving the economic livelihood of women by encouraging income-generating activities that can be developed within the village itself (P. Ahmad, 1982). Here, the notion of income-generation through village workshops is to transform existing natural resources into handicrafts and household decorative and utilitarian commodities that appeal to the urban populations in Malaysia and which have export potential. The making of embroidered cushion covers, pot rests and food covers and some other aesthetically appealing handicrafts seem to be the focus of Karyaneka activities in Kedah. Ideally, besides handicraft training, women are also supposed to develop business and managerial skills. Hence, the ideal goals of Karyaneka suggest that when production has expanded sufficiently, women may obtain opportunities to organize and manage the organization at the grassroots and develop their potential as organizational leaders. However, here again, the scope of involvement is limited to the goals and needs of the organization rather than those of the rest of the community.

The Karyaneka programme was created by top-level administrators and foreign consultants who introduced it to women in the village during a brief meeting. In the village of Penia in Kubang Pasu, Kedah, very little was done in the early stages of the conception of the programme in August 1982, to bring in views, ideas and comments from the women or village leaders themselves (Lochhead and Ramachandran, 1983). Although the activities of Karyaneka have now commenced in other villages, there is a tremendous amount of obscurity, confusion and anxiety about it. The village women who are actively providing the labour for the production of the handicrafts remain unsure about their future role in Karyaneka. The rest of the villagers remain detached or alienated from it and, judging from the initial organizational and administrative problems which Karyaneka has already projected, do not seem to express great confidence for it. Indeed, Karyaneka is now projected in Kuala Lumpur as a highly successful export-oriented business consortium. Again here, a programme which was initially designed as a co-operative and conceptualized as a 'People's Programme' appears to be having the opposite effect of reducing village women into productive labour units for a commercial enterprise in which they have no part.

In the same way as KEMAS activities have converted the majority of female participants into government extension workers and functionaries of the government, so has Karyaneka achieved the same results by transforming poorer women into a public labour force. Only when Karyaneka implements its co-operative principles of management and provide rural women with complete access and control over the stages of production and distribution will the programme be seen as a 'People's Programme'.

The conversion of women into government functionaries and waged labourers is possibly the main obstacle to their future development as community leaders and workers. Potential women leaders continue to be produced from the families of the rural elite. Since these organizations invariably create differences in social priorities, interests and goals, they separate women and youth according to political ideology, social rank and class. What could otherwise be organized into a wider movement for women becomes a concern for political party goals and class interests. Here, it is apparent that what is needed is an overall effective radical philosophy of community development, team spirit and dedication which unites women across political and class frontiers. Generally, it appears that in the context of public policy, it is not so much gender which becomes the basis of extension or discrimination of power, but class, social rank and politics reinforcing earlier deep-rooted schisms in Malay rural society.

Female Leadership in Islamic Political Parties

The current position of Malay women in political parties like PAS, which use Islam as their ideological strategy, is significantly different from when Islam was part of a strategy for nationalism. Currently, in PAS, women only assist men in their campaigning and are not allowed to stand for elections, a situation different from the earlier days when women like Khatijah Sidek were allowed to contest a seat. This strategy of male leadership through Islam and female domestication is reinforced by the party's concept of 'restructuring society' in accordance with an Islamic state system. This political manifesto rejects Malay *adat* as a legitimate basis of social organization and, together with it, leadership roles in women. It is probably for this reason that PAS has never been able to win massive support from Malay rural and urban women the way UMNO has over the last three decades.

Before the 1982 General Elections, campaigning in PAS's strongholds in the state of Terengganu, particularly in Rusila and Marang, was accompanied by the marked increase in female participation in fund-raising activities geared towards the production of goods like the mini *telekung* or *tudung* (veil), skull-caps (*ketayap*), cassette tape recordings of speeches or *ceramah* of PAS leaders and pre-packed food items.[12] Also, in the *ceramah* organized by PAS before the election, the audience comprised substantial numbers of women, sometimes exceeding the men. At a particular *ceramah* delivered by *Ustad* Haji Hadi Awang, a highly skilful orator and charismatic politician from Rusila, Terengganu, the audience comprised about 20,000, more than half of whom were women. As before, women maintained an active interest in political affairs. Yet they were banned from direct participation in politics, at both the state and national levels. In the August 1986 General Elections, PAS's defeat in Terengganu and Kelantan clearly demonstrated the limitations of an Islamic rhetorics which spoke of the Islamization of a multi-ethnic community and the non-involvement of women in public life. Although Barisan Nasional's control of mass media was a contributory factor, Barisan women in their anti-PAS campaigns used the issue of women's unequal political representation, withdrawal of voting rights for women and veiling to discourage women from joining the PAS camp. These anti-PAS campaigns were rather successful, as the results of the election showed.[13] PAS won only a single Parliamentary seat out of 177 (148 went to the Barisan) and 13 in State Legislative Councils (out of 351). In comparison, the Chinese Opposition did better, in DAP, which fielded 24 Parliamentary seats and 37 State seats (*New Straits Times*, 5 August 1986).

The state of Kelantan was returned to PAS in their stunning victory in the October 1990 General Elections. This victory has been partly attributed to Tengku Razaleigh who left UMNO to form Semangat 46, maintaining a united opposition coalition with PAS, DAP and PBS (Parti Bersatu Sabah). Local opinion in Kelantan suggests that voters followed Tengku Razaleigh and stopped supporting UMNO when he quit the party. Others, however, express parochial ethnic sentiments suggesting that to be Kelantanese and Malay are two different things. Women voters in Kelantan swung their votes accordingly, to PAS and Semangat 46. That UMNO's campaign in Kelantan did not have the same desired result as the 1986 elections was significant proof of the people's desire to reconsolidate their identity through cultural and religious sentiments. By 1990 the rights of Muslim women and women in general in the state assumed a secondary role as the Kelantanese revived an earlier political consciousness which had become diffused under UMNO rule.

The sexual politics of PAS, articulated through Islam, ironically reflects the history of politics in the West — of women's marginality from public office and struggle for equal public and political representation. According to Foucault (1978: 83), 'power acts by laying down the rule: power's hold on sex is maintained through language, or rather through the art of discourse that creates, from the very fact that it is articulated, a rule of law'. The comparison with Foucault stops here for this rule of law expressed through Islam is alien to most Malay women. They had achieved a starting advantage in political activity through Islam, during the nationalist movement. They were able to establish relations of power through the traditions of *adat* in the post-nationalist period. The history of participation of Malay women in formal and informal politics from the fifteen century to the period of nationalism and modern times expresses a continued concern for political activity and sexual representation. Occasionally however, the frontiers of politics turns sharply away from gender concerns as political consciousness is shaped by a larger overriding concern for ethnic-cultural sentiment, expressed through 'state' rather than 'Malay' symbols of identification.

Reflections of History

Over many decades, the push towards domestication through Islam has been apparent, yet women have managed to demonstrate their political interests as successfully as men, striving towards literacy and professionalism and acquainting themselves with both bureaucratic and grassroots techniques and strategies of extending power. Like their male counterparts, they continue to use kinship, family and affinal networks as a basis of support and popularity, lacing it with formal education and professional training to establish social credibility and prestige. Nevertheless, the deployment of sexuality in party politics using the language of Islam is a fundamental attempt at redistributing power through men. If it is successful, Muslim men will eventually control the trends of development of power politics in Malay-Malaysian society. However, if history repeats, Islam can also be used to produce intellectual liberation for women. These opposing forces in Islam — towards women's intellectual liberation or domestication will probably continue to be reproduced in history, the importance of one over the other being dependent on the social and political realities of the day. This suggests that in some periods in history, ideological fusion between Islamic and *adat* constructs on the position of women and women's power will occur, and it is in these situations that Malay bilaterality is particularly reinforced.

What makes Malay women's participation in public or political life a manifestation of pre-defined cultural forms? The answer rests on the general argument in this volume that Islam and Malay *adat*, though ideologically conflicting, may when convenient or necessary, jointly construct a formula for woman's power in society. Indeed, the symbolic fusion of *adat* with Islam in critical periods of history (example, nationalist movement, and formation of Kaum Ibu) has reduced some of these ideological differences, offering bilaterality as a mediatory mode of thought and action. The deliberate separation of the two gives rise to the theory of female domestication in Islam but this appears harder to achieve, at least for Malay Muslims, since it requires the cultural system to be split down the middle, deconstructed rather than reconstituted. In modern history, women activists have with the support of men, attempted to develop their own political image, by utilizing Islam and/or modern educational experiences to their advantage. Yet, as the example of PAS may show, Islam is also deliberately used to suppress their independent public and political contributions to society. It is possible for this reason that Malay women seem more drawn to the politics of Wanita UMNO than PAS.

Like most modern bureaucracies, the UMNO bureaucracy is not free from male domination, but at least here, Malay women find some opportunity to express their own views publicly without passively emulating the thoughts of men.[14] A woman veteran in politics, Puan Sri Puteh Maria, stated that she was surprised Wanita UMNO women did not speak out more 'bluntly' with 'more guts' to whip up massive support for women's issues (*New Straits Times*, 3 August 1987). They had an impressive stage and audience but were reluctant to use the microphones.

Finally, it should be noted that as a massive political force, their strength in mobilizing the populace to support any issue cannot be understated. The future directions of power of Malay women lie in their ability to use the political machinery to their advantage. Indeed, without the women's branch in UMNO, it is possible to speculate that the major portion of UMNO's grassroots support would be seriously undermined. This is obviously something the women in UMNO have not formally articulated or seriously thought about; otherwise, it could be a potentially effective weapon for further consolidation of their power within the party.[15]

Malay *adat* emphasizes the vital role of women in politics in different ways. The saying 'young men are the hope of the nation, young women the pillars of the state' expresses the dynamism of women in social and political decision-making. Another Malay expression 'the strength of a man lies betwixth a women', expresses the power of sexuality in politics. The recognition of women's power was also shown in other ways. Unlike the situation in England, France and the United States where the suffragette movement developed to assure women of their voting rights as citizens, Malaysia, like other countries in Southeast Asia, automatically gave Muslim and non-Muslim women the vote with independence. Women now enjoy 'equal pay for equal work' within the government administrative machinery though discriminatory wage practices continue in the private sector. Equal tertiary educational opportunities are also given to women, including professional education in medicine and law; however, economic constraints may prevent some from utilizing existing opportunities for higher education.

Comparing the situation in Malaysia to that in more advanced countries like the United States and England, the patrons of Western democracy and freedom, it is obvious that in the latter, the women's movement still suffers the onslaught of conservative government policies which undermine women's valuable contributions to change and development. In the United States, the Abortion Bill, sex-discrimination in education and non-protective measures to ensure equal opportunities for working women, continue to undermine the efforts of women's groups to elevate the status and working conditions of women.[16]

Significantly, during the Democratic Party Primaries in July 1984, women's rights became a 'minority group' issue, campaigned along with the position of black minorities. These were two important issues which had not received the full attention of the Reagan administration. Consequently, for the Presidential campaign, the Democratic Party elected a woman Vice-Presidential candidate in an unprecedented decision in the United States history. Geraldine Ferraro, Catholic ethnic with a working-class background, symbolically reaffirmed the minority status of women in America. 'A Star is Born', exclaimed the press and once again the American dream was reconfirmed in the victory speech of Presidential candidate Walter Mondale that 'America is for everyone who works hard and contributes to our blessed country' (*The New York Times*, 13 July 1984).[17] Ferraro's dismal failure to uphold this dream reconfirmed the dubious position of women in American politics and their inability to effectively contribute to or change political trends in American history. Meanwhile, England, boasting of a woman Prime Minister in Margaret Thatcher, had increased female representation in Parliament in a significant way. In the Parliament election of 1987, 41 women, including Thatcher, won seats in the House of Commons, an improvement over the 26 who held seats before.[18] Nevertheless, it was only a very small fraction of the 650 seats available. Yet many women were assigned as token candidates to constituencies their parties knew would be difficult or impossible to win. There was a record 327 women candidates running for office compared with 276 in the previous election in 1983 (*New Straits Times*, 30 June 1987). The Alliance of Liberal and Social Democratic Parties led with 105 women, Labour 92 and the Conservatives 46. The rest ran for smaller parties.

Despite these somewhat positive trends in politics in the United Kingdom, the position of women in industry continues to be bleak with the recent upsurge of home-based and piece-rate workers, poor unionization, discriminatory wage practices for women and retrenchment, which hit women workers the same way as the Third World. The British Department of Employment (DE) and the Equal Opportunities Commission have revealed a number of problems facing women, both as entrepreneurs and managers. Generally they face obstacles in raising capital; customers and suppliers lack confidence in them. Many who have made it to the top are self-employed (*Sunday Star*, 19 August 1990: 3). In the United States, a study conducted by the Graduate School of Management at the University of California at Los Angeles revealed that women and minorities are discriminated against in the same way in the corporate sector and that 95 per cent of the top management jobs at the largest corporations are held by white males (*Sunday Star*, 19 August 1990: 14). This suggests that women's power is not naturally derived from Western democracy and modern education but their solid determination and effort to fight tokenism and charity. Japan's 'Madonna Politics' expressing the phenomenal rise of women in party politics through the mass media splurge on male dishonour and the public shaming of male politicians is a fine example of how women use culture to permeate political ideology and action, and eventually sway public opinion in their direction (*Asiaweek*, 4 August 1989; *New Straits Times*, 11 August 1989).

In social research, part of the problem of understanding women is perpetuated by social scientists who continue to view women through Western paradigms of power relations (Overing, 1986). Overing argues against writers like Ortner (1974) who believed in women's real and symbolic devaluation and subordination. This, she argues, is an extension of Western notions of hierarchical opposition of culture over nature, man over culture, and pragmatism over emotion. Yet others, as briefly (Mac-Cormack and Strathern, 1980), have attempted to avoid this paradigm by stressing the difficulties of imposing Western universalisms over a people's world-view. In truth, if scholarly research continues to perpetuate the ideology of women's subordination and inability to penetrate pre-existing systems of power or to reconstruct it to their advantage, the research process itself is self-defeating, not to mention its ultimate self-destructive character in upholding a morality derived from early European machoism and ethnocentrism. Researchers should perhaps examine more deeply, indigenous constructs of power relations between women and men to understand how relationships are ultimately sorted out in the long term.

Notes

1. *Pondok* schools under the patronage of renowned *guru* sprang up everywhere in remote areas where the British were less concerned with implementing Malay and English medium education for Malays.

2. The majority of these were Irish Roman Catholic Teaching Orders (Convent of the Holy Infant Jesus). Latin, French, History and English were some of the more important subjects taught in the convents.

3. Based on an interview with Datin Paduka Aishah Ghani in 1982, the former Minister of Social Welfare, who was one of the pioneer students of the school from the Peninsula.

4. AWAS, together with the newly formed youth organization API (Angkatan Pemuda Insaf) teamed up with the Malayan National Party to form PUTERA (Pusat Tenaga Rakyat) under the leadership of Dr Burhanuddin al-Helmi. The PUTERA organization was formed mainly to oppose the Malayan Union proposed on April 1946 by the British. It allied with UMNO, the United Malay National Organization,

which was formed on 1946 for the same reason. The more radical Malay nationalistic spirit of PKMM, which not only opposed the principle of *jus soli* for citizenship but also wanted to see the end of British rule immediately, together with the termination of the sultans' powers in Malaya, was too much for UMNO to accept. UMNO was against the *jus soli* principle but upheld the sanctity of the sultanate system. They were also prepared to work with the British as long as it was necessary to bring about independence in Malaya. A month later, in June 1946, the PKMM broke their merger with UMNO.

5. A number of the members of the MCP were formerly in the AMCJA which was formed on December 1946 under the leadership of Tan Cheng Lock in reaction to the protest of the Malays against the Malayan Union. Although AMCJA agreed to the sovereignty of the sultans, it was more concerned to protect the interests of the non-Malay communities in Malaya, particularly the Chinese, who were not represented in UMNO.

6. In the 1960s, Samsiah Fakeh escaped with Ibrahim Mohammed (a radical trade unionist in Johor in the 1950s) to Jakarta where they established the MNLL. Along with Ibrahim, she was arrested by the Indonesian army during the abortive coup of 1 October 1965. After a year's detention by the Indonesian military government, they went to Hanoi, where they were given political asylum in North Vietnam, before finally moving to Beijing.

7. Based on personal commentaries of Begum Bismillah Munawar, the author's mother, one of the early founders of the Women's Institute in Johor Bahru in the early 1940s and a co-founder of the Pan Pacific and Southeast Asian Women's Association in Kuala Lumpur in the 1950s along with Toh Puan Saadiah Sardon. She said that in the welfare activities of the Kaum Ibu, all Women Institute members were solidly united with their Malay friends. In fact, all Muslim women of the Women's Institute became members of the Kaum Ibu in Johor although their activities were non-political in nature. Interviews were also conducted with (Senator) Datin Athinahapan and Puan Sr. E. N. Chong, two women veterans in the early women's movement in the country.

8. The personal interview with Tan Sri Fatimah took place in 1982, when she was also president of the National Council of Women's Organizations in Malaysia (NCWO). It is reported that during her term in office in UMNO, the membership of Kaum Ibu increased by 100,000 from 1956 to 1966. She was defeated by Aishah Ghani in 1972. Other women politicians who were interviewed were Datuk Paduka Rafidah Aziz, Puan Marina Yusoff, Datin Rahmah Othman, Datuk Paduka Zaleha Ismail and Datin Rosemary Chong from MCA.

9. Other prominent women UMNO leaders such as Datuk Paduka Rafidah Aziz, Puan Marina Yusoff and Datin Rahmah Othman were also professionally trained in economics, law and journalism, respectively. The latter two resigned from UMNO and are now in Semangat 46, a splinter group of UMNO. Similarly, Datuk Paduka Zaleha Ismail is a graduate from the University of Malaya. Personal interviews were also conducted with these women politicians.

10. Based on in-depth interviews with sixty Malay women leaders in Kuala Lumpur, Alor Star, Penang and the villages of Mawang and Tasek in Seberang Perai in 1982. Fifteen represented Wanita UMNO leaders at national, state and district level, ten were members of KEMAS, ten more were women professionals

from various ministries and twenty-five from voluntary organizations. Those interviewed in the villages were either members of KEMAS or Wanita UMNO. Two of them were members of the Village Development and Security Committee (JKKK). This study was part of a larger KANITA study on the development of female leadership conducted amongst all ethnic groups. This study was repeated in 1989, as part of a UNESCO funded research on 'Women in Political Activity and Public Life' and much of the earlier findings were consistently borne out.

11. Within the Malaysian Chinese Association (MCA), the Chinese branch of the Barisan Nasional, the women's branch was established as an independent unit only in 1981, while the women of the Malaysian Indian Congress (MIC) are still subsumed under the dominant male leadership of the party. Over history, only one woman candidate has been fielded by the MIC for the General elections.

12. The author visited Rusila and Marang a few weeks before the election in 1982. At this time, a number of young girls were also recruited through ABIM and Arqam to aid PAS in the elections.

13. Other strategies used to appeal to the Malays were employed by the Barisan with the help of the media. These were the non-feasibility of PAS's manifesto of the Islamic Republic in a multiracial country and their undisguised hypocrisy in collaborating with the Chinese (PAS formed the Chinese Consultative Committee before the 1986 elections). Other harsher examples of anti-PAS slogans were 'In an Islamic state, the Chinese will be circumcised, and would lose their voting rights.' The theme of hypocrisy of Malays collaborating with the Chinese continues with the coming election campaigns for 1990 except that this time two Malays political parties have come under attack, Pas and Semangat 46. The Chinese-based party under attack is still the DAP.

14. Thus, although the percentage of women members in UMNO is 55 per cent compared to 45 per cent male (526,716 out of 957,667), they occupy only 2.2 per cent (8) of the total number of seats (35) in Parliament (Dewan Rakyat). The figures of Wanita UMNO members were obtained from the Wanita UMNO Head Office in Kuala Lumpur in 1983 and refer only to those women who have paid membership fees. This probably implies that the total membership is much more. The membership of women in UMNO Baru will probably remain the same since UMNO and UMNO Baru merely express the 'deregistration' and 'reregistration' of a similar organization as endorsed by the Registrar of Societies.

15. In this context, observers argue that they should probably have asked for more Parliamentary and State seats in the August 1986 and 1990 General elections.

16. The National Organization for Women in July 1984 conducted an anti-Reagan campaign for his unprecedented assault on women's rights. Some of their justifications for the campaign were as follows:

1) Ronald Reagan was the first US President in 35 years to oppose the passage of the Equal Rights Amendment (ERA).

2) He opposed women's constitutional right to choose, by supporting proposed laws which would ban all abortions plus some birth control methods including the Pill and the IUD.

3) He was dismantling the federal programmes and agencies designed to project working women's right to equal opportunity.

4) His budget cuts forced two and a half million more women and two

and a half million more children into poverty, while his spending on defence continued to rise steadily.

5) The Reagan Justice Department convinced the Supreme Court that sex discrimination in education should be legal again.

Excerpts from the anti-Reagan campaign brochures distributed on July 1984 at Hyde Park, Chicago.

17. In the United States, the first female Cabinet Officer was Frances Perkins, Secretary of Labour under Franklin Delano Roosevelt, but nearly a decade passed before a second woman was named and twenty more years before there was a third. In all, eight women have served in the Cabinet, often only in health and education posts. There have been no women Attorneys-General or Secretaries of State, Treasury or Defence. The first and only woman Justice of the Supreme Court is Sandra Day O'Connor, appointed in 1981 and secretary of Labour, Mrs. Elizabeth Cole, appointed at the same time. Only 2 per cent of Senate Seats, about 5 per cent of seats in the House of Representatives and two of the 50 State Governorships belong to women who make up 51 per cent of the nation. (Russel Warren Howe, *The Observer Magazine*; reprinted in the *New Straits Times*, 21-22 January 1990). To compare, in the 27 years since Independence in 1957, Malaysia has had three Malay women Cabinet Ministers, three Deputy Ministers, and one Malay woman Justice of the Supreme Court appointed in 1983.

18. Twenty-one of the women represented Labour, 17 Conservatives, two the Social Democratic Alliance and one the Scottish Nationalist party (*New Straits Times*, 30 June 1987).

5

Contemporary *Adat* and Islam in a Malay Village: Gender Relationships and Power

Air dicincang tidak akan putus
Water that is cut cannot be broken

— *Malay proverb*

The Village of Mawang at the Seberang Perai-Kedah Border

Significantly, Kedah (Queddah) already existed as a pre-Islamic Malay state before the formation of Melaka in the fifteen century. Archaeological evidence from the ancient sites of the kingdom of Kedah and Province Wellesley date back at least to the middle of the fourth century while the sacred site of the *Kandis* of the Merbuk Valley date between the fifth and the eighth centuries (Braddell, 1980: 201). Using sources from the *Kedah Annals*, the *Hikayat Marong Mahawangsa* and archaeological excavations, Wilkinson confirmed present-day Kedah to have been a territory under the ancient Buddhist kingdom of Langkasuka (AD 115) in Ligor. Hence, it probably existed from as early as the second century AD (164-165). Relating Braddell's work on Kedah pre-history to the period of Melaka, Wilkinson suggested that Kedah in the thirteenth and fourteenth centuries must have been part of the Kataha-Sri Vijaya Empire, a dependency with local hereditary chiefs, the founder of whom was an immigrant from Sambroon (Braddell, 1980: 164-165). After the collapse of Sri Vijaya, the Kedah chiefs were left independent. This explained why the raja of Kedah sought recognition of royalty from Sultan Mahmud of Melaka. Wilkinson concluded:

If we wish to believe the literal truth of the traditions, we may suppose that the early chiefs were personally Moslems, coming originally from Sambroon, that they bore Sanskrit (Sri Vijaya) and Indo-Chinese (Ligor) titles, and that the conversion of the whole state to Islam occurred in 1474 AD (Notes in Braddell, 1980: 164) Descendants of this Chief from Sambroon probably acquired the title Raja after mythically elevating his status to that of a prince' (1980: 164).

In the sixteenth century, Pires (1967: 107) described it as a small kingdom, flourishing with Thailand (Siam), Pasai, Pedir, Gujarat and Melaka. It exported rice and pepper in significant quantities and received textiles from Indian traders.

Towards the end of the year 1784, Captain Francis Light, representing the East India Company, arranged to lease the island of Penang from the Sultan of Kedah for a sum of six thousand Spanish Dollars(as an indemnification of the loss he might sustain in his revenues, from the trade to Queddah being diverted into another channel (Leith, 1804: 2). In 1786, the island was officially called 'Prince Wellesley Island' but because the sum agreed upon was not paid to the Sultan, the latter launched a series of attacks on Penang, eventually necessitating the signing of a treaty in 1791 to compensate him for his losses.

At the same time, Seberang Perai on the mainland was acquired by the British in 1791 from the Kedah ruler. It was named Province Wellesley and functioned mainly as a hinterland for the colony of Penang, which was not self-sufficient in food production. In 1836, Captain James Low, writing his thesis on the Soil and Agriculture of Penang, observed that the province was already producing fish, rice, sugar, plantain and coconut in large quantities, with the annual surplus disposal agricultural produce being valued at not less than 80,000 Spanish Dollars.

Culturally and politically, the Malays of Seberang Perai are more closely affiliated to Kedah than to the island of Penang, although the continuous pattern of in-migration of Kedah Malays into the island has removed some of these cultural and political differences to a certain extent. Today, the patterns of settlement and nature of land use in Seberang Perai is similar to that found in the southern districts of Kedah and northern Perak, though rubber and oil-palm estates and plantations dominate the economic development of the region unlike the surrounding areas in Kedah which subsist on intensive rice farming and mixed cultivation. Generally, this reflects the more thorough penetration of the colonial cash economy in the province where rice cultivation was maintained by rural Malays to a more limited extent.

Historically, land-ownership in Seberang Perai expressed a curious mixture of *adat*, Islamic and British colonial law. Between the years 1829 and 1833, it was found that the largest land owners were, in terms of single personal ownership, the British followed by Malay elites (male), and finally the Chinese (Hill, 1977: 80-81).[1] Officially, women owned a very small portion of land in Seberang Perai (7 per cent), but these figures may not be indicative of the actual land ownership by women since they only accounted for registered titles and did not include informal transfers. Furthermore, land registered in the name of a male sibling could in reality also be owned by women under rules of *pakat* or informal agreements. Again, *wakaf keluarga*, indicating family group ownership as provided in Islamic law was another popular system of ownership in Seberang Perai and Kedah. In this case, the owners both men and women are members of the immediate family, and no single person has personal or legal jurisdiction over the administration of the land itself. The family, however, may appoint the eldest sibling male or female to preside over any transaction concerning the land. Generally, the relatively small percentage of land officially owned by women in this northern region was offset by the disproportionately large units of land cultivated by women. The mean size of farmland under rice cultivation was largest for women, showing an imbalance between female land ownership and productivity in agriculture.[2]

The Malay village of Mawang in Seberang Perai is located at the Kedah border in the district of Kulim (Map IV). Informants date it back to more than a century, locating the early pioneering families as those living along the areas which now form the road front. It has road accessibility to the nearest town, Simpang Ampat, which is about 6 kilometres away from the village. In 1983, the village contained 214 households with a population of approximately 1,500, most of whom are engaged in agricultural activities relating to rubber and padi cultivation.[3] Its close proximity to the towns of Simpang Ampat, Bukit Mertajam, Kulim, Butterworth and Georgetown, on Penang Island, has encouraged rapid urbanization, manifested in the emphasis on tertiary education and training, the increasing importance of non-agrarian-based activities and wage employment of youths in the Free Trade Zone at Bayan Lepas in Penang and its neighbouring towns. In this sense, Kampung Mawang is not unlike most present-day villages in Peninsular Malaysia which are being rapidly affected by national development policies focusing on agricultural modernization and industrialization.

Women, the Household Economy and Land

The land tenure system in Mawang is generally similar to that found in the northern states of the Peninsula. Land is usually distributed

Map IV: Penang and Seberang Perai

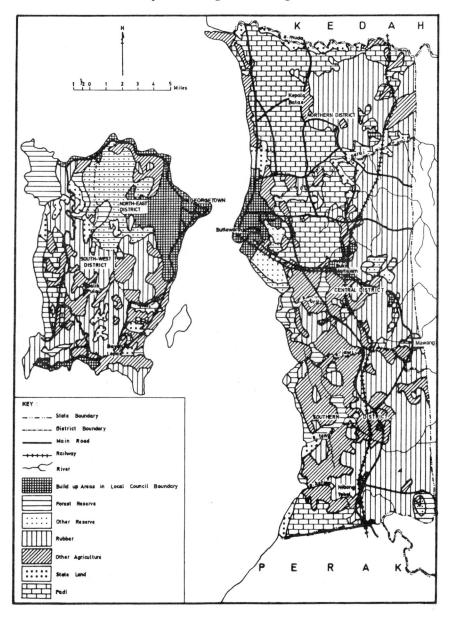

according to the personal preference of parents before their death, and there is still a general tendency to allocate it equally between daughters and sons. However, if both parents are land owners, they may agree (*pakat or janji*) to allow daughters to inherit land from the mother and sons from the father, in which case, it is not so much land values but 'units' which are accounted for. Each child is given an equivalent unit of land and where only a piece is available, it is divided equally among them. In families where the mother is a second wife or a divorcee (*janda*) who has remarried, she may prefer to give all her property to her children from her first marriage (including sons), should she feel that her second husband has enough to divide amongst their children from their marriage. Similarly, if her husband has been previously married, such an arrangement is also upheld for his children by his first marriage. These systems of property distribution may be officially sealed through legal land transfers in the Land Office but sometimes they are based on *janji* and the children are expected to agree to uphold their parents' decision after death.

Conflicts may consequently arise, in which case the matter may be settled informally with the help of the village headman or may be brought to the local district office for further consideration. At this stage, Islamic laws of inheritance may be applied so that women may theoretically be at a disadvantage if a prior settlement cannot be agreed upon by the siblings or kinsmen concerned.

According to the villagers, distribution of property before death usually follows *adat* law, rendering Islamic law meaningful only when a person dies intestate but many women feel that today, men are beginning to interpret Islamic laws of inheritance in its literal manner, so that *adat* preferences cannot be easily catered for. Generally, they believe that men are getting more aware of the advantage of observing Muslim laws of inheritance, not only for personal gain but because it prevents land segmentation and ensures greater economic viability in farming. In such situations, consanguines normally agree to divide the profits of the produce from the land, so that it is not so much ownership which becomes an issue of concern but equitable distribution of profits according to time and labour invested in the land. However, in families where major or permanent rifts have already occurred between parents and child or children, a son or daughter who is disfavoured may lose his/her rights completely. In the same way, a more caring son or daughter may be favoured above the others, particularly if they are in a position to take care of their ageing parents and to maintain the farms. Generally, sentiments continue to be an important consideration, rendering a fair amount of arbitrariness and flexibility to rules of land ownership in the village.

Although approximately 40 per cent of the land in the village continues to be owned by women, they represent the oldest or earliest residents and land owners in the village. Most of them are between the ages of 50 to 75 and state that they had inherited the land from their parents (mother, father, or both). Their parents or grandparents had resided in the village not as new migrants but as the original pioneers or settlers.[4]

The more recent land owners in the village represent the rural gentry of *Haji*, headmen (former *Ketua Kampung* or *Penghulu*) and contractors who have recently acquired land. Despite the high percentage of land owned by men, male land owners represent less than 30 per cent of the households (70 per cent are landless and rent land from these land owners (*sewa tapak rumah*) to construct their homes and maintain a small orchard or farming plot. The arrangement to *sewa tapak rumah* is a common practice in Malay villages and may be done privately between the two parties concerned or formally through a letter of agreement officiated by the headman. In Kampung Mawang, the sum is usually extremely small, amounting to less than MR\$5 a month (US\$2 a month) and is regarded more as a symbolic token of recognition of ownership rather than rent as such. Produce from trees cultivated on the land (usually fruit trees) before or after the period of tenancy commences is normally divided equally between the two parties, but if the tenant does not pay rent regularly, he or she will give much more, to compensate for the default in rents or irregular payments.

Rice lands (*bendang*) are also commonly farmed out and this is usually done according to a shorter term period of between 5 and 10 years.[5] The land owner and tenant again agree to a stipulated sum, which usually amounts to MR\$50 per season. The oldest land agreements made are of this nature and currently stand to benefit the tenant rather than the owner, since the price of rice has increased radically over the years while the tenancy terms remain the same. Furthermore, government quit rents on the land are paid by the owner and not the tenant. Thus, for new tenancies or more recently acquired rice land, the agreements are based on a rice season (*disewa musim demi musim*) and a sum of approximately 150 gantang (approximately 47.5 kilogrammes) is agreed upon. Even so, this amount may be reduced if the rice harvest is exceptionally low but it is not increased if the rice harvest is very bountiful for a particular season.

It is important to consider that most of these transactions are based on old friendship ties which often develop into fictitious kinship relationships expressing the continuance of long term social relationships within the village (Banks, 1983; Wilder, 1982). A land owner who maintains an easy or generous arrangement often gains in social standing and esteem within the village community. The older residents of the village have an added obligation to maintain these socioeconomic ties and it is here that the image of old women as benevolent land owners contrasts sharply with more recent immigrant male land owners, particularly *Haji* and schoolteachers, who have sharper entrepreneurial skills and business sense, and regard village tenancies as commercial enterprises (Scott, 1985b). For this reason, the distinctions between *orang asal* (the original people) and *orang asing* (outsiders) stand even more sharply today, blurring basic prestige or status distinctions attached to wealth and land ownership. Those in the *orang asing* category may be land owners or be more enterprising, but they have relatively lower social standing compared to the earlier residents. Generally, however, it is the newer residents rather than the earlier residents who are landless and their tenancy status renders them a low social position in the community if it is not compensated by hard work or professional and economic attainment in some form.

The conditions in Mawang are representative of those found in other rural villages where women continue to have an important role in maintaining the household economy and resources within (Hill, 1977; Banks, 1983, Heyzer, 1986; Ong, 1987). Table 5.1a shows the majority of the women as housewives (67.3 per cent) but these women spending considerable time in farming and food-processing for household consumption, though would not classify themselves as 'farmers' since their farm work is part-time rather than full-time. Generally, only 'waged' workers (labourers on the farm or estates of others) said that they were working (full-time 3.3 per cent and part-time, 6.6 per cent).

Women's productivity in agriculture is possibly even more important today in view of the rapid out-migration of young men into towns and cities in search of regular or waged employment. This problem will be discussed further in Chapter 6 but is necessary to observe here that a consequence of this has been to reduce to some extent women's control over labour resources within the household, particularly from their own sons and daughters, though hired help from the kindred unit and village is often resorted to. However, increased mechanization in farming is a growing feature of the Malay rural economy, and it is an area where women have not yet shown their participation, except in the case of established land owners who engage private entrepreneurs who have invested in agricultural machinery. Those who have not done so have abandoned their rice fields, a situation normally referred to as *tanah terbiar*. It is interesting to note that these fields have not been taken over by the men of the family and household so that a transfer to male providers is not apparent. However, with the increasing application of new concepts of farming management techniques, mechanization and expansion of integrated land schemes, the agricultural economy is gradually being 'privatized', operated and controlled not so much by land owners but by outsiders with the capital and skills to lease disused farmland as a business venture or to accumulate and lease farming machinery as a commercial enterprise. Significantly, apart from the government, most of these companies are owned and operated by non-Malays.

TABLE 5.1   Women's Occupation, Marital Status and the Socioeconomic Profile
of Kampung Mawang, Seberang Perai, 1983

a. WOMEN'S OCCUPATION

Occupation		No.	Per Cent
Farmer	(full-time)	7	(3.3%)
Waged labourer	(part-time)	14	(6.6%)
Waged labourer	(full-time)	42	(19.6%)
Professional		5	(2.3%)
Housewife		144	(67.3%)
Others		2	(0.9%)
TOTAL		214	(100.0%)

b. MARITAL STATUS

Married	Divorced or Widowed	Polygamous Union	Others	TOTAL
159	51	4	0	214
(74.3)	(23.8)	(1.9)	(0.0)	(100.0%)

c. HOUSEHOLD STRUCTURES

Male Heads of Household	Female Heads of Household	Others	TOTAL
163	48	3	214
(76.2)	(22.4)	(1.4)	(100.0%)

d. FAMILY TYPES

Nuclear	Extended	Single Parent (mother)	Others	TOTAL
140	35	23	16	214
(65.4)	(16.4)	(10.7)	(7.5)	(100.0%)

e. HOUSEHOLD INCOME AND EXPENDITURE

	$100	$100-$300	$300-$500	$500-$700	$700+	TOTAL
Income	75	120	18	1	0	214
	(35.0)	(56.1)	(8.4)	(0.5)	(0.0)	(100.0%)
Expenditure	88	111	11	2	2	214
	(41.1)	(51.9)	(5.2)	(0.9)	(0.9)	(100.0%)

In this sense, it would be difficult to apply the usual argument maintained by writers like Boserup (1970), researching mainly in Africa, that the consequences of mechanization and privatization in agriculture are female domestication and encapsulation within the household. In the case of the Malays, women have derived significant power in owning, controlling and managing land, labour and capital. With the current instabilities within the household economy, displacement is not so much demonstrated in terms of gender variables but rather class and ethnicity. True, men own machines but women with sufficient farmland and capital can hire them to mechanize their farms. The domain of hiring and firing is not the monopoly of Malay men. It might be possible to envisage the growing phenomenon of private or co-operatively owned farming machinery but the current situation is a displacement of the parental unit in agriculture and men, more than women, within the household. Women's diversification techniques in agriculture are extensive. Their skills and labour in household management, where agriculture and farming is a fundamental feature of the household, has not been significantly displaced or replaced. In the northern region, diversification into tobacco, maize or vegetable cultivation and the establishment of agro-based village industries is dependent on female labour. Kampung Mawang has not diversified in this way, but in other villages in Kedah, the displacement of women in rice has been counter-checked by their employment in the wider agriculture sector.

Many of these developments within the Malay household economy may be better analysed if modes of social relations, as ordered by *adat*, are properly understood. In this context, Islam, as operationalized in the past or present, has had little relevance to the household economy either in terms of reordering gender roles within the Malay family or of restructuring the rural economy through Islamic principles of co-operation and sharing. Significantly, while Islam is not incompatible with capitalistic modes of production, the patterns of capital transfer within agriculture are not even discussed or reviewed in terms of Islamic notions of profit-sharing or business management, except in the area of *zakat* where produce from farming has always been taxed according to Islamic principles of reckoning surplus and profit (Scott, 1985a, 1985b).

The issue today is not so much the diminishing value of Malay women in agriculture or farming but the continued participation and control of the peasantry over the rural economy. Here, the current challenge of bilaterality in the Malay household as a mode of organization of land, labour and capital within farming and agriculture rests on the capacity of the Malay peasantry to participate in processes of mechanization, capital transfer and penetration of capitalism in the rural economy on the same level as the non-Malays. One of the consequences of these socioeconomic developments is the transfer of capital, labour and management to a non-peasant-based population challenging the existing continuity and survival of the Malay household economy. The trends are obviously there but the present concern of observers is whether it has produced an irreversible disintegrative effect on women's position in general or on their economic productivity in particular. This is obviously a question that needs further thinking and cannot be properly sorted out here. Chapter 6 discusses this problem in some detail. For now, it is worth commenting that trends towards urban employment of young Malay women (who have not been previously employed) can be seen as a process of regenerating female labour and indirectly the productivity of the rural household. It is also accompanied by a continuous flow of remittance to the rural household from daughter to mother or son to mother (Karim, 1987b). Women then maintain some control over household income, even if they do not produce it themselves, after being displaced in farming.

However, whether the young rural female worker in the factory is accorded the same value as her mother in agriculture depends on the extent to which she is able to demonstrate social mobility in a variety of ways. From an emic perspective, a woman's (mother or daughter) increasing accessibility to goods and services that are rated highly in the village is a good measurement of socioeconomic mobility (Karim, 1987b). It provides women with a sense of self-worth and satisfaction that they have purchasing power and can compete with the upper classes in the acquisition of new goods. Another is advancing educational or professional standards of women and men within the family (Ayse Nurlifer, 1986). A third in rural and urban areas is the amassing of fixed assets and property. If visible changes are seen in a family's standard or style of living in the village as a result of new forms of employment, then personal status (i.e. prestige) increases with family or household status increase (Papanek, 1979; Karim, 1987b). On the other hand, factory work associated with impoverished landless families may only be a means to obtain basic income for food and rent and this does not necessarily change personal or family status. Employment only caters for basic needs, not surplus. The importance of measuring women's value and power in relation to the family and household cannot be understated since economic activities, motives and decisions are invariably intertwined with group family concerns and obligations. Economic choices designed to upgrade living standards of the family have implications on women's value and power in both a personal and group sense. In rural areas in particular, an analysis of women's value and power cannot be easily made without a contextual reference to the family or household.

The Kindred Group and Status Ranking

Pioneering anthropological studies on the Malay family, kinship and marriage were mostly undertaken in the 1950s and 1960s in the works of Djamour (1959), Swift (1965) and Firth (1966). More recently, other writers have contributed significant research on Malay kinship (Wilder, 1970, 1982; Banks, 1972, 1983; Mckinley 1983; Carsten, 1987). These studies have been instrumental in confirming the principle of bilaterality in Malay culture and the overt importance of age, seniority, siblingship and equalitarian principles in ordering roles and relationships within the family and kinship order.

Despite the fact that Djamour's study was undertaken amongst urban Malays in Singapore, Swift's in a Minangkabau village in Jelebu in Negeri Sembilan (administered according to *adat perpatih*) and Firth's in a fishing community in Kelantan which in terms of modes of social relations differs somewhat from mainline agrarian-based Malay communities in the Peninsula, generalities of structure and organization were observed in all these communities in bilaterality as a fundamental principle of Malay culture. Sex or gender differentiation as a basis of social analysis was further attempted by Wilder (1970), who sought to demonstrate certain structural inconsistencies in sex differentiation rules, in the phases of adolescence and marriage. He argues (p. 250) that 'the tendency to sexual equality that develops in marriage appears to contradict the clear separateness and contrast of male and female roles prior to marriage'. Sexual asymmetry may be related to sexual status but not marital status, where 'complementarity is not maintained as strictly'. Here, Wilder defines complementarity in terms of inequality in role differentiation rather than balanced statuses within role differentiation.

The argument in this study appears partly to support Wilder's ideas for it is shown here that rules of sexual differentiation in the pre-adolescent and adolescent periods do clearly exist. However, a point not brought out by Wilder is that, despite their complementarity roles, both sexes are subject to comparable codes of social and moral behaviour, rendering their status to be more balanced and equal than that assumed. Clearly, *adat*, as a powerful agent of socialization, does not encourage radical gender differences for those in the pre-marriage category. In the pre-marriage category, both sexes suffer from ritual exclusion. Also, Islam as practised in Malaysia and *adat* do not confine adolescent women to domesticity nor do differential roles lead to sexual segregation. The only advantage young men enjoy is physical freedom. Men are physically more independent and free to move about with minimal social restriction but they continue to be bound by the same codes of morality and economic behaviour as women.

Distinctions of women's and men's 'peripheral' and 'central' status based on the pre- and post-marital phase of relationships appear to be more meaningful. Ritual power through matrimony and the accompanying standards of adulthood and seniority it provides for men and women describe Malay ways of ascribing values in accordance with matrimonial functions, rather than gender. Conversely, the 'peripheral' position of single women is shared by single men, except that they could be more restricted physically.

While the kindred system preserves equalitarian values of gender, the system of status differentiation within the kindred network is again based on principles of seniority within and across generations. The system of address and references of members of the kindred group emphasizes principles of cognatic descent which pervade Malay social structure. The example of Kampung Mawang is very much representative of the Malay kindred system in the northern region.

Generally, ego addresses members of his generation within and without his immediate family according to classificatory terms denoting differences in sex and age; those elder to him as *kakak* or *abang* ('elder sister' or 'elder brother' respectively) and those younger to him as simply *adik* ('younger sister' or 'brother', Figure 5.1, Ego 2). Seniority is again further distinguished by terms reflecting their order of birth; *long* from *sulong* (eldest), *ngah* from *tengah* (middle) and *su* from *bongsu* (youngest). These terms of address are also terms of reference for both sexes within ego's family and are usually extended to members of his generation within the kindred groups. For example, ego will refer to and address his eldest brother as *abang long* (or, if the first born was a sister, *kak long*), and may also extend the same terms to his elder first cousins parallel or cross, male and female, respectively. When there are too many siblings or cousins to address by these main categories, shortened versions of names or descriptions of a person's attributes will be used instead (e.g. *Kak Tam*, 'elder cousin with a dark complexion'; *Bang Jang*, i.e. 'elder brother who is tall', *Bang Ngah*, 'cousin of middle-birth order [*tengah*]). These terms are normally retained for life and members of the succeeding generations would merely change the classificatory kinship reference (while retaining the pseudonym) to denote differential generational status. For example, *Bang Jang*'s nephew or niece would call him *Pa'Cik Jang* or *Pa' Jang* (Uncle *Jang*).

Members of ego's (Figure 5.1, Ego 1) father's (*bapak, ayah, abah*) and mother's (*emak, ibu*) generation are addressed and referred to by terms reflecting their sex and seniority in relation to their order of birth within that generation. As with ego's generation, the same three levels of seniority are recognized, *long, ngah* and *su*. Again, the term *mak (emak)* or *pak (bapak)* will be added before these three terms denoting seniority, so that a mother's/father's eldest brother is called *pak long*, and a mother's/father's

132

FIGURE 5.1 Malay Kinship Bilaterality and Terms of References and Address

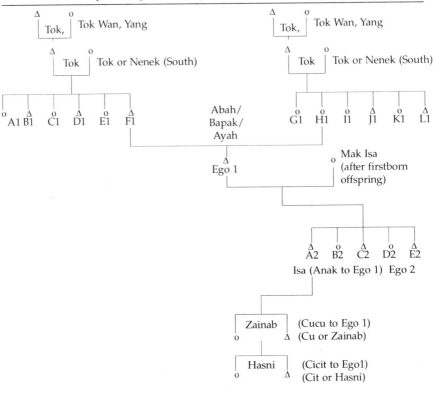

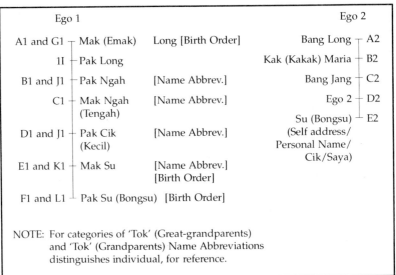

younger brother, *pak su*. If his parents are the youngest offspring of their generation, the second uncle in order of birth will be addressed and referred to as *Pak Ngah*. A wider range of uncles and aunts will again necessitate the introduction of naming variations (*Pak Teh*, *Mak Siah*, etc.) to avoid confusion in both address and reference. Finally, members of the grand-parental generations are referred to and addressed as '*tok*' for both sexes (shortened from '*Dato*'), a term denoting seniority and reverence, or regularly in the South, '*tok*' for men and *nenek* for women, with the same emphasis on terms of differentiation according to order of birth. Members of the great-grandparental generation are in the North referred to and addressed as *Tok* or *Tok Wan* regardless of sex, and in the South, *Yang* or *Moyang* (ancestor).

The generation below ego are commonly referred to and addressed by personal names to express the honorific and senior positions of the parental generations as a whole while those of the succeeding generations of 'grandchildren' may be simply addressed by their personal names and referred to as *cucu*. Great-grandchildren are also addressed by personal names but referred to as *cicit*. Generally, when grandchildren and great-grandchildren are addressed by personal names, it may be because there are too many of them for the simple generic term to be used.

In marriage, daughters-in-law and sons-in-law commonly refer to their spouses' parents as *emak* (mother) and *ayah* or *bapa* (father) and this absolute reciprocity is also marked by the way in which the classificatory titles of either spouse (for example *Mak Siah*, 'Siah' shortened from 'Samsiah', female; *Pak Mat*, Mat, shortened from 'Mohammad', male) is extended to their new wife or husband. Thus, *Mak Siah*'s husband is referred to and addressed as *Pak Siah*. He assumes his wife's name within her kindred group. Among his own kin, however, she automatically assumes his name. Thus, if he is known, referred to and addressed as *Pak Mat*, his wife would, among his kinfolk, be known, referred to and addressed as *Mak Mat*. Malay bilaterality is best expressed in these classificatory naming systems which disregard gender to highlight generational factors, seniority and affinity.

Marriage Patterns and Preferences

Despite the multi-ethnic structures of Malaysian society, marriage preferences of the Malays continue to be subject to values of *adat*. The criterion of ethnicity is imposed in both rural and urban areas, for both arranged marriages and those based on romantic attachments. Arranged marriages are exceedingly uncommon today, but when they do occur, it invariably reflects a preference for ethnic and cultural homogeneity. This seems to be the situation in Kampung Mawang and the neighbouring village of Tasek. The parents of the prospective bride or bridegroom tend to seek out another 'Melayu' (Malay) family of approximately the same socioeconomic background where social ties are already consolidated or can easily be established through a close coparents-in-law (bisan) relationship. This implies that such marriage arrangements are based on social and cultural familiarity, where to be 'Melayu' is the first criterion, followed by the preference of choosing individuals within the same sub-ethnic and linguistic category — example, Javanese, Minangkabau, Bugis, Baweanese. Strong cultural variations continue to exist amongst these communities, upheld by variations of adat, language (bahasa) and dialect (laurat). Malays who are unable to trace their origins to any particular region or sub-cultural group do not place much emphasis on these socioeconomic differences and may only emphasize marriage with another Malay.

Although all Malays are Muslims, the converse is not always true and urban Malay populations may stress on Islam as a unifying force, rather than ethnicity. It may be acceptable for families to arrange or accept marriages with Indian Muslim families or Chinese converts though these marriages are usually avoided in normal circumstances when other choices are available from the Malay community. Marriages which are based on personal selection rather than family arrangements, tend to follow the same religious criterion. Despite the increasing choices for mate selection which the younger generation enjoy today, Malay men and women gravitate to members of their ethnic group and continue to regard inter-ethnic marriages as socially problematic even if the non-Muslim spouse converts to Islam. Highly romantic attachments may show a disregard for ethnic homogeneity, but even so, strong parental social pressures may be exerted upon the man and woman concerned, leading to a dissolution of the relationship or continued misunderstandings after marriage. Children may succeed in bringing about stability to the marriage but only after the married pair and their parents have achieved a certain degree of mutual adjustment and compromise in the marriage. Thus, though adat and Islam are inseparable on the level of ethnicity, adat tends to permeate preferential rules of marriage much more strongly than Islam.

Another important consideration besides ethnic homogeneity is selection of marriage partners according to the same state (negeri) boundary which, again, appears to accommodate variations of adat negeri within the boundaries of the state. Though this is not always possible with increasing geographical mobility and selection of residence according to place of employment rather than village of origin, significant prejudices and negative stereotypes are revealed when interstate marriages or potential marriages are contracted. These prejudices and stereotypes are more commonly directed against women than men, but men do receive a significant share of these sentiments. Most of these explicit statements directed against men and women from other states refer to cultural incompatibilities and varying standards of morality. To illustrate, one of the more common stereotypes in Kampung Mawang about marriage to a Kelantan woman is that she is obsessed by jewellery, will freely use love spells and potions (*tangkal pengasih*) to keep her husband in tow and will not hesitate to leave her husband should she capture a man with more wealth or social standing. It is also the belief in the kampung that marriage to a Perlis woman invariably leads to female dominance and tight control over household finances. Similar views are expressed against Minangkabau women from Negeri Sembilan who are said to make bad wives because they have a need to dominate on all matters. A Johor woman is said to be cold and unapproachable and not very accommodating to her spouse's kinsmen.

These views, which are frequently circulated by both sexes, are directed towards women from another *negeri* or state. Often, men and women may reject the views others may have of their womenfolk and retaliate by saying something negative about women from other states so that more prejudices are revealed and developed in this way. A Kelantan man, for example, stated that while he did not believe the vicious comments directed against Kelantanese women, was willing to take a solemn oath that women from Selangor possessed the very same traits of which his women were being accused. Generally, these prejudices are more often upheld by women of the older generation who may utilize them to direct their son's choices back to their own state.[6]

In Mawang, views expressed of men usually centre around standards of cultural refinements (*bersopan santun, berbudi pekerti, kehalusan*) and ability to provide for their wives and family (*bertanggungjawab, memberi cukup makan*). Women believe that men from Melaka and Kedah are crude and loud (*kasar*) in contrast to those from Negeri Sembilan and Johor who are said to be soft-spoken and refined (*halus*). However, in terms of economic support and responsibility towards the family, men from Kelantan, Terengganu and Negeri Sembilan are supposed to be the least dependable. Generally, social differences and incompatibilities widen according to physical distance so that North-South and East-West cultural prejudices are the most clearly expressed and upheld. For example, it would be more common to hear a person from Johor criticizing the men and women of Penang and Kedah rather than Pahang or Melaka. A person from Mawang may have more misgivings marrying someone from Terengganu or Johor than someone from Kedah or Perlis. These cultural variations are also expressed in terms of differences in wedding rituals (*adat-istiadat perkahwinan*), methods of payment of bridewealth (*bayaran hantaran; letak belanja*), and terms of references of the marriage contract (*perjanjian kahwin*).

Kinship preferences, expressed in marriages between close or distant consanguines, continue to be strongly maintained by the elder generation. First- or second-cousin marriages are approved of although second-cousin marriages are preferred since coparents-in-law in such cases can achieve a compromise between familiarity and in-breeding. Marriages between distant relatives (*saudara bau macang or adik-beradik jauh*)[7] are definitely preferred to marriages contracted with non-consanguines or affines, for the latter evokes feelings of uneasiness and doubt about the potential social ties that may evolve between the two family groups concerned. However, here, it should be emphasized that the preference for marriages based on kinship ties is not always shared by the younger men and women involved, partly because their association may not be as close or harmonious as that enjoyed by their prospective coparents-in-law. This is particular so where these young kinsmen have established their own peer groups through relationships established in schools, colleges or associations. Opposition to these endogamous marriages within the parental unit may take place when such families are embroiled in personal disagreements or disputes. When this occurs, it is hardly likely that such marriages will be encouraged, even if the young man and woman involved agree to marry each other. It appears that although marriages within the same kinship circle are greatly encouraged, it is very much dependent on the existing amicable relationship between the prospective coparents-in-law so that social sentiments very often override kinship preferences. Furthermore, considerable disagreements may arise between parents and their children which may make such marriages difficult to contract or to maintain.

The importance of social sentiments is clearly expressed amongst men and women who may not be related to one another but who happen to maintain very close friendship ties. Such friendships often lead to the extension of fictitious kinship ties (*saudara angkat*) in which one or both persons may wish to strengthen their friendship by encouraging their children to marry each other. The progress from friends to fictitious kin and finally co-parents-in-law is something clearly seen as desirable and ideal.

In certain instances, close affinal ties between spouses of consanguines (*biras*) may encourage co-affines to marry one another, with a certain amount of prompting and encouragement from a sister- or brother-in-law (*kakak ipar, abang ipar* respectively). When the younger siblings of co-affines are already familiar with one other, this may not be such a problem and marriages along this pattern often arise in villages where endogamy is prevalent. The motivation behind such marriage arrangements is not only to restrengthen affinal ties but also to ensure that the kindred network could be smoothly maintained with sociocultural and economic differences reduced to a minimum. This principle applies to extremely well-connected or wealthy families where *bisan* and *biras* ties are constantly utilized and reinforced within the kindred network to ensure that the standard and style of living of each family unit be approximately similar. Thus, socializing behaviour, expenditure and consumption patterns are predictable and easily accommodated or adjusted to, bringing misunderstandings down to a minimum.

The selection of marriage partners along class lines applies to both urban and rural Malays, but is again most clearly expressed in situations of extreme wealth or poverty. As mentioned earlier, families who are exceedingly wealthy, titled and landed have a strong preference for selecting marriage partners from other families of similar socioeconomic standing. Children from such families quite often socialize together so that it is not altogether true to say that such marriages are usually arranged and lack personal contact or romantic attachment.[8] However, since the social milieu provides the optimum conditions for mutual compatibility, personal differences and preferences are not given such importance.

Marriage alliances are more commonly expressed in families with political connections and interests and is most clearly expressed in the marriage patterns of national Malay politicians and their children. When women from such families contract a hypogamous marriage, they normally do so with men who have a certain amount of professional status and this serves to bring about greater social acceptability. Hypogamous marriages are generally more common for men than for women since men of this class do not look upon women as economic providers and may marry for other qualities such as domesticity, beauty, obedience and fidelity. Women, on the other hand, regardless of their wealth, expect their husbands to shoulder a fair amount of domestic and public expenses and this makes it more difficult for them to marry down. Nevertheless, such marriages are avoided as far as possible and even when they do occur, affinal ties, based on *bisan* or *biras* relationships, are weak and in some cases completely severed.

The difficulty in making personal, social and economic adjustments in such marriages discourage men and women from rural and non-professional backgrounds to marry others with dissimilar socioeconomic status. This pattern of marriage is particularly important in Mawang which comprises mainly poor or lower-middle working-class families. Women from these families have a greater tendency to marry hypergamously than men, particularly if they have the right combination of qualities which Malay men often look for — a fair complexion, a gentle disposition and domesticity. Within the region, it frequently happens that a number of the rural elite, comprising schoolteachers, religious specialists, landed and titled farmers and local political leaders, take in lovely but poor young girls as their second wives. Mawang has three such marriages, one to a contractor, another to a schoolteacher and a third to an *imam*. Such marriages are acceptable, particularly since both parties stand to gain from the union; social standing and economic benefits for the girl's kinsmen, and for her spouse, added prestige and glamour in taking a younger and beautiful wife. Socioeconomic mobility through marriage is clearly more commonly discerned among males and female children of the rural elite who are better able to acquire professional training through tertiary education and have greater access to the noveau-riche Malay society in towns and cities. Marriages based on similarity in professions or income are fast becoming the standard marriage style for urban Malays and it is increasingly uncommon for young men and women to return to the village to look for marriage partners.

In rural areas, while the majority of marriages continue to be contracted between young men and women from the village or surrounding villages, the trend towards seeking waged-employment in the nearby towns and cities has enabled the younger generation to seek spouses according to place of employment. Women who marry men in this way invariably indulge in virilocal residence except in cases where both spouses originate from the same village. Women who marry hypergamously are the selected few who manage to contract marriages with regular waged or fully employed men, usually those holding jobs within the teaching profession and armed forces. In Mawang, a girl who marries a man from the army, regardless of his rank, is considered fortunate since he is able to provide for her regularly (*gaji tetap*), and obtains special allowances for his wife and children. However, someone who marries a schoolteacher is considered even more fortunate since her husband's profession carries an added prestige and social standing in the village.

Within the existing ranking system of hyper- or hypogamous marriages, marriage to a farmer, whether he works part or full-time, is probably ranked the lowest for such an occupation does not guarantee regular income, is not physically 'glamorous or sophisticated' (*pekerjaan comot, kotor*) and conveys low geographical and occupational mobility. Thus, the preference for blue-collar or white-collar careers on the part of men is indirectly prompted by women's low preference in wanting a farmer as a spouse. Men are strongly intimidated by this prejudice, for the fear of not being able to procure a wife is as strong as a woman's fear of not being proposed to at all (*tak kena minang*); the former situation places a man in the derogatory position of a *bujang lapok* (a disused, ragged bachelor) and the latter, places a woman in the position of an *anak dara tua* (a spinster). This seems to suggest that choice of marriage abide by the status definitions of the day. While economic stability, materialism and regularity of employment have always been value considerations in marriage, they are now neatly formulated in blue-collar and white-collar categories. Parents may well prefer their daughters to be the second wife of a highly established entrepreneur, religious specialist, schoolteacher, or civil servant, than to be married to a full or part-time farmer or waged farm labourer. However, if the person happens to own land, is extremely industrious and enterprising and shows entrepreneurial skills,she may be persuaded to marry him since he is industrious and landed (*rajin dan bertanah pula*).

As mentioned earlier, arranged marriages are becoming increasingly uncommon although occasionally a worried mother, fearing her daughter's selectiveness of a marriage partner will leave her on the shelf (generally selectivity is synonymous to 'fussiness' or *cerewet*), may nag her to make up her mind about a particular man who has expressed his wish to have her as a bride. The same applies to men who procrastinate a decision on marriage. They may be constantly advised to 'get a wife' (*cari bini/isteri*) or in the most desperate of situations, may be nagged to marry a particular girl who has been 'viewed' or 'screened' (*dah'menengok*) and is approved of by both parents and close kinsmen. In Mawang, the ideal marriageable age is between 16 and 25 years for women and between 20 and 25 for men but women more than men are pressured to conform to this ideal age-group pattern, particularly if they are unemployed and are not pursuing courses or careers. More shame relatively is attached to a family with unmarried daughters than to those with bachelor sons though the position of an unmarried woman or man is equally marginal in Malay rural society. The unmarried are excluded from numerous social and ritual activities which are organized by the married and the village elders, merely because they are conceived to be immature and inexperienced. The married, having raised families are seen to be more experienced in the social dynamics of community life.

In the village, marriage choices based on standards of religiosity are not often abided by. The religion specifies that a man chooses a wife for four reasons — beauty, property, family background and religiousness. Of the four, the most important criterion is religiousness and it is for this reason alone that a Muslim man should marry a woman. This argument is sometimes articulated in Mawang but a man seldom selects his wife because of her religiousness unless it is accompanied by other personal attributes. For example, he may be inspired by a woman who does public recitals of the Qur'an (*mengaji Qur'an*) but may decide to marry her not so much for her piety as for the melodious quality of her voice. Then again, a man may marry a woman who is a religious fundamentalist (*dakwa*) and allow her to 'reform' him, to follow the 'true path of Islam', but in such a case, he may have already been attracted to her in the first place to allow her to do so. He may also realize that it is the best way to get closer to her. Another common situation is when a man attempts to develop a sense of religiousness in his wife after their marriage, in order to control her more effectively or to ensure that she maintains a high standard of social propriety and decorum which meets the approval of his kinsmen. Her piety or wantonness before marriage is not really the issue here. It is only her overtly expressive personal behaviour after marriage, towards him and his kinsmen, which is of importance.

Polygyny and Divorce

Polygynous marriages continue to be upheld by the relatively more wealthy urban or rural elite Malays. However, men normally indulge in polygyny for the following reasons:

1. When a wife is barren (*mandul*) and a man desires to have children of his own. Since this is a provision for polygyny in Islam, such marriages are seldom criticized though a fair amount of sympathy and compassion may be expressed for the first wife, particularly by women.
2. When a man's wife has reached menopause and desires to have more children. Such polygynous marriages are normally frowned upon by women for they normally interpret this as an excuse on the part of the man to have a better sex-life or to prove his continuing virility. Criticisms levied against the male are mainly expressed by women who point to the wide age difference between the two. Remarks like *dia tak sedar umur* ('he does not realize his age') and *boleh buat anak* ('she could be his child') are frequently made in relation to age differences. Sometimes the reason given is an abnormally high sexual drive and this is framed in rude expressions like *nak cuba pakai yang muda pula* ('he wants to use a young one now'), *yang lama jadi barang kondem dah* ('he has made the old one a condemned item') or *dia mempunyai nafsu anjing* ('he has the sexual appetite of a dog'). All these comments have been heard in Mawang but the most vicious comments directed against such a man makes reference to his 'impending death state' or *hilang tabiat* which expresses the Malay belief that a person, regardless of age or sex, indulges in extraordinary or strange forms of behaviour prior to death. However, the wide age differences in such marriages may actually work to the advantage of the younger wife who may be more kindly rewarded by her co-wife. In the best of circumstances, an older woman will not attempt to compete sexually or materially with the younger wife and may even come to regard her as her daughter.

In these circumstances, a likely solution for the man concerned is polygyny, although it may not meet the approval of the wife and woman with whom the man has had a liaison. The man may be reluctant to divorce his wife for many reasons, the most important being the fear of losing control and custody of his children. He may also still love and care for his wife and may not want to see her being married to someone else, a situation which may eventually severe his close relationship with his children. His wife may also not want a divorce because she feels unable to cope on her own, either emotionally or financially. A divorce is only likely in circumstances when the wife is anxious to have the chance of a second marriage. In this case, even if the husband is unwilling, she may attempt to pester, nag or plead with him to divorce her. Alternatively, a divorce may be a condition imposed by the new wife who is unwilling to be a co-wife. Under such circumstances, a man may divorce his first wife for fear of losing his newly found partner.

Often, polygynous marriages are traumatic for the husband and co-wives because of constant quarrelling, misunderstandings, jealousy and favouritism. Conflicts are greatly lessened when the wives do not live together in the same house or if they live in separate villages or towns. However, both marriages may continue for years with increasing or decreasing stability, depending on the kinds of compromises or hardships faced by the husband and his co-wives, with each successive year of marriage.

In Mawang, as it usually is amongst the Malays, polygynous marriages are limited to two wives. The full Islamic provisions of marrying four are not abided by freely because of economic, emotional and personal constraints. In contrast, members of the Malay royalty or men with wealth and social standing may marry more than two but the Islam rule of treating and providing for each wife equally is seldom met or observed. Again, men with strong religious convictions may be reluctant to marry more than one wife or may restrict themselves to two mainly because they feel they cannot meet the commitments and responsibilities laid down in Islamic law for the four wife polygynous system.

Divorce in Malay society adheres to Muslim divorce procedures following the principle of *talak* (Ar. *talaq*).[9] A simple statement of 'I divorce you' is equivalent to a first *talak* but it is legitimate only if pronounced in the presence of a witness, normally a *kadi*, or is soon afterwards confirmed in the presence of a *kadi*. The latter may attempt to advise the man or the couple to reconsider but if the husband or both parties are adamant about it, he will issue the wife a written statement confirming the divorce, which becomes valid only after the period of *iddah* of three months and ten days. The *iddah* serves as a period of reconciliation or trial separation and is imposed to enable the man to reconsider the decision or to ensure that the woman is without child.[10] A Muslim man may not divorce his wife during her pregnancy. He has to maintain her till the end of her period of confinement after which he has to agree to make adequate provisions for his child (and previous children, if any), and provide alimony if she is not economically independent.

The high rates of Muslim divorces in the Peninsula is not simply an indication of Malay or Muslim men abusing the simpler rules of Muslim divorce procedures to start a new life or to be rid of a financial burden.[11] In the majority of divorce cases registered in the *Pejabat Agama Islam* or the Religious Department in Kelantan and Terengganu, divorce procedures were initiated by women rather than men. These decisions against the continuity of marriage conform to more universal patterns of social preferences where women feel that it is better to terminate a bad marriage than to maintain one which brings on mental anguish and unhappiness. Amongst the more common reasons for divorce are inability of the husband to provide economically for the family, sociocultural incompatibility, personal differences pertaining to styles of living, sexual behaviour or physical needs, polygyny and adultery. Men usually divorce their wives on the basis of socioeconomic incompatibility and personal differences since the majority prefer to maintain the first marriage rather than terminate it in the face of polygyny or adultery (which is seldom made public).

It has been mentioned before (Djamour, 1959: 115-117; Firth, 1966: 29) that Malay women exercise a certain amount of prerogative in divorce and resort to numerous informal procedures of procuring a divorce when the husband is reluctant to give her one. Other than appealing to the *Kadi* in the Syariah Court, she may resort to nagging her husband for a divorce and, if that fails, cause him much public humiliation and agony by exposing his lesser qualities to others, particularly his general state of bankruptcy, lust or cowardice. This strategy works rather well and eventually results in the woman obtaining a divorce. A woman who is divorced at a fairly young age has a good chance for remarriage and may prefer to take this chance than to carry on with a marriage she can no longer endure. In the village of Mawang, of the 23.8 per cent women who are divorced or widowed, above half have remarried (mainly to divorced men), since the period of the survey in 1983 (Table 5.1b). There is little stigmatization in being divorced or remarried and in fact is more socially acceptable than not marrying at all.

Normally, such marriages lead to a compound family structure with three sets of children (from both spouses' first marriage and their own children together) calling one another *adik-beradik* (here to mean siblings). They do not however necessarily form a single household but attempt somehow to establish sibling relationships within the freedom and con-straint of multiple parentages. Table 5.1c shows households to comprise mainly nuclear families (65.4 per cent) but many of these may contain half-siblings within the same household or different households. The degree to which children are able to adapt to half-sibling relationships depends greatly on the physical and social conditions of interaction imposed by parents and close kinsmen.

It appears that generally Malay monogamous or polygynous marriages seldom reflect the ideal marriage rules laid down in Islam. Choices and preferences are dominated by *adat*-ethnic, sub-ethnic, and socio-cultural values rather than religious norms. The Islamic religion is upheld only in a formal ideological sense in the application of Islamic rules of polygyny and divorce or when property is divided according to Islamic law.

Sexual Relations Between Spouses

In a typical Malay marriage, it is common for both spouses to attempt to seek sexual satisfaction from each other in the best possible way (Banks, 1983). It is as important for a man to know how to please his wife sexually as it is for her to please him. A Malay husband would go to lengths to improve upon his sexual performance, by seeing traditional medicine-men or the *bomoh* for sex therapy, or by trying out some of the many local and Indonesian *jamu* herbs and potions which are believed to increase a man's virility and sexual potency. Some of the more common sexual anxieties Malay men suffer from concern sexual fatigue, impotence and premature ejaculation. Male preoccupation with sex therapy and use of *jamu* to resolve sexual problems or to improve virility is linked to notions of manhood and honour.

Older men in particular become the butt of male and female joking behaviour if their wives' complaints of their low sexual performance became public knowledge. Women have a way of ventilating their frustrations to other married women who seldom hesitate to disclose the intimate details of the story to their husbands or close female friends. The story soon reaches the male circle and the consequences are humiliating for the person concerned but hilarious for his friends. Premature ejaculation is referred to as *tumpah bubur* or *nasi* (literally, 'to spill porridge' or 'rice') and a married man who constantly disappoints his wife in this way is considered by women to be a highly undesirable sexual partner.[12] The perfect sexual partner is someone who can perform well sexually every time. In addition, for a man, an ideal wife is one who can also produce as many sons and daughters as they can afford. In idiomatic Malay, a man *berenang* ('swims') when he can perform well sexually but *tenggelam* or *mati lemas* ('sinks' or 'drowns') when he performs poorly and is unable to satisfy his partner. Thus, though the issue of sexuality and reproduction is a function of both sexes men bear the added burden of proving virility at all times. Writers like Bouhdiba (1985) and Sabbah (1988) have discussed female sexuality in Islam as a male discourse fashioned and designed by men. Men interpret female sexuality as passive. Desire, lust and sexual provocation should be down played, thus allowing the female body to be an object of love and desire. One can quite clearly say after reading such lengthy discourses on male notions of sexuality in Islam how powerful are the pulls of culture in Islamic societies. Islamic ideals imposed upon Arab-Muslim society, as a reaction to pre-Islamic *Jahiliah* times when sexual norms were different are not upheld in Malay culture. Malay men and women do not prescribe to these ideals in sex and marriage.

In the same way as a Malay man constantly strives to improve his sexual performance with his wife, so does the woman attempt to make herself as desirable as possible to her husband. An idiomatic expression for a wife is *lawan*, literally a 'sparring partner', and the same term is used for a husband. A woman who participates actively in lovemaking is said to be a good 'sparring partner' (*melawan*). For the Malay woman, sexual desirability is perceived not only in terms of maintaining an alluring personality, a good, well-proportioned figure, a flawless complexion, and even well-toned muscles, but also the ability to participate actively in sex. She too resorts to numerous traditional tonics, herbs, *jamu* and *majun* which are believed to have the effect of shrinking the uterus and stomach and tightening the vagina. In Mawang, as with most other Malay women, post-natal rather than pre-natal food taboos and preferences are decidedly given more attention. The care which a woman takes to restore her own beauty and vitality may be said to exceed that shown for her infant's nutritional needs in terms of effort and money.

Significantly, with the modernization of the health services and increasing health and education, pre-natal food taboos which adversely affect the nutritional status of the infant have been mostly discarded except in the more rural and isolated villages, but customary food practices which negatively affect the nutritional and health status of the mother have been retained. This pattern of selectivity of pre- and post-natal food taboos and preferences reflects the importance and priority given by the Malay woman to body-care. Most of the food taboos are allegedly designed to reduce bleeding, to prevent tearing of the vaginal tissues, to tighten the vagina, to revitalize the body and to tone up muscles after pregnancy and delivery (Laderman, 1983).

One of the many fears and anxieties the author heard about is the possibility of a prolapsed uterus (*jatuh tempat beranak*) in the post-partum period through negligence and poor physical care. Restrictions on body movements after pregnancy is partly an attempt to prevent this dreaded condition from happening. To the majority, a prolapsed uterus implies the inability to conceive again rather than death. Women in Mawang confide that barrenness may prompt their husbands to marry another. These fears indirectly suggest that Malay women are hostile to the idea of polygyny and accept it only when they have no alternative. The preoccupation with body-care rather than infant-care after delivery need not be mutually exclusive but it appears to be so amongst many Malay women in Mawang. Although one may suggest that this may be directly or indirectly linked to polygyny, it nevertheless expresses a value on the maintenance of sexual desirability generally supported by various animistic ideas and ritual practices.

In comparison, urban Malay women may maintain an equal emphasis on body and infant-care if they deliver in hospitals. Here, they are subject to a different set of instructions and guidance from those given to women who have home deliveries. The attempt at maintaining a harmonious balance between physical appearance and sexuality and the health of the infant has caused many to occupy the post-natal care period with body massage, skin and muscle-toning, and weight reducing while the infant is entrusted to a midwife or an elderly woman who functions as a baby-minder during the period of confinement (*dalam hari*). For the large number of urban Malay women who continue to return to the village for delivery, practices relating to traditional forms of post-natal health-care continue to be administered by the midwife or *bidan*.

In Mawang, it was disclosed that one of women's biggest anxieties after delivery was having loose vaginal muscles, probably for fear of being unable to satisfy their husbands. However, women's poor sexual performance does not lead to public joking as in the case with men who suffer from certain sexual problems. If they are fat or obese and are visibly bigger than their husbands, they may be laughed at by the men who would express mock terror at being 'swallowed up' (*telan*) by such women. A certain amount of mock sympathy may be directed towards the husband when he is not around. He may, however, in his better moments, joke about it himself, saying that he likes 'being swallowed up' or simply that she may be fat but is a good sparring partner in bed.

Such forms of joking behaviour are more commonly expressed by middle-aged or elderly men who feel freer in being candid about their own sexual performance or that of their wives. Men of the younger generation usually avoid such topics in public. Within the elder generation, male and female reservations on sexuality are not clearly differentiated and a woman is free to rag or ridicule her husband in public in the same way as he is free to tease or taunt her for not wanting to co-operate with him sexually or, conversely, for being too sexually demanding. He may say with undisguised candour and amusement that he has no more sexual ardour (*dah tak larat lagi*) but has to do something about it because she nags him about it and still wants it (*bising; mahu lagi*). Such forms of bawdy humour between the sexes are always taken in good fun and considered to be a sign of a happy, well-adjusted marriage.

Conclusively, it may be said that Malay marriage norms and rules of behaviour emphasize fundamental *adat* principles of the mutual needs and concerns of men and women. The maintenance of equal roles and duties in a Malay marriage reflects the principle of bilaterality — mutual responsibility and rights between men and women on the domestic and community level. The traditionally strong economic position of Malay women is reflected in their role in mate-selection and marriage where they control a fair amount of the decision-making.

Pregnancy, Child-birth and Child-care

Once it is known that a woman has conceived, she is subject to a variety of *pantang-larang* or taboos to ensure continued health and a safe delivery. Extra care and precautions are taken with regard to her physical and mental condition because of the belief that a pregnant woman is particularly vulnerable to spirit-attacks and spirit-possession, leading to physical and mental illness and other forms of mystical retribution that are likely to cause harm to the mother or foetus. Pregnant women are believed to be particularly prone to spirit-attacks from malevolent spirits like the *pelesit* or *hantu raya* which is expressed in mental states of dissonance through violence, unintelligible speech and a state of physical disarray. Spirit-possession, if unchecked or untreated by the *bomoh* or shaman, has been known to be fatal to the mother or foetus. Spirit-possession during pregnancy exists within the domain of pre-Islamic, animistic beliefs. Taboos involving the kind of food, place and time a woman should avoid are guided by beliefs of witchcraft and sorcery. Since most places outside the house compound are mystically dangerous after dusk, she is physically confined to the house in the evening but in daylight may move about freely. Places that are avoided include the compounds and houses of villagers who are rumoured to rear spirits, grave-sites, river banks and forest areas beyond the *belukar* or forest clearings. She should also avoid receiving food from villagers with whom she is not well acquainted or kinsmen who are strained from her immediate family for fear that they might place a charm in the food and cause her to become seriously ill and eventually to lose her baby.

During her pregnancy, numerous symbolic associations are made between the physical state or appearance of foods and a woman's health and physical condition during and after delivery. These animistic food beliefs continue to pervade the socialization patterns of women during and after delivery and compete with other food practices which are derived from non-Malay or Western notions of health and medicine. Within the animistic system of food classification, foods which are avoided during the period of conception are those which contain sharp stings or spikes, such as the catfish (*ikan sembilang*), the mud skipper (*ikan tembakol*) and the stingray (*ikan keli*). Meat which is obtained from hunting or sport when the particular animal is wounded or killed in a trap is also avoided. This is related to the belief that such sources of food have powers of 'contagious magic' whereby the sting, spike or state of suffering of a wounded animal is magically associated with the occurrences of complications during pregnancy such as abortive pregnancies, bleeding, difficulty in labour and excessive labour pains. Laderman (1983) gives a detailed account of this through the Malay humoral system.

The system of logically relating physical acts or physical characteristics in a food item to an act of human suffering during pregnancy is complicated by the fact that certain physical activities of other members of the household have to be restrained, particularly acts relating to the injuring or killing of animals. It is believed that when such acts are committed, the infant will be born with animal features or adopt animal-behaviour characteristics as it gets older. This form of mystical retribution, known as *tekanan* or *terkena*, is still a strong source of anxiety amongst both men and women and rather seriously upheld in many Malay villages. In Mawang, the avoidance of *tekanan* is as seriously adhered to as food prohibition since both sets of ideas are closely associated with physical complications during child- birth and with birth abnormalities.[13] Numerous other *pantang* guide a woman's behaviour during pregnancy but they are not all adhered to and depend very much on the influences of elders on the younger generation and the persistence of animistic ritualistic practices, oriented around *adat*.

In Mawang, many taboos relating to physical movements tend to be upheld. These include the taboo against passing behind a pregnant woman, for fear that she might be subject to witchcraft, the taboo against a pregnant woman entering a house by the front door and leaving from the back, for fear that she might have a difficult delivery, and the importance of avoiding negative comments relating to other children and adults, for fear that her child might acquire the same traits. Since everything she does is said to have an indirect effect on her baby's physical health and personality development, she should cultivate only good traits during her pregnancy. For example, it is believed that if she constantly looks beautiful, her child will be so, and if she is demure and pleasant, so will her child be. Thus, all forms of physical behaviour and attributes of a pregnant woman have a direct physical effect on the child. A regular symbolic association is made between the state of well-being of the mother, and the foetus, and actions which are conceived as 'dangerous'. Women observe the *pantang* as much as they can, even in urban areas, since these taboos have the effect of influencing a woman's conception of her child's physical and psychological state.[14]

In Mawang, as with other Malay villages in the North, the rationale for food preferences and avoidance based on *adat* notions of traditional medicine, appear to be particularly important during the period of confinement or *dalam hari*. Generally, these pre-Islamic food categories are derived from the Malay notion of 'heat-giving foods' (preferred) or 'cold-giving foods' (avoided), referred to as 'hot' and 'cold' foods (*makanan panas* and *makanan sejuk*, respectively).[15] There appears to be a tendency to treat high-calorie foods as 'heat-giving' and low-calorie as 'cold' but this principle is not closely adhered to at all times. For example, women strongly believe that bananas are *sejuk* (cold) and, as such, bad for the mother during the period of confinement. All fruits except for the *durian* (durio fruit) and *rambutan* are 'cold-giving' and are thus avoided during the period of confinement for the same reason. Included within the category of cold foods are foods which cause 'wind' such as tapioca, sweet potato, pumpkin, and grapes.

Then again, many varieties of fish are believed to be 'cold' and are singled out because they are said to be harmful to the mother. Within this category are included the *ikan kembong* (mackerel), *ikan keli* (ray fish), *ikan todak* (garfish) and *ikan sembilang* (catfish). In fact, in Mawang, most women during the 44-day confinement period resort to eating only *ikan pelotan* (a fatty variety of catfish found in the brackish waters) which is usually simply fried. This fish cannot be prepared with tamarind, which is again *sejuk* and believed to cause the woman's veins in her stomach and feet to become distended and swollen. A very important category of food which is avoided on the basis of *sejuk* is seafood such as prawns, shrimps, crustaceans, squid, bivalves and univalves. Seafood is also believed to cause skin rashes and discomfort.

Generally, then, only 'heat-giving' foods are encouraged during the period of confinement and these revolve around certain varieties of fish, eggs, meat and chicken. Meat and chicken, however, are luxurious sources of protein for the Malays and it is a highly privileged woman who gets to taste these meats during her confinement. It is obvious that the Malay concept of 'hot' and 'cold' foods is not fully based on the 'yin-yang' principle of 'hot' and 'cold' foods which has a strong scientific rationale though it is possibly derived from the latter in some way. This category of food beliefs is further complicated by customary side-effect theories that certain sources of protein cause rashes or itchiness, or that certain 'flavour giving foods', like tamarind, cause distended veins. The belief that 'cold' fruits cause early conception also adds greater confusion to the problem.

During the period of confinement, concepts and ideas about what restores energy and promotes good health again do not reflect a good knowledge of nutrition, nor are they based on sound medical evidence. An important category of energy-giving foods outside the normal range of foods comprises herbs (*ubat akar*) and several varieties of Indonesian *jamu* which are believed not only to restore a woman's vitality but also to shrink her stomach and uterus, eventually helping her to restore her figure and maintain her sexual attractiveness. As mentioned earlier, the restoration of a woman's figure to its former shape and size is given great emphasis and it is obvious that a significant amount of time and money is devoted to this activity. Most women would also hire a traditional midwife or *bidan* to *urut* or massage her body back to its former shape. In many cases, the treatment stops after the first three days of confinement, but a number of women carry on with the *tunku* (heat therapy administered by means of a heated stone), *jamu* medication and therapeutic massage.

The Malay customary emphasis on physical appearance probably becomes more acute in the post-natal period when women feel less attractive and show considerable depression over it. Also, as mentioned earlier, it is closely bound to a deep anxiety felt by Malay women that child-birth could lead to a prolapsed uterus (*jatuh tempat beranak*) though the actual occurrences of such a condition is rare. It is nevertheless true that this fear encourages the practice of post-natal ritualistic therapy such as the use of the *tunku*, massage therapy and an assortment of *jamu* to shrink the uterus.

Malay food categories that concern women are maintained at different phases in a woman's cycle of conception, child-birth and post-natal care. They are conceptually separated and serve different functions which are compatible on the operational level. On the other hand, Islamic notions of food avoidance and food preferences are valid in daily acts of feeding and eating, but with the exception of the taboo on pork, does not have a significant role ritually during the pregnancy and delivery processes. They may, however, be more strictly adhered to during Islamic ritual festivities such as ceremonies of ritual blessing (*membaca tahlil*), thanksgiving (*doa selamat*) or acts of breaking the fast (*membuka puasa*). Animistic beliefs and practices relating to the system of *pantang-larang* only become meaningful in 'life crisis' situations or periods relating to pregnancy, illness or eminent death. Notions of 'hot' and 'cold' foods are generally applicable to adults and children alike but are strongly adhered to only during the period when a woman is recovering from child-birth or when a child or adult is recovering from a particular illness. The practice of food preference and avoidance according to *adat* (animistic), Islam or western medical sources is demonstrated in Table 5.2.

It will be seen that Islamic food taxonomy does not play a role in the period of pre- and post-natal care and that it is mainly animistic ideas

TABLE 5.2   Food Taxonomic Systems Relating to *Adat*, Islam and Western
                   Medical Sources

Food Category	Ideological Explanation	Relevant Situations or Periods
Allowed/Prohibitive Avoidance/Preferred	Islamic	Daily meals Islamic rituals (Praying and Feasting)
Physically dangerous Pysically safe and Heat-giving/Cold-giving	Adat/Animistic	Pregnancy and Conception (Pre-natal) and Child-birth (post-natal)
Nutritionally valued	Western/Medical	General illness in infants, children and adults

(*adat*) which are upheld during the period of pregnancy and conception. The categories of heat-giving and cold-giving foods based on traditional medical notions of food contents and combination appeal to the post-natal period when women are more concerned with body care and other restorative problems. The notion of nutritional value is usually described by the term *zat* (vitamins) and is a source of knowledge mainly acquired from maternal and child health clinics and hospitals. However, food with *zat* is given 'special attention' during illness rather than in periods of good health. Notions of preventive health or nutritional care are not generally well developed in Mawang.

The cycle of beliefs relating to physical and mystical dangers in the environment during the period of conception is in the post-conception period transferred to the newly born infant (*bayi*). The infant is believed to attract not only ghosts (*hantu-syaitan*) and vampires (*pontianak, langsir/langsiak*) desiring its blood but also medicine-men (*bomoh*) who require newly born infants as sacrifices to their helping spirits. A newly born infant is protected from such mystical dangers by certain sharp physical objects like the *kacip* (betel-nut cracker), scissors or small knife which are placed under its head to ward off spirits, and it is felt that once such mystical forces are combated, the physical and mental development of the infant will be non-problematic. Food is not an important consideration at this stage because infants are normally breast-fed as long as it is possible for the mother to do so.

During the 44-day period of confinement, a woman may obtain considerable assistance from her husband, mother and siblings in household tasks and may need only concern herself with the restoration of her health and the feeding of the infant. It is common for a Malay husband to clean and dress the infant, sooth it to sleep or carry it about the house to relieve his wife from such chores. He may also play a bigger role in the care of the older children, if any, although this task is often left to a grandmother or family elders if they are available. Although it generally happens that termination of the period of confinement is marked by a sudden end to the husband's general activity and participation in domestic matters, some men attempt to continue to assist their wives in housework, particularly when there are other children to care for.

Child-rearing and Socialization

In the evaluation of infancy, Vygotsky argued for the crucial role of biology in the formation of human mental processes (1978;1986). Others (Leontiev, 1981; Sinha, 1989) see infancy as the emergence of 'culturalized' features of human biology with universal psychological rules of operationalization. The Malay material suggests pregnancy, child-birth and infancy as an evolutionary chain of important correlated biological events where human survival and development is at its most crucial testing point, necessitating an elaborate symbolization of nature through anthropomorphic ideology and language. From these three phases, the child-rearing and socialization of toddlers and children up to the age of six suggest a transitory period of 'acculturation of biology', where formal rules of behaviour are ignored to encourage a spontaneous, casual transition into adulthood. It may be said that the most significant factor governing child socialization in the one to six years age group is their freedom from formal ritualization (Karim, 1980). This is reflected in the complete abandonment of all rules of social behaviour relating to age and sex differentiation and codes of morality. This ritual marginality becomes less apparent from the age of seven to puberty.[16] The process of formal education through primary schooling and *adat*-Islamic socialization normally begins at the age of six or seven and it is only then that children of both sexes are trained and disciplined in basic rules of moral and social conduct. Amongst the rural poor, the relative indifference to socializing toddlers and pre-school children in formal rules of conduct lies partly in the fact that mothers can devote very little time and consideration to such matters, being fully occupied in domestic and economic activities. Fathers also do not bother to assume this role though they may devote considerable time to the social and mental development of older children. Generally, however, the indulgence and passivity shown to the behaviour of younger children reflect fundamental Malay cultural beliefs in child-rearing that children in this age group are too young to be trained and disciplined and hence are best left alone to discover their own devices and interests. Their freedom from ritualization and discipline derives from the idea of young children as still being 'immature' (*budak lagi*), i.e. close to 'nature' — spontaneity is encouraged with the knowledge that formal learning and discipline will come later.

Regardless of their sex, toddlers of between one and three years equally stand to enjoy the physical and emotional comforts of care from their mother.[17] As long as the mother does not conceive again, she will continue to breast-feed her toddler if her breast milk is still sufficient even if the child is already on solids and supplementary milk foods. Occasionally, when children of this age category display temper tantrums, their mothers may attempt to pacify them by allowing them to suck at their breasts even when their milk is insufficient. During my fieldwork, the mother of a two and a half year old toddler died of throat cancer. The toddler was still being breast-fed and cried endlessly for its mother. The grieving widower said that the toddler would surely become ill because it was still being breast-fed (*masih lagi menyusu dengan emaknya*) and sought a *bomoh* for a talisman (*tangkal*) to make the toddler forget. Men and women believe that breast-fed children are more closely bonded to mothers than fathers, not only in a physically way but also emotionally and psychically.

The indulgence and maternal comforts which women display to children of this age may gradually wear off when they conceive again and are unable to take care of their children properly. The children are then weaned to lead a wild, capricious life in the compounds of the neighbourhood within the village boundary and are left to discover the world and all that it contains on their own. They normally gather together in small bands of three or four and roam in the village area. Children from the same neighbourhood or *jiran tetangga* (explained earlier, 'kinsmen sharing the same door steps') normally group together even if they are not bound by close kinship ties. Their activities comprise any perceived sport or adventure that is related to or imitative of family social relations and economic or physical activities of adults. They roam the village, locating mud-holes, water pools, rivers or streams to wade and bathe in or to capture fish, tadpoles, insects and frogs, catapult birds to win some game or attempt to construct shelters which function as houses in which to play out parental roles. Mock marriages, cooking and serving are some of the major sports attempted and they return to their houses only when home food seems more appealing. Sexual segregation at this stage in child development is uncommon and only begins at six or seven, particularly through formal schooling when peer group behaviour based on age-sets become more crystallized. Informal Islamic instruction in the village is another important source of socialization which encourages sexual segregation during Qur'anic lessons and prayers.

The playing activities of Malay pre-school children follow informal physical and social boundaries which are instilled in a child from the time it begins to play in the house compound. This may occur immediately after the infancy period, when a child is able to move and walk about on its own. Its parents may rebuke or chide it gently for wandering too far from the house compound or touching and eating objects which are likely to cause physical harm. The teaching and learning processes here mainly pertain to things which are regarded to be physically or mystically dangerous rather than socially or morally wrong (Karim, 1980). Children are told not to wander near grave-sites, nor to venture into the forest or play in rivers because these areas are believed to harbour vengeful spirits and ghosts that prey on both adults and children. They are also told to avoid playing near or in the compounds of houses of village medicine-men who are believed to rear preying spirits or ghosts known as the *pelesit*, *hantu raya* or *hantu toyol*. The physical dangers of swimming without surveillance, playing near wells, climbing trees and playing with fire are normally known since parents rebuke those who indulge in such activities when they actually see them at play. However, since children are generally not supervised during play, such activities are indulged in anyway and children manage to do just anything they can think of during their play hours.

The supervision of a child's personal health and hygiene is also not taken very seriously and this applies to pre-school and school-going children as well. Children play in mud, dirt, sand and water and often do not wash their hands but are only advised by their mothers to do so when they actually see the kind of things their children have played with. A child who defecates in the bush or river may make an attempt to wash his or her hands when water is available but since they are seldom supervised, their hands are never properly washed and they become prone to a number of parasitic ailments. Children normally go about bare-footed not only because it is a financial strain on their parents to keep on replacing their slippers and shoes which are constantly lost, damaged or outgrown, but also because the children themselves prefer not to wear any for ease of movement and play. Climbing for fruit is a popular activity while collecting snack food along the way from women who are busy preparing them is another reason to wander aimlessly about the village. When they return home and announce that they are hungry, a plate of rice with some fish and occasionally vegetables is dished out for them and they eat immediately, without changing their clothes or washing their hands.

Often, nursing mothers do not even have the time to supervise their older children's personal needs and food requirements so that these children quite often eat what is cooked for adults but in smaller portions. Schoolchildren who return home later often have to wait for the meals to be cooked because their mothers are busy attending to the needs of infants and toddlers. Left-over food, especially curry or salt fish or boiled shoots from the previous day, may be served with some freshly cooked rice. Because of the irregularity of meals, children harass their mothers for money to buy junk-food such as sweets, synthetic chocolates, sweetened fruit preserves, artificially-flavoured prawn or fish crackers or some locally made ice-cream prepared by enterprising women of the village. Mothers normally give in to these demands since they are generally unable to cope with the temper tantrums and sulkiness which follow when such demands are not immediately met.

School-going children begin to be formally socialized in codes of social conduct and morality by both parents and their teachers. Eventually, the most important forms of conduct which are emphasized pertain to *adat* values of how parental and child relationships and child and adult relationships should be ordered. Conduct according to Islam concerns the relationship between child and God or *Allah*. Values of consistency on good behaviour (*Buat baik berpada-pada, buat jahat jangan sekali*; do good constantly, do bad never at all) and gratitude (*Hutang emas boleh dibayar, hutang budi dibawa mati*; debts of gold can be repaid, debts of good deeds are carried to the grave) are derived from *adat* though these are in no way incompatible with Islamic values of conduct. Teaching a child about God or the Prophet Muhammad, however, is seldom undertaken at home, but when it is, it can serve to provide an alternative reference to authority without involving parents directly in the exercise of disciplining. References like *nanti Tuhan marah* (God will be angry) or *Tuhan nampak* (God saw you) are useful and these are intended to force children to behave without making parents the centre of authority and discipline.

Sex differentiation begins when young girls can be disciplined to assist their mothers in domestic chores and young boys in the chores of their fathers when the latter are engaged in heavy work in the house compound such as housing construction or chopping firewood. Fathers also frequently bring their sons along with them to their place of work within the village or to the local sundry or coffee-shop; young girls stay at home to assist in the care of a younger sibling. They function as 'young mothers' carrying a child about, or rocking a young infant in a *sarung* cradle (*buayan*). They also feed their younger siblings with milk, cereals or snack food, sometimes without much supervision from their mothers. Children who disobey their parents when delegated such tasks are chided for being *nakal* (mischievous), and in extreme cases called *derhaka* (lit. 'treason' against parents. Though they are seldom beaten, they may be threatened with severe punishment. These threats, however, are rarely carried out since feelings of pity and remorse (*kesian*) often override all other considerations.

The beginning of formal socialization into Islam reinforces preferences for sexual differentiation which have naturally developed during processes of early socialization. Islam widens these forms of sexual differentiation rather than create them. Religious training is often conducted separately, particularly for prayers and Qur'an reading, although other religious activities relating to the teaching of the *sunna* or choral singing in praise of *Allah* and the Prophet (*Nasyid*) may be conducted jointly. In the context of these religious activities, sexual differentiation implies sexual segregation to a certain extent. The practice of religious knowledge pertaining to sexual segregation may also widen boundaries of sexual behaviour. For example, other than the formalities of sexual segregation imposed by religious teachers in schools or informal religious classes, parents may ensure that their young daughters of pre-puberty age (between the ages of six and twelve) do not sleep in the same room as their young sons in accordance with Islamic codes of behaviour. However, in Mawang this rule is not strictly imposed except in families which are rather religious or where the father or mother is a religious teacher or specialist. Generally, principles of sexual differentiation in Malay culture do not necessarily lead to sexual segregation though it may reinforce differences in the conceptions of the role behaviour of boys and girls.

Rituals of male circumcision (*sunat* or *masuk jawi*) or clitoridectomy in young girls may ideally and symbolically express Islamic values of sexual differentiation but they do not in reality lead to sexual segregation.[18] Circumcision in boys is done any time between six and fourteen years, during or after the school-going period (in cases of early school drop-outs), and does not indicate initiation into adulthood or puberty, that is, a transference to the status of a *dewasa*. The *budak* and *dewasa* distinction in fact is prompted by something even more basic than circumcision, which is marriage. Thus, the transference from the status of *budak* to that of a *dewasa* is symbolically similar to the shift in the status of a *bujang* (bachelor) to that of a married person (*sudah kahwin*). They convey similar differences in social rank and esteem. Marriage significantly breaks down the cohesiveness of age-sets which are integrated by their single or *bujang* status. It is not so much Islamic ritualization through circumcision rites which determines social boundaries of rank and status between children (for youth) and adults but, rather, fundamental principles of marriage.

Social Relations in the Village and Town

It was mentioned in the early part of this chapter that status ranking is ordered by both historical and social factors relating to origin, marital status, economic wealth, material acquisition and political standing. It invariably follows that Malay villages usually contain a core group of residents who can separate themselves from newcomers by imposing 'outsider' and 'stranger' distinctions. The kindred system is capable of absorbing newcomers quite neatly by being ego-centred and expanding its overlapping networks of nuclear families so that eventually everyone appears to be related to one another, but in reality, without other economic and political compensations, it is difficult for newcomers, including spouses of local residents, to be fully integrated with the community. There have been many instances in Mawang of affines being called 'not one of us' (*bukan orang sini*) or 'outsider' (*orang luar*) even though they have lived there for a few decades. An extreme example was an old woman from Perak who married a man from Mawang 35 years ago. She was even once accused of harbouring spirits. Such accusations are more likely directed towards those in the *orang luar* category. This reflects a stereotype, that 'outsiders' are less society conforming. In the case of some village *bomoh* with 'outsider' status, this may actually be true, reflecting a vicious cycle of non-acceptance, alienation and further non-conformity. In Mawang, as will be discussed later, a *bomoh* with 'outsider' status freely indulges in witchcraft practices which have alienated the village folks further. Hence integration within the kindred system does not necessarily imply acceptance within the village community. Nonetheless, there are numerous ways in which acceptance can be achieved and some of the most important of these necessitate participation in and commitment to village community affairs relating to *adat* social customs and rules of local politics.

Members of the younger generation are generally excluded from formal ritual responsibility. Instead, the parental generation is given the leading role in ritual responsibility, symbolically expressed in the euphemisms of being 'already cooked' (*sudah masak*) or having 'tasted salt first' (*sudah makan garam dulu*), in contrast to the young and single who are still 'raw' (*mentah*) or have not 'tasted salt' (*belum rasa garam*). Significantly, 'insider' and 'outsider' distinctions are structurally similar to youth (unmarried) and elder (married) categories. Despite the existence of a loose kindred pattern of networks, relationships are eventually pooled or separated according to 'central' and peripheral 'action-set' groups. At this level of social relations, differences in social conformity and participation according to gender are insignificant.

These symbolic categories are not as clearly defined in neighbouring towns, which receive residents from many surrounding villages. Here, since origin, descent and seniority cannot be so easily established, economic and political attainment become the more important criteria of status. Wealth and political power are usually accumulated from business or professional attainment rather than land. In the village, people within the 'central' set of relationships are usually also the more established members of the kindred who have managed to acquire or accumulate economic wealth through land and political roles through reverence (*kehormatan*) over a period of time. It follows that men and women with influence and authority are invariably the earlier residents of the village. Competition and rivalry may arise between earlier and newer residents if they are of equal economic and political standing but villagers usually demonstrate their allegiance to the former if a choice has to be made. Within the central core of members, similar states of dissonance may arise over support of rival or incompatible systems of ideology; these usually pertain to religious differences or party politics. In this context, women are seldom involved in the conflict except indirectly in the way they render their support or rejection of specific individuals or groups. This intermediary role, however, can have important social consequences for the community, for it can influence the trend of public opinion and decision-making processes in the long term.

In the village of Mawang, conflicts between the group of *ulama* and traditional *bomoh* have been apparent when the latter have refused to follow the advice of the former in matters of Islam. Although there are four *bomoh* practising in the village, the one who is most censured by the local *imam* is the spouse of a woman of the village who came to the village about fifteen years ago. He receives his clients from several neighbouring villages as well and is regarded to be an extremely reputable and potent shaman since he has five 'helping spirits' (*hantu bela*) to aid him. His shamanistic skills are also feared by the villagers but those who need his services will not hesitate to consult him. The *imam* claims that his conflict with this particular shaman is on account of the latter's practice of *ilmu syirik* (sorcery and witchcraft) which is prohibited in Islam. The shaman himself claims that it is on account of him being an 'outsider' and not recognizing the *imam*'s authority in other ways like attending Friday prayers and religious ceremonies in his neighbourhood.

Obviously, both arguments bear weight and express the complexity of overlapping sets of ideals and value preferences in Malay society. Nevertheless, it is obvious that the shaman is treated with a certain amount of social ambivalence since his skills at healing and curing render him helpful and yet potentially dangerous and threatening to the members of the village. This ambivalence is generally demonstrated in many cultures but amongst rural Malays, the shaman's peripheral role stands in sharp opposition to the more central position of the *imam* as the symbol of social and divine authority. What is being emphasized here is that many reasons may account for such conflicts between traditional medical practitioners or shamans employing animistic methods of curing and healing and Islamic religious specialists or leaders.

It is important to note that men who do not originate from the village may feel more free to practise the kind of medicine (or politics) they want even though it goes against those norms of behaviour which are regarded as 'acceptable' (*patut*) in *adat*. Significantly, in Mawang, the treatment techniques of the three other medicine-men who are originally from the village are not regarded as effective since they use only mild forms of chanting (*berjampi-jampi*) employing verses from the Qur'an. Yet, they are more often consulted than the. *bomoh* mentioned earlier. They lack the necessary 'fame' to attract clients from other villages but receive most of their support from local residents. Generally, these central and peripheral boundaries of membership reflect 'insider' and 'outsider' distinctions. Animistic practices appear to be contained within the domains of individuals who for certain reasons, one of which is an 'outsider' status, feel fewer social inhibitions in practising or utilizing this craft. Significantly, the 'marginality' of the practitioners gives them more impetus to disregard or defy religious authority or normal Islamic congregations like the *Jemaah*. It also does not prevent them from attracting a large clientele, within and outside the village, and to gain the confidence of the religious but sick.

The withdrawal of animism to the periphery may be reinforced by Islamic revivalism when villagers attempt to make distinctions between acceptable forms of treatment within Islam and *ilmu syirik*. This withdrawal, however, is only on the level of public 'ritual practices' surrounding techniques of healing and curing. Belief in animism and private seances continue to be an integral component of Malay rural and urban life. The phenomenon of the *bomoh* practising as an 'outsider', receiving clients from other villages, towns and cities, reflect their continuing popularity within the wider general population. The differences today is that this peripheral status of the *bomoh* is even more strongly emphasized than before with Islamic leaders and villagers attempting to sort out fundamental differences between custom and religion.

Although most *bomoh* are men, midwives are sometimes consulted for specific problems and illness relating to sex, pregnancy and child-rearing. Their clientele are usually women. In *adat* traditions, there is no expressed taboo (*pantang*) or shame (*malu*) attached to women who consult a male *bomoh* so that a significant portion of the clientele of male *bomoh*, are women. The extensive patronage of traditional midwives and medical specialists by women is a major factor in their continued effectiveness in the rural and urban community. It may be concluded that the uninhibited independent way with which women consult these specialists contributes to the maintenance of the traditional health-care systems in Malay society.

In the same way as animistic rituals reveal social dissonance within the community, so does political party allegiance and loyalty create factions amongst supporters. Conformity to one of the two dominant Malay political parties, UMNO (or UMNO Baru), one of the components of the Government coalition, the Barisan Nasional (National Front), or PAS (Parti Islam SeMalaya), appears to be a necessary condition to remain in the central core of relationships within the village. Supporting a political party which is not supported by the majority of the people in the village is believed to be arrogant and flaunting and may actually result in ostracism of the non-conforming few. When the village is split between the two, factions develop which serve to disrupt social relationships amongst kinsmen and neighbours.[19]

Women play an important role in these events for their participation in party politics both intra- and inter- village, is as dynamic as their male counterparts. Although women are not usually central figures in party leadership, these parties would not have acquired the membership or influence they enjoy today without the continued support of women. The villagers of Mawang are almost completely UMNO supporters. Here, the most active campaigners for UMNO are women. Since the village is an UMNO stronghold, religious leaders and members of the Village Security and Development Committee share similar political ideals, so that when a person appears to be sympathetic to PAS, as it occasionally happens when the spouse of a local woman with opposing ideological convictions resides in the village, the event is viewed with much apprehension.

In Mawang, parents also attempt to prevent their children from associating with men and women whose parents are active supporters of PAS and divorce has been known to occur when a spouse actively supports the opposing party. In these cases, women are as capable as men of disrupting family and community relations in support or rejection of a particular political party. Where it exists, party factionalism is seldom resolved through Islam. If any, the allegiance of a certain party like PAS, towards Islam, has in fact contributed to factionalism within the village. Also, Islamic specialists like the *imam* cannot always be centrally authoritative or politically powerful unless they can also monopolize formal political activities within the village. In the same way as they derive their authority by opposing animistic rituals, so can they hope to expand it by participating in party politics. Formal exclusion from party politics may help a religious specialist maintain his position through personal influence but such a person would not go far, in terms of formal leadership. Authority and power are defined relative to dominant political ideologies rather than absolutely in relation to Islam. It will be shown later how Islamic revivalism which has mainly permeated the social activities of the younger generation Malays, again introduces further splitting processes within the rural and urban Malay population. Since the younger population attempts to derive its religious knowledge from outside sources rather than local religious leaders, it further threatens the central role position of religious specialists within the community. An even more basic consequence of religious fundamentalism is the process of cultural splitting within the urban milieu. In a sense, *adat* as a system of ordering basic social relationships and behaviour maintains a continued relevance, for as alternative models of utilizing Islam are being introduced, these serve to compete with one another rather than develop into a cohesive force which can revoke *adat* tradition altogether. As long as *adat* is effective in regulating conflict and change, Malay women can successfully continue to be active participants of the social system. The following discussion on cultural splitting among the younger generation reflects this argument to a significant extent.

Notes

1. It was found that James Low, Director of the East India Company, was the largest single landowner, with land totalling 63 *orlong* followed by Sir Francis Light and a John Sneider who owned 20 *orlong* of rice land at Permatang Penaga (Hill, 1977: 81).

2. The median was 5.8 *orlong* and the mean 4.0 for rice land under female ownership.

3. Based on a Census Survey conducted in July 1983. Detailed information on land-ownership was obtained six months later through in-depth interviews with key informants.

4. This suggests that the present village has a history of approximately a century, although it is likely that the area was opened up much earlier, before the acquisition of Province Wellesley from Kedah. The presence of old Buddhist cemeteries in the plains and constant discoveries of Hindu relics in the region, suggests a fair amount of population movement within the area in the period before European rule.

5. The average size of rice land is 4 *orlong*, though some land owners may have acquired land elsewhere in the district.

6. It is interesting that of all states, women from Kelantan bear the most prejudices and cultural stereotypes, relating to use for witchcraft, overt materialism, promiscuity and sexuality. These views are partly reinforced by belief in their frequent utilization of Thai charms, which are considered to be more potent than Malay love charms, but are also aggravated by the traditions of Kelantan women to be economically independent through trading and small-scale business. The high divorce rates in Kelantan (in 1989, 30% in Kota Bharu and 25% in other districts in Kelantan) and frequent re-marriages of divorcees (*janda*) are also taken to be indicative of their emotional and social independence and sexual desirability.

7. Close kinsmen are in the southern states generally referred to as *saudara-mara*, while the term *adik-beradik* is used in the North. *Adik-beradik* in the South generally refers to siblings or consanguines.

8. Generally, in the Peninsula, Johor upper-middle and upper class families are believed to be the most conservative and 'clanistic' in designing marriage partners

for their children, often preferring first-and second-cousin marriages to preserve or improve upon social standing, wealth or political alliances.

9. The first *talak* is normally resorted to for the first divorce and the second *talak* when a man remarries his former wife. If he divorces her a third time and pronounces the third *talak*, and wishes to remarry her (for the fourth time) she would have to marry another man first (and consummate the marriage). Only with the consent of his former wife's husband can she then be divorced to remarry him. This principle, which subjects a man to considerable ridicule and humiliation, is an attempt to prevent rash spontaneous decisions of divorce and to impose a sense of responsibility and commitment to a marriage. In Malaysia, this principle of *talak tiga* is referred to by the derogatory phrase of *Kahwin Cina buta*, literally 'to marry a blind Chinese', presumably since a man may only obtain non-Malays to consent to such an undesirable experience. See Djamour (1959: 110-114) for a more detailed description of Malay divorce in Singapore.

10. If sexual intercourse is attempted during the period of *iddah*, the divorce is automatically null and void. Thus, the *iddah* rule refers to a serious exercise of rethinking rather than an excuse for sexual intercourse, so that if it is attempted, it is taken to be an indicator or reconciliation, not lust or mere sexual desire.

11. The divorce rates in Peninsular Malaysia vary from state to state and it is difficult to attain national figures since records are only kept by the State Religious Departments and are not systematically co-ordinated and compiled to project national trends. However, of the eleven states in Malaysia, the Muslim populations of Terengganu and Kelantan on the East Coast have the highest divorce rates, amounting to 25-30% in Kelantan and Terengganu in 1989. See Sarina A. Rani (1990), *Perlaksanaan Undang-undang Keluarga Syarak Dalam Konteks Perkahwinan, Poligami dan Perceraian di Negeri Kelantan*.

12. It is a condition associated with Malay youths who are believed to be without sexual control because they lack sexual experience with women. Men who have recently married and suffer from this problem eventually seek sexual therapy from a *bomoh*, who usually provides technical advice and massage (*urut*) to cure the problem. Homeopathic medicine is increasingly popular for this reason.

13. Malay women from the village occasionally recall children with animal characteristics and attribute this to *tekanan*. An extreme case was seen in a six-year-old child who died recently. She refused to wear clothes, would play with the chickens the whole day and climb up trees. She would eat her food like a monkey and could not sit still in the car whenever her parents took her out. She died of pneumonia after being exposed to rain one evening. Her parents forgot she was playing in the garden and did not bring her in.

14. Refer to Karim (1984) where an analysis of Malay pregnancy taboos is described in the context of Malay midwifery practices in Kedah in Peninsular Malaysia. See also Laderman (1983).

15. Generally, food classifications surrounding Islamic notions of *halal* (allowed), *haram* (prohibitive), *makroh* (preferred avoidance) and *sunnat* (promotive) are upheld by all adults and children alike but no special treatment of foods based on Islamic principles of classification is adhered to by pregnant women. Islamic food taxonomy exists in a completely different conceptual and ritual sphere from animistic food categories which are mainly concerned with maintaining a har-

monious balance between elements in nature and the prospective mother's physical and mental state of health. Malay 'hot' and 'cold' food categories are more closely allied to Chinese 'hot' and 'cold' foods derived from 'yin-yang' notions of harmony and balance between man and nature.

16. Puberty is here defined as the period of adolescence when a child is transferred to adult status (*dewasa*). The terms for adolescent girls is *anak dara* or *pemudi* and boys, *teruna* or *pemuda* (general terms for both are *belia remaja* or *pemudi-pemuda*).

17. Toddlers are generally referred to as *kanak* (pl. *kanak-kanak*) or *budak kecil* (small child) while older children regardless of sex between four years and adolescence may be generally referred to as *budak*. The toddler age group is here defined as children between one and three years. Children between four and six years are currently referred to as *kanak-kanak pra-sekolah* or pre-school children, mainly because of the increasing pre-school facilities in rural areas in Malaysia.

18. An analysis of child socialization with an emphasis on male circumcision rites and socializing processes has been previously undertaken by anthropologists like Wilder (1965) and will not be attempted again here. Rather than provide a detailed analysis of rituals, this discussion merely attempts to demonstrate the patterns and phases of ritualization and non-ritualization within the life-cycle processes which render certain age groups to be more integrated and others more 'marginal' within Malay social structure.

19. In extreme situations when both parties are equally dominant, as in certain constituencies in Terengganu and Kelantan, the effect of these factions has been to create the phenomena of *kafir-mengafir* (to accuse opponents of being infidels), separate Friday prayers and even the construction of separate mosques.

6

Islamic Revivalism, Gender and Power

Bersatu teguh, bercerai roboh
Strength in unity, crumbles in dissension
— *Malay proverb*

The Islamic Movement in Malaysia

The Kaum Tua — Kaum Muda Conflict

Time and again, the continued importance of *adat* in Malay popular life has been questioned by the *ulama* and attempts have been made to reorder laws and statuses according to Islamic principles alone (Roff; 1974: 58). One of the earliest reformist increments began in July 1906, with the publication of a periodical called *Al-Imam* (The Leader). Amongst the small group of men who started the *Al-Imam* were Shaykh Mohd Tahir b. Jalaluddin Al-Azhari, a Minang and the first editor Sayyid Shaykh b. Ahmad Al-Hadi, a Melaka Malay of Arab descent and an active contributor, Hj Abbas b. Mohd Taha of Singapore, a second editor and Shaykh Mohd Salim Al-Kalali, an Achehnese and director of *Al-Imam* for the first two years (Roff; 174: 60). They attacked Minangkabau *adat* traditions as being contradictory to Islam and the mystic *tarekat* traditions in Sumatra, Singapore and Malaya. Of these men, Sayyid Shaykh Al-Hadi was most concerned for the emancipation of women in Islam and translated Kasim Amin Bey's *Tahrir ul-Mara'ah* (The Emancipation of Women), published collectively under *Alam Perempuan* (Women's World; Jelutong Press: Penang, 1930)[1]. A series of debates erupted in the 1920s between old and young religious specialists, on issues relating to the validity of the Hadith, commercialization of funeral rites, the legitimacy of Nakshabandi Sufism, interest payments and the relevance of European clothing. Usually called the *kaum tua* (old faction) and *kaum muda* (young faction) conflict, this was another attempt to introduce Islamic fundamentals by 'deculturizing' Islam but it did not achieve a consensus amongst Muslim populace or leaders and ultimately lost its appeal. The *kaum tua* and *kaum muda* conflict went on for more than a decade and may be seen as a symptomatic expression of the nationalist movement in West Asia from the early decades of the twentieth century. Writings by Jamal al-Din al-Afghani and Sheikh Muhamad Abdul were the main reference sources of the *kaum muda* who followed the ideas of these scholars by demanding a return to doctrines of *salafiyya* which heightened fundamentalist ideas from the Qur'an and Sunna (Mohd. Sarim Haji Mustajab, 1979). The movement in the Peninsula is normally referred to as the *Islah Islamiyyah* Movement (*Gerakan Islah Islamiyyah*). This movement created a general feeling of discontent amongst the younger, new graduates in Islamic philosophy and jurisprudence from Al-Azhar University and Mekah al-Mukarramah, who mobilized their followers to create a wave of anti-British sentiments amongst the Malay population. The movement was not supported by the older religious scholars who were for the most employed by the British as teachers and administrators, and a conflict between national sentiments and religious priorities led to massive public slanderings and accusations, through local bulletins and newspapers (*Suara Benar, Saudara, Al-Ikhwan, Idaran Zaman* and *Semangat Islam*)[2]. A central theme of these publications by the *kaum muda* was that Muslims should use reason (*akal*) to determine the truth of religion rather than accepted customary authority (Roff; 1974: 77).

In this sense, although the movement developed as a show of concern for issues of contradiction between custom and religion, or redefinitions of modes of living, its ability to challenge the existing colonial government (and the religious authorities promoted by this government) converted it into a new political force. Thus the 'restructuring processes' it called for began to be aligned to issues of culture, ethnicity and nationalism rather than concrete issues of reinterpretations of the Qur'an or Hadith. Religious issues began to be associated with piece-meal external symbols of religiosity like the usage of the correct headgear or robe during prayers, the relevance of the *surat tauliah* issued by the government to religious heads (*imam, kadi*) to practise their professions, or the importance of traditional religious-type schools (*pondok*) administered according to an apprenticeship system of devout leader and follower (Mohd. Sarim Haji Mustajab, 1979).

Current Sectarian Movements and Associations

The current trends of Islamic revivalism are again monitored through 'cultish' strategies developed by religious organizations and associations and through various *ad hoc* Islamic programmes and legislation on the part of the government (Kessler, 1980; Nagata, 1984; Chandra Muzaffar, 1986). The short term effects of these have significantly affected the image of Muslim women in Malaysia, at least in symbolic terms, in representing a social and cultural system which is different from the West.

Generally, the Islamic revivalist movement in Malaysia commonly referred to as *dakwa* ('to respond to a call'; fundamentalist), is dominated by groups which vary in their ideological and ritualistic interpretations of the Sunna, the set of texts describing the rules of conduct and behaviour of Muslims as observed from the personal behaviour, sayings and activities of the Prophet. Because of the nature of their formation and organization, these groups evolve into cults which gradually lose momentum when their members question the leadership structure and attempt to establish a separate movement elsewhere. One such *dakwa* group is the Al-Arqam or Darul Arqam which upholds the idea of an Islamic community. It derives its name from Arqam, a man who opened his home to Muslims as a sanctuary during the time of the spread of Islam in Mecca, when the religion was regarded as heresy. It represents an attempt to fully implement the principles of syariah, the total involvement of mind, spirit and body and the integration of the spiritual with the practical realities of living. In its self-containment, it expresses a rejection of government policies towards Islam, which is based on piece-meal integration within a cosmopolitan, multi-ethnic society. All socioeconomic activities are channelled towards community needs and services through the administration of the *bai' tul-mal* or central treasury.

The movement is contained in several communes throughout the states of Malaysia, including Sabah and Sarawak. The original commune at Sungai Pencala in Selangor was replaced by Kampung Sempadan in Temerloh, Pahang. It operates its own pre-school classes, schools and clinics. At present, it has some twenty factories located throughout the country (Ustaz Ashaari, personal communication, Universiti Sains Malaysia, 28 March 1988). The Darul Arqam also maintains an extensive network of sympathizers in Kuala Lumpur (approximately 6,000 — Ustaz Ashaari, personal communication) and draws its support heavily from the group of middle-class professional Malays who offer financial contributions and social services to the group. A number of college and university students also claim allegiance to the group in a more informal sense, by supporting the ideals of the group, purchasing *halal* food commodities and other products manufactured by Al-Arqam or emulating the principles of communal sharing of property and strict discipline in religious learning.

This group has come under severe attack from religious departments, in particular The Research Bureau of the Religious Affairs Department, for spreading teachings of the Sufi-based *Tariqat Muhammadiah* (Arabic *tariqat*, 'religious brotherhood')[3]. The *Tariqat Muhammadiah* is based on writings of the life of Asy- Syeikh As-Sayid Muhammad bin Abdullah As Suhaimi ('The Book of Praises'), a Javanese born in Kampung Sudagaran in the Wonosobo district of Java, whose teachings led to the development of a messianic cult (the 'leader', popularly referred to as *Imam* Mahdi)(Ashaari Muhammad, 1986). This Muslim idealist who was prone to Sufi ideas of holy retreats and mystical communication with The Almighty was believed to be endowed with the special power of being able to see the unseen, including the ability to converse with the Prophet Muhammad. The Syeikh came to Malaysia at the turn of the century and converted many Malays to his ideas and teachings.[4] When he died in 1925 in Klang, Selangor, Malay followers of this *Tariqat* believed that he was the *Imam* Mahdi or the 'chosen' leader who would rise before the Apocalypse.

According to the Religious Affairs Department, Malay followers of this *Tariqat* number nearly 2,000, most of whom are members of Al-Arqam. Approximately 500 more are scattered in isolated groups in Pahang and Selangor. The leader of the Al-Arqam in Selangor, Ustaz Haji Ashaari Muhammad, is believed to have led his followers into the *Tariqat*. The retreat of many members of this group to Kampung Sempadan in Temerloh, Pahang, has been construed as an attempt on his part to implement more thoroughly ideas from 'The Book of Praises'. The leadership crisis in Al-Arqam, between Haji Ashaari and his deputy, Haji Moktar Yaakub, in 1985 is said to have been on account of disagreement by Haji Moktar and some followers of Arqam on the teachings of Ashaari. Ustaz Haji Ashaari, however, has accused the media of exaggerating these differences between them in order to convince the masses that the movement is splitting up. Haji Moktar Yaakub's subsequent death in 1987 and the gradual disbanding of his followers has been one of the trump cards of government religious authorities to show Muslim Malaysians the fragmentation of leadership within religious movements in the country. Currently, Ustaz Haji Ashaari's continuing attempt to defend the *Tariqat Muhammadiah* in Darul Arqam has confirmed his determination to work for a new Muslim Malaysian society which, in his words, 'should emerge in a hundred years from now' (28 March 1988, Universiti Sains Malaysia lecture; see also Ashaari Muhammad, 1986). In 1991, all activities of the Darul Arqam were banned and their permission to publish withdrawn by the Ministry of Home Affairs. In order to survive, this movement will probably resort to activities which are more sectarian in form, including a change in external dress codes, patterns of gathering and fund raising.

The Dakwa Tabliqh comprises a movement of zealous Malay and Indian Muslims who are part of the wider Jemaah Tabliqh movement in India and Pakistan. The followers generally focus on missionary activities, lead very simple lives bearing an image of piety and impoverishment in the way they move about, carrying very few personal artifacts and generally sleeping in mosques whenever they are allowed to do so. Unlike Arqam, they spread their teachings in traditional villages rather than create their own. They are not always tolerated by villagers and cases have been known, in the villages of study in Seberang Perai and Kedah, in particular, of Tabliqh men being refused permission by the local *imam* to sleep in the *madrasah* or mosques. Rural women who frown upon the activities of the Tabliqh missionaries state that their general unkempt appearance and dirty clothes seem to be contrary to the principle of cleanliness in Islam (although they conceded that it is difficult for travellers to stay clean). Also, their tendency to act as destitutes *(fakir)*, asking for food and shelter, is regarded as parasitic by some, who allege that such behaviour is contrary to the Islamic principles of initiative and industry.[5] The author's own observation of Tabliqh activities in Mawang and neighbouring villages at the Seberang Perai and Kedah border saw them as self-reliant, clean, quiet, and unimposing. It is probable that the villagers resent such personal intrusions and so create convincing reasons as to why they should not be entertained. The Tabliqh also seek donations to travel to India and Pakistan to meet leaders of the Tabliqh movement in New Delhi, Karachi and Lahore, and villagers see this as a preference to Mecca, a factor which is believed to be another *penyelewengan* or deviation from Islam.

Generally, however, the way in which the Tabliqh operates through a quiet network of kinsmen, friends and associates, is not regarded to be overtly threatening or intruding, except that many villagers, particularly elders, claim that they are already versed in the teachings of the Qur'an and that it is arrogance on the part of the younger Tabliqh members to assume that they know more. The Tabliqh movement is well patronized amongst middle-class academics and teachers. In the early eighties, it gathered momentum among young professionals of the lower middle income level in Kota Bharu, in Kelantan, Alor Star in Kedah, and the island of Penang.[6]

A large number of those in the *dakwa* movement identify closely with ABIM or *Angkatan Belia Islam Malaysia*, a national body which represents the activities of Muslim youths in the country. PERKIM (*Persatuan Kaum Islam Malaysia* or the Muslim Organization of Malaysia) is another large organization which represents the general interests of Muslims in the country. Its focus is on welfare and charitable activities while the conversion of non-Muslims to Islam is a fundamental part of its missionary work. All these organizations have strong international links with other Islamic groups and organizations in Asia and the Middle East. Anwar Ibrahim, a former prominent student leader from the University of Malaya who became the charismatic leader of ABIM and developed ABIM to its present strength, was made a deputy Minister, and soon afterwards full Minister after having being persuaded by the Prime Minister, Dr Mahathir

Mohamad, to participate in the UMNO elections of 1982. This is a striking example of the swift conversion of a *dakwa* leader into national politics, a move speculated by many to be aimed at transferring the popularity of ABIM into UMNO. Since ABIM was after all very closely identified with Anwar Ibrahim, the organization lost much of its appeal when Anwar became a public leader within the government coalition, the National Front or Barisan Nasional. Previously, ABIM's activities had been closely associated with the dominant Malay opposition party, PAS, and this was viewed as an added calculated move on the part of the government to remove an important basis of mass support from the opposition party.

Students who identify with ABIM, support it in many ways by being actively involved in its tasks, seminars, Islamic teaching, training courses and fund-raising activities, or merely by reading its newspapers and bulletins. The organization also has links with the Islamic Associations of the various universities in Malaysia, and very often leaders from these associations are active members of ABIM. It also maintains a woman's branch, HELWA (*Hal Ehwal Wanita ABIM*, Women's Affairs of ABIM), which attempts to promote women's activities in Islam, particularly the observance of the Islamic form of dressing and the importance of education and proper conduct in marriage and child care. Its impact on the rural areas is negligible (Nagata, 1984: 91) considering that its membership is mainly drawn from urban Malays of the lower and middle income brackets. ABIM's activities, however, are well known in the villages (particularly during the time when Anwar Ibrahim was the leading spokesman of the organization) and although it is often seen to be closely associated with PAS, it also draws the interest and support of members of the UMNO Belia, the youth branch of the UMNO Party. Compared to Arqam or Tabliqh, the activities of ABIM are probably most widely known amongst the populace, mainly on account of its wider circulation of materials on Islam.

Thus, currently, the *dakwa* movements represents a 'mix bag' of activities and responses ranging from the establishment of bureaucratic organizations like ABIM and PERKIM to smaller commune-type movements like Darul Arqam in Kampung Sempadan. The movement is also individualized since a large number do not identify with any of these groups or organizations but believe that they should 'correct' their way of life and be 'more Islamic' in one way or another.

The main factor behind the government's condemnation of independent *dakwa* movements is its concern to control and guide Islamic teachings and practices according to its formulations of religious ideology and practice. Supporting the government's stand on *dakwa* are the UMNO-appointed state religious leaders (*Mufti, Imam, Ustaz, Ustazah*) who continue to believe that they should monopolize the dissemination of knowledge and information on Islam, including its media of communication to the Muslim masses. Their interpretation of Islam as a religion contained in a society which upholds freedom of worship of all religions is to 'nationalize' it, symbolically and ritually, by introducing *ad hoc* programmes based on Islam, such as Islamic education in schools and colleges, sponsoring Qur'an-reading competitions, introducing strict dress codes (*tidak menjolokkan mata*, that is, 'does not provoke temptation'), levying fines on Muslims who do not fast during Ramadhan or imposing marriage or fines on couples who are found in close physical proximity to each other, outside wedlock (referred to as *khalwat*). A much more serious move with long term consequences is the attempt to integrate Islamic Law more closely with Civil Law and the increase in the powers of judges of the Syariah Court to impose heavier fines on sexual offences, gambling and consumption of alcohol. Needless to say, these policies do not attempt to restructure the political system in any significant way, except to create a general atmosphere of 'religious consciousness' amongst Muslims in the country. Existing political structures (Sultanates, Western political party system, Parliament [based on a Federal Constitution]), are allowed to remain with minimal changes in political leadership and control.

It is mainly for this reason that the titanic conflict between UMNO and PAS continues to divide Muslims who either find UMNO's version of Islam more convenient or PAS's idea of establishing an Islamic state more positive. In addition, the government attempts to control interpretations of the Qur'an and Hadith by allowing only a selected number of books on this subject to be read. For example, the controversy over the Hadith as an authentic source of reference of Islamic law and theology (Fazlur Rahman, 1981) has served to aggravate differences between the government-sponsored class of *ulama* and independent scholars and writers on the subject. The former continue to preach the importance of the Hadith alongside the Qur'an while a number in the latter group see the Hadith as the primary source of misinterpretations and deviant thinking in Islam, particularly in Malaysia.

Subsequently, government authorities in July 1986 banned Kassim Ahmad's book on the subject, *Hadis, Suatu Penilaian Semula* on account of its major premise that Muslim disunity, particularly that between the Sunnis and Shias, has been caused by the *ulama* placing far too much emphasis on the Hadith as a source of reference and as a text as important as the Qur'an. In a way, this can be viewed as a local response to a wider intellectual movement led by Ismael al-Faruqi, and others, to use basic Qur'anic concepts to pave the way for a global Muslim community. Al-Faruqi, in his last intellectual contribution written a few days before his death, wrote:

'Islam is committed to the idea of the universal community as an integral part of its vision. The absolute unity and transcendence of God affirmed by *tawhid*, necessarily implies that all creatures are one in relation to the one and only God.' (Inquiry, London, 1986)

Malaysian Muslims who have come out in support of this line of thinking, have been mainly concerned over the way in which individualistic interpretations of the Hadith have in fact sponsored the fervour of religious movements in the country, including *dakwa*-labelled groups like Arqam and isolated movements which support ideas of *Imam Mahdi* (resurrection of the Messiah). A. Ghani Ismail (12 June 1986) suggests that banning and censoring religious texts only serves the *ulama* with more powers to subdue the population while encouraging 'illegitimate' religious groups to thrive by developing Islamic ideas derived from the Hadith. He suggests that 'Islam is getting out of control in more ways than one in Malaysia, be it "official Islam", "the Sunna movement or *dakwa* Islam", and of course PAS Islam' which considers UMNO Islam *kafir*. In this sense, the government's attempt to control knowledge and information on Islam by introducing an 'official' version of it merely succeeds in encouraging others to develop their own versions, in defiance of the existing government practices which are said to be truly 'Islamic'.

The overwhelming global impact of Islamic revivalism has indeed made its mark in Malaysia through these sporadic religious movements which are either part of international networks of religious activities or local community-based activities under the control of charismatic leaders. Political parties which employ Islam as the basis of party ideology like PAS or HAMIM also accelerate the general mood of participation of Islamic revivalism. However, despite these current trends, it does not appear that Islam is rapidly displacing *adat* values or activities. Articulations of apparent contradictions between the two have not made Malays ashamed or reluctant to support ideas and activities based on *adat*. If any, increasing ethnic consciousness in Malaysia amongst the major communities has heightened the concern for preserving and maintaining customs and traditions and the Malays have been as much concerned in maintaining ethnicity through cultural heritage as well as through Islam. Political issues relating to the creation of a 'national culture' or 'national identity' have in fact the opposite effect in encouraging not only the Malays but also the other ethnic communities to seek greater public exposure for ostentatious rituals and cultural activities. The 'national culture' that has emerged is a revival of different ethnic and cultural sentiments projecting an abstract cohesiveness in ethnic pluralism. Significantly, by early 1990, numerous Malay intellectuals refer to the *dakwa* movement in the past tense, to indicate that the fervour of Islamic consciousness is over and that the Malays are once again concerned for the 'nitty-gritty' of practical life-party politics, power groups and public scandals.

Heralding the trend of multi-culturalism are the Malays who obtain maximum exposure in national television networks, radio and the press, in displaying courtly and folk *adat* rituals which are both festive and entertaining. The idea of *maksiat* in Islam, that public entertaining and singing is both carnal and wasteful, does not seem to receive much attention except perhaps in certain specific contexts, such as when entertainment is brought before the attention of a group which is predominantly *dakwa*, as in certain universities and colleges.[7] Thus, the external symbolisms of *adat* projecting notions of social refinement, grace and education are widely extended to the populace, including non-Malays audiences, to create awareness of the strength and vitality of Malay culture. One this level, *adat* symbolically ensures cultural continuity in some form. To know of and to practise *adat* makes a Malay hierarchically superior to someone who ignores it. Positive or negative references of Malays are made accordingly with terms like *orang beradat* (person 'with culture') and *orang tidak beradat* (person 'without culture'). These categorical definitions bear more social significance than those concerned with differentiating the religious (*halim*) from the non-religious but even when piety and spiritual knowledge is given priority over the customs and traditions, the two categories are not presented as mutually exclusive. A Malay who is *beradat* yet *halim* fulfils the social prescriptions of ideal-type behaviour and on a cultural continuum of *kasar* and *halus* ('from vulgarity to refinement'), such a person occupies the uppermost position of reverence in Malay society.

The Malaysian model of Islam is inherently contradictory in that it supports ideas of a cohesive Muslim *ummah* on one level while, on another, reinforces ideas of *shu'ubiyyah* or the value placed on culture and ethnicity above the Muslim *ummah*. The latter transpires dramatically in the association of Islam with Malay culture and ethnicity rather than univer-salisms of welfare, charity and social justice for all, be they Muslims or non-Muslims. According to Al-Faruqi (1986), the force of *Salafiyyah* or traditionalism (which Malaysian *dakwa* attempts to emulate) 'has not yet succeeded in translating the vision of Islam into a model capable of proving itself and holding its ground, nor has the *Mu'asarah* (modernism) model succeeded in shaking itself free of Western forces of power and creativity'. Thus, Muslim countries are left with their own brand of patriotism and particularisms. He concludes that true Islam does not seek to destroy culture but merely to 'tame it' to make it work for the good of all (*tawhid*). The author's personal viewpoint is that culturalisms work in Islam not because but in spite of it.

In rural areas, although *dakwa* groups are not in any way popular, the integration of sainthoods (*keramat*) with Islam has recently become more apparent. Formerly, these local sainthoods evolved around the memories of renowned *ulama* or traditional healers (*bomoh*) who were believed to possess mystical powers like *kebal* (invulnerability), the ability to change or substitute bodily forms into other humans and animals (*menjelma*), to disappear and have replica representations of themselves remain in the village (*kadam*), or to have powers of premonition (*menengok*). Eventually, the graves of these masters of mysticism and supernatural healing became shrines or *keramat* for the population to offer food sacrifices and to pray (*niat*) for things to happen. Currently, local sainthoods have devolved upon men and women who suddenly undergo ecstatic experiences and become living embodiments of 'sainthoods'. In the Peninsula, these 'saints' are not necessarily people who are religious or learned in Muslim theology, but those who are usually suddenly inspired (*ilham*, to guide others along the 'true' path of Islam). In this sense, they are not Sufi mystics or descendants of renowned religious leaders but more closely resemble the kind of miraculous or charismatic sainthoods described by Rabinow (1975: 7) to have been common in Morocco during the *Maraboutic* (saint) crisis before French rule. When these 'sainthoods' are associated with pious men, they are referred to as *Tok Wali*, a term generally bestowed on religious specialists (trained in Islamic theology either locally or abroad) with unusual gifts of communication with God (*Tuhan, Allah*) or the Prophet. As mentioned earlier, the founder of the *Tariqat* associated with *dakwa* Arqam was said to possess such a gift. This gift is 'divine' in the sense that it comes directly from Allah (*berkat*) to certain men to preach and to guide others towards proper moral conduct. Rabinow (1975: 25-29) similarly describes these miraculous saints as being given the gift of *baraka* which is the conception of divine grace and supernatural power, best translated as 'the manifestation of God's grace on earth'.

One such person in the state of Kedah is in fact, an extremely effeminate individual with tendencies towards transvestism. He is impoverished and uneducated and had not appeared in any religious congregation or *jemaah* in his village. However, he suddenly took the villagers by surprise by skilfully repeating verses from the Qur'an in Arabic. His friends claim that he receives 'callings' (*Panggilan Ilahi*) from God to help others 'reform' in the same way. His religious callings are fervently believed by Muslims who travel for miles to pay homage to this devout individual to obtain his ritual blessings and to be inspired in return. Such 'local saints' may assume tireless catatonic positions, spouting verses in Arabic to the awe and wonder of devotees.

The immense personal satisfaction which devotees obtain from the experience is strongly related to the fact that these inspired individuals usually come from the same socioeconomic background as they do. They have little material wealth, formal education or occupational skill and yet have managed to acquire certain mystical attributes without practice or skill. For this reason, they become highly ranked individuals in the rural areas and may be occasionally called upon by other Malay villagers to give sermons in the local religious hall or *surau*.

The phenomena of *keramat* and *walism* are not peculiar to the *dakwa* movement, having an older history in Malay peasant culture and politics, but they render greater significance in contemporary history since they are perceived by some groups to be yet another indication of the power of Islam — its ability to excite mystical experiences in the common man. In an atmosphere where certain individuals and groups attempt to search for explanations of dissonance between the 'self' and 'other', such phenomena have the capacity to reaffirm the role of spiritualism in change.

These sporadic cults occasionally assume forms which are more militant. One such example was the Crypto Cult discovered in Jelutong, an urban district of Penang in 1981. It was led by a Malay who believed that his group and the Jewish population were chosen to rise in arms against governments (beginning with the Malaysian government) to prevent further destruction and death. The conditions in the world were now similar to those described in the Apocalypse and it was up to this group to rescue it from further turmoil. The Malaysian government broke up this group even before it was known to many to exist. Another important group of this kind was that led by Ibrahim Libya in the remote village of Memali in Kedah. With support from PAS, this group, developed the notion of *mati syahid* or martyrdom in opposing the government. The police stormed the village on November 1985 and many villagers, including Ibrahim Libya himself, died in the violent onslaught.

Followers of the wider *dakwa* movement have also broken away from these groups and attempted to establish their own, usually for reasons of bringing about rapid political changes in the country. A keen follower of the Arqam recently said that he was setting up his own group since the group was too slow in bringing about political and socioeconomic changes. He did not know yet what he was going to name his group but was certain that it would stand to oppose the government and its haphazard policies in integrating Islam with development, which he felt were too slow and erratic, and contrary to his expectations of an Islamic nationhood.

As mentioned earlier, cultish groups were known to exist even in the periods before this particular phase of Islamic revivalism. They were formally viewed as harmless; however, they are now immediately categorized as 'dangerous', a security risk and contrary to the national policy of 'multi-culturalism'.[8] The Internal Security Act has created extra problems since it defines behaviour and activity relating to religion and politics as 'extremism' if the government defines it as such. It is significant to note that in the simple village of Memali, once it was recognized that the villagers were closely allied to PAS, the image of the movement changed, from a local peasant cult to a movement which was politically threatening.

Briefly, the Islamic movement in Peninsular Malaysia supports two basic modes of participation: one surfacing in cultish movements like those described in this chapter, and the other, demonstrating trends of ritual or symbolic conformity to Islam, usually manifested in speech rhetoric and dress codes, and new interest in the scriptures. Of the two, the former is a minority movement of Muslims who, for some reason or other, obtain greater satisfaction from participation in a cohesive brotherhood. They number a few thousand and are transitory in the sense that splinter effects often diminish the strength and vitality of the cult movement in the long term. The second is possibly more visible and is more easily manifested in men and women of the younger generation. Much of it is a result of peer group conformity, in schools, dormitories, colleges, universities and governments offices. Its effect on the young will be discussed in greater detail in this chapter. The Malaysian government's policy on Islam probably reinforces this latter movement, since teaching and learning institutions often organize Muslim students according to current Islamic modes and trends.

Significantly, over history, such revivalist movements express the transformation of Islam from a self-critical movement in the pre-modernist phase (expressed in *Wahhabism* in the Middle East and India and the *Sanusi* movement in North Africa), when attempts to reimpose orthodoxy grew in the wake of ecstatic Sufism and orgiastic sainthoods, to a reactionary criticism of Westernism in the spirit of nationalism, self-identity and self-rule. Attempts to seek political redefinitions of this kind usually swing to the extreme, making orthodoxy almost acceptable.

Self-containment and anti-Westernism may assume many forms in Islam. According to Fazlur Rahman (1979: 216), the Muslim modernist, Jamal al-Din al-Afghani (1939-97), approached the issue of fundamentalism through educational reform because he was essentially concerned with intellectual modernism, an approach he believed would strengthen the World of Islam politically against the West. The movement evoked humanistic ideals of self-thought and autonomy through an appeal for self-rule, a challenge to the moral denunciation of the religion by French critics like Renan that Islam was the incurable enemy of Reason and the Obstacle to Science. In this way, as Said (1978) argued, the message for self-rule and expression revealed European writers to be the enemy of Reason and the colonized population their victims. Such thinking coveted in Islamic ideology swept through Muslim nations colonized by European powers, sending ripples in Indonesia and Malaysia in the early decades of the present century, the period when anti-colonial sentiments were overtly manifested.

The *dakwa* movement in Malaysia is yet another attempt at de-orientalism but it is hardly an expression of intellectual modernism of the kind expressed by Rahman. However, its attempt to revive pristine or orthodox Islam through various ritualistic ways is again in direct opposition to the current trends of Westernism now nourished by capitalism and free enterprise. It is not surprising, then, that those who favour it are mainly middle-level urban workers, student groups or professionals without social status or power, who are marginally involved with modern development processes and generally incapable of acquiring an important platform in decision-making concerned with the government machinery or economy. Urban Malay women of this category invariably become part of these trends of change and although the formal leadership is monopolized by men, they support the movement by joining in the various activities organized and providing support to friends or spouses. The penetration of *dakwa* by the adolescent age group evokes inter-generational conflicts which are expressive of the marginal role of young unmarried women (and men) in ritual activity. The negative reactions of rural and urban Malays towards them is a rejection not so much of Islam, but of the new trends of *dakwa* leadership which challenge earlier forms established through eldership and discipleship. In a sense, it reintroduces the earlier *kaum muda* and *kaum tua* conflict through a similar rejection of Westernism and neo-colonial ideology.

The Constructions of Revivalism in Men and Women

Islamic revivalism has affected Muslims who participate in the movement, whether seriously as leaders, preachers and missionaries or marginally by conforming to the external symbols of the movement in the form of dressing or through acts indicating new religious awareness (like attending religious classes [*usrah*], eating only food cooked and served by Muslims or avoiding physical or eye contact with the opposite sex). For women, veiling in the form of the *telekung* is the most obvious indicator of participation in *dakwa* while men who wear the *songkok* (fez) or *kepiah* (*ketayap*, colloquil North) (similar to the Jewish skull cap) or Arab headgear (*serban*) and robes (*juba*) are immediately categorized as *dakwa*. Women seldom adopt the full *purda* dressing seen in other West Asian regions like North Pakistan or Saudi Arabia but when they do, justify it as *aurat* (the observance of modesty as stipulated in the Qur'an). Extreme cases of women covering their faces completely with a veil or exposing only the eyes occur in the Al-Arqam movement. For men, the Arab tradition of dressing and robing is justified through Sunna, although it confuses Arab with Sunna traditions since dressing the way of the Prophet has nothing really to do with Islam but with Arab customs of dressing. Government religious authorities treat the confusion between Arab custom and Sunna as an expression of the distorted (*songsang; bida'ah*) practices of some groups.[9]

In urban centres, references to *purda* styles of dressing are usually derogatory though the short veil or *telekung* has more or less become acceptable in schools, colleges and offices in the public and private sectors.

Many of these women adorn the *telekung* to be more fully integrated with peer group activities and it is for this reason that veiling is most commonly seen in secondary schools, colleges and universities.[10]

Still, it can be said that the majority of Muslim women remain unveiled in urban centres. Very few are veiled in villages though in ceremonial activities, whether of a religious or a cultural nature, most women and men cover their heads in some form. The *selendang*, a long scarf wrapped around the head loosely and worn in numerous skilful and attractive styles, continues to be popular amongst older married women, while men usually wear the *songkok* or fez.

Participation in *dakwa*, both superficially by merely adopting the external symbols of the movement (usually in the form of veiling or dressing) and more intensively through participation in cultish movements has been significantly important in urban ares (Kessler, 1980; Nagata, 1984; Chandra Muzaffar, 1986; Ayse Nurlifer Narli, 1986). Here observance of *dakwa* does not contradict basic patterns of social relationships relating to courtship, marriage, family and peer group socialization. Indeed, these institutions are often reinforced through greater ethno-centrism and rejection of Western values. Many demonstrate their piety by avoiding public and formal activities associated with states of exaltation and intoxication (*khayal*) such as Western dancing, shows by popular entertainers and 'socials' with members of the opposite sex.

On *adat* forms of cultural entertainment, the opinion is usually divided. Some believe that it is proper to continue with Malay forms of entertainment which are culturally important like the *joget, ronggeng*, forms of group dancing performed by both men and women and the *dondang sayang*, a classical Malay operatic form of singing *pantun* originating from the early Chinese immigrants of Melaka (*baba nyonya*) in which men and women deliver alternate verses while dancing. Others, however, believe that such forms of entertainment are *maksiat* (wasteful acts which are unproductive or immoral) and should be avoided at all costs. Generally, the 'morality' of forms of entertainment and behaviour is subject to varied modes of interpretation, depending on which particular line of cultish behaviour is encouraged by a particular group.

Importantly, for women at least, standards of behaviour demonstrated through *dakwa* seem to have brought clearer distinctions between public and private expressions of *haram* or prohibitive acts. In colleges, veiled women prefer not to eat publicly with men but many have steady boyfriends and go riding together on motorbikes or stroll in the campuses at night, hand in hand. I recall a student of mine saying that although she was veiled and rode on her boyfriend's motorbike in close physical proximity, she had one sin less than other girls who did what she did but did not *tutup aurat* (veil themselves). Often, the act of veiling and unveiling is observed situationally. To illustrate, a Malay girl stated that she turned up for an interview for the job of a receptionist in a cosmetic line, heavily made up, in an elegant, fitting *kebaya* with her hair worn loose, falling below her shoulders. The excited American director on the panel of interviewers selected her immediately. On her first day of work, she turned up wearing a veil and a dull coloured *baju kurung* (loose Malay dressing, similar to a long *kurtah*, with a sarung, much to the dismay of the American and the others who had interviewed her. However, the director was reluctant to sack her for fear of being labelled anti-Islamic and she kept her job.

Events to the contrary are also observed when girls remove their *telekung* after a while in offices where the majority of Malay women are unveiled. Thus, it is important to note that such forms of external symbolization are more characteristic of the Malay *dakwa* movement than personal revelations or enlightenment.

For many men, the cultivation of Islamic verses in speeches and letters of correspondence is another important symbol of participation in *dakwa*. Speeches invariably begin with *Bismillah al Rahman al Rahim* (In the Name of God, the Merciful and Compassionate) or *Assalam u 'a alaikum, wa rahmatullah hi wa barakatuh* (God be with you, may the mercy of God be blessed upon you), punctuated by comments of approval by Allah and ending on the same notes as the opening. Indeed, a circular was issued to government heads of department to reduce the number of quotations from the Qur'an because it distracted the attention of listeners from the actual contents of the speeches.

However, this style of social rhetoric continues to be popular among government political leaders who may not support the *dakwa* movement but wish to convey a general image of religiosity. While the oratory style attempts to evoke group emotion and cohesiveness, the text of speeches is secular and usually relate to practical problems of implementation of government programmes and policies. The success of industrialization and other forms of development is linked to God's willingness to see it happen (*insya'lah*) and while this may distract attention away from social realities, it nevertheless emotively reduces the burden of politicians who make promises that are not carried out. Many political leaders who are trained in Arabic adopt these forms of social eloquence rather skilfully by combining them with Malay metaphors, imagery and quatrains (*pantun*) and the total effect is the conveyance of an effective new form of social communication which evokes images of artistic finesse and flair (*kehalusan*) guaranteed to win admiration and approval from the masses. In a sense, it attempts to combine the language of the Malay *ulama* with that of the former colonial leaders and Oxbridge Orientalists (Winstedt, Wilkinson and Swettenham, among others) who used the *pantun* with skilful flair and elegance to convey their knowledge of and involvement with Malay culture.

The revivalist forces in Islam have affected different nations in a variety of ways. The model of Iran in the reconstruction of the state system along the lines of an Islamic Republic differs from Pakistan, which maintains a democratic-style government while simultaneously restructuring its civil laws according to the Syariah. On a different note, young Muslim students in the West see it as a period of intellectual enlightenment under the leadership of scholars like the late Ismael al-Faruqi and Fazlur Rahman. Attempts towards Islamization of knowledge as an alternative to Western scientific models and paradigms have led this movement to achieve an international following transcending political and ethnic sentiments and boundaries. Malaysian Muslim responses to Islamic revivalism has overtones of this distinctly anti-Western sentiment in the attempts of leaders to revise physical and social modes of communication and relationships according to the ways of Muslims in the Arab world.

Ideologically, the movement is anti-Western; codes of dressing, communication and socialization seem to move away from Western models to those which are distinctively Eastern. Economically and socially, its appeal to Muslims in towns and cities seem to lie in its provision of an alternative life-style which can soften the strain of conformity to urban modern values, aspirations of social mobility, existing socioeconomic inequalities according to class and ethnicity and intense individualism. Overtly, there seems to be some rejection of public activities which are anti-Islamic, particularly those which belong to the realms of animistic and anthropomorphic interpretations of behaviour and phenomena. However, on the level of interpersonal relationships, the movement is characteristically 'ethnic' or 'Malay' in the way in which it accommodates pre-existing Malay values and forms of socialization. As shown earlier, its emphasis on grassroots conformity, mysticism, discipleship and cultish leadership patterns based on charisma or in extreme situations, sainthoods go hand in hand with earlier modes of male power and authority derived from Islam.

The strategy of imposing modesty and domesticity in women is, however, more apparent now than before. It attempts to strengthen male cults while dissolving earlier images of the *Seri Kandi* or female heroism. In this sense, it has systematically selected a version of *adat* and Islam that is more patriarchal than bilateral. Yet men and women who follow rather than lead manipulate the rules of revivalism to their personal advantage and do not seem to suffer much from it.

Symbolic conformity, contextual selectivity, and situational logic, all denote shrewd pragmatism as a survival strategy in a rapidly changing world. Malay response to this mode of conformity in both Islam and *adat* is articulated in *syarat*; going along with the basic principles of both systems to avoid the problem of choosing or rejecting either system. This will be explained in greater detail in the last section of this chapter but it is important at this stage to see Islamic revivalism in Malaysia as a predictable Malay response to global and Malaysian issues of change and development.

Dakwa in the Village

In Malay rural life, religious training and teaching is the formal responsibility of men of the category of *ulama*, here meaning the *imam* and established religious teachers (with the titles of *haji/hajah* or *ustaz/ustazah*) who have maintained their influence by being part of a prestigious line of established scholarship in a particular area (*keturunan keluarga a'lim*). Conventional religious institutions which are performed in groups such as *mengaji* Qur'an (Qur'an reading), *nasyid* (hymns) and *kelas agama* (religious classes) are normally presided over by religious teachers (*ustaz* or *ustazah*) but intense Islamic training under the *guru*-following system (*mengaji pondok*) is performed by *ulama* with established family genealogies (*isnat*). In Mawang, religious training of this form is unheard of but in villages in Kedah, Kelantan and Perak, this form of training is a common practice.

Among adolescents, religious activities adhere to the conventional forms of sexual segregation in Islam except that sometimes men and women may partake in complementary activities that necessitate the presence of both sexes during the same occasion. For example, in Mawang, although *nasyid* is normally organized for women, it is not uncommon for men to participate in it, particularly when the group is organized by youth organizations or government agencies which are concerned with community or social development. Group prayers on Friday or the *Jemaah* are usually performed only by men in the *surau* (prayer-house), *madrasah* (prayer-house and meeting-hall) or *masjid* (mosque) but there is an increasing tendency on the part of women to pray in the *surau* or *madrasah*. Generally, young girls continue to pray in the privacy of their own homes unless they are accompanied by older female relatives at the local prayer house. Other forms of community praying which are performed from time to time because they are sunnat, such as the *Sembahyang Aruah* (prayers for the dead) and *Sembahyang Doa Selamat* (generally, thanksgiving prayers), are always conducted and performed by the men. Women have the role here of preparing the food and supervising the children who accompany their parents on such occasions.

The traditional role of the *ulama* in villages in ensuring that Islamic values and practices are upheld at all times has over the last two decades, been obscured through Islamic revivalism which obtains its leaders from different sources — popularly trained individuals without established genealogies (*salahsilah*, *keturunan*) of Islamic scholarship or *isnat*. Emulating the *kaum muda / kaum tua* conflict of the 1930s, many of them are also much younger than the established group of *ulama* and derive their inspiration from different sources (Mohd Sarim Haji Mustajab, 1979; Nagata, 1984). These are usually external figures rather than local *guru* and include theologians and politicians like the late Mau-du-di, the late Ayahtollah Khomeni and Gadaffi.

Dakwa and Conflicts Between Youth and Elders in the Village

The Anak Dara Sunti

The Islamic revivalist movement has had its widest impact on young Malay women with rural backgrounds who are in the process of acquiring new educational standards or professional skills in towns. Among the adolescents, these influences begin from secondary schools and colleges and are mainly a consequence of the social exclusion of young women (and men) from village community life (Ayse Nurlifer Narli, 1986). Their marginality and ritual exclusion lead them into new systems of ideas dictated by external forces, be they religious or modern. Industrialization pushes young women into the urban labour force while conformity to *dakwa* threatens to encapsulate them into domesticity. In order to better understand this phenomenon, a brief background of the Malay *anak dara* group will be provided.

The *anak dara sunti*[11] age group, comprising young girls who have reached puberty (usually between the ages of 12 and 18), has been neglected by anthropologists and other researchers on Malay social structure, possibly because they seem to comprise an insignificant group within the Malay ritual order. Significantly, the marriage of a girl within this age group changes her status immediately from that of a young girl to a woman.[12] Like their younger counterparts in the *kanak-kanak* (toddler and pre-school) age category, they experience a rather anomalous marginal status within the family, kindred and wider culture.

Although an *anak dara* is expected to perform most of the domestic tasks that cannot be undertaken by her mother because the latter is busy attending to the needs of the younger members of the household or earning a supplementary income from agriculture or trading, her domestic role is something that is more or less taken for granted. Since she is also of school-going age and therefore also burdened with homework and school examinations, she has very little time to socialize except in the evenings. One these occasions, the girls will visit their friends, often bringing along a younger sibling in their care. After a while, a group of two or three will be joined by many more along the way. Laughing and holding hands, they attempt to draw attention to themselves by calling out to kinsmen and neighbours en route; they make funny comments now and again and dissolve in fits and giggles, much to the concern of the older village members looking on. They are quite frequently labelled as unreliable, lazy, or stubborn, and it is common for a mother to pronounce her daughter stupid and not fit for marriage, though not in unaffectionate terms.

The *anak dara* group is regarded with grave importance only by the *teruna* of the village. These single young men, mostly in their adolescence, share a similar position with the *anak dara* group in having a significant lower status compared to married men. Being unmarried and therefore *mentah*, they cannot be included in the core of traditionally Malay or Islamic rituals reserved for the married and the older men of the village. However, these men enjoy considerably greater physical freedom than the *anak dara*. Not only are they free from domestic chores, they are also less confined by social conventions which make them more obstrusive in public. Though generally respectful of elders, loud chatter, open joking and gang behaviour are common to men of this age group. They form peer groups and have close companions, the local expression of which is 'member', with whom they organize various group activities — social or income-generating or both.[13] They are also free to leave the village in search of alternative employment in the towns and cities, and very often do so whenever the need or opportunity arises. Young girls normally leave the village when they pursue a course of study or career elsewhere. Factory work is another reason for leaving the village, when gainful employment is not available there or in neighbouring towns and their parents are dependent on them for supplementary income.

Generally, unmarried girls within this age group are not encouraged to converse freely with their male counterparts but they often meet socially during ceremonies and festivities and increasingly so during formal meetings organized by youth organizations (*Kumpulan Belia*) which are based in the village. These youth organizations, like the MAYC (Malaysian Youth Council) and the 4B (*Belajar, Bersatu, Berusaha, Berkhidmat* [Learn, Unite, Strive, Serve]), have permeated villages like Mawang and are often headed by married men in their thirties (still very much a *belia* category according to formal political definitions of 'youth').[14] Although these 'youth' leaders generally supervise the behaviour of the younger members of the organizations, the *anak dara* and *teruna* may gather together to discuss issues or club projects either before or after the meeting proper, and friendships may blossom amongst them. That some of friendships may blossom into romance cannot be discounted.

Young men and women find it difficult to show their mutual liking for each other during ritual ceremonies and festivities. At these events, women and men are segregated according to their various domestic and ritual functions in a *bentara* — a voluntary labour group organized for special functions, usually headed by elder women. Generally, in a ceremony that involves cooking and feasting (*kenduri*), the young girls will assist the older women in the kitchen or communal cooking centre, preparing vegetables, stirring the pots, fetching water or washing dishes. The food will be laid out in small dishes and arranged in trays (*hidang*). These will be passed over to the *teruna*, who have the main function of serving and clearing dishes to be handed back to the women in the kitchen. The point of social contact between the young men and the young girls of the village occurs at this juncture when both groups are involved in the task of sending out and returning food trays. Young men and women who prefer not to take part in these tasks may be soundly rebuked. Some of these young girls and boys may be seen chatting idly with members of their peer groups during such festivities. Idle talk and gossip is not encouraged but grudgingly allowed as long as the normal social conventions of discreet sexual segregation and moral conduct are observed. It is on these occasions that young girls become noticed by older women who reflect on their personal behaviour and pattern of conduct. Positive comments evolve around notions of gentle behaviour and femininity (*manis*, lit. sweet, gentle) or proper standards of morality and virtue (*bersopan santun*). Negative observations concern loud or coarse behaviour (*kasar*, *kasak*) or overt flirtatiousness (*gatal*, *gatai*). There are certain ways of speaking, gesturing and sitting, for example, which are regarded to be proper or which make a woman 'feminine' and it is advantageous for a young girl to conform to them, lest she be labelled as unfeminine by the womenfolk. These comments might deter older women from 'viewing' them (*menengok*) as potential wives for their own sons or those of their relatives or *adik-beradik/saudara mara*.

Although these rules of femininity apply to all women regardless of age, it is significantly the *anak dara sunti* rather than older married women who are forced to conform to these social conventions. This is partly because the former will contract marriages in the near future and the breach of social conventions may reduce a girl's chances for a good marriage. Generally, young men of this age are also expected to show respect and obedience to their parents, to be gentle and religious, and to aid their immediate family and kinsmen in whatever way they can. However, they may not be bound by such strict codes of decorum as the women, and may adopt extroverted manners without being categorized as *tidak bersopan* (improper conduct). They should not, however, breach codes of morality relating to sexual conduct, and may be as severely censured as women when this happens. Wilder's comments (1970) that women more than men (pre- and post-marriage) are subject to rules of sexual morality and social exclusion is not entirely untrue, except that in rural areas, differentiation according to marital status rather then sex is the more important rule of social conduct. Moral censorship on the behaviour of young male adolescents is usually overlooked by researchers who might assume that this group can do what they want and how they please.

Although an *anak dara* is expected to be economically productive, she does not face as strong a pressure as male youths to achieve economic independence and earn a supplementary income for the family. However, with the increasing reluctance of young men to partake in farming, families compensate for their lack of income by encouraging daughters to seek jobs in the cities. Hence, economic responsibility is now transferred to young girls. Although numerous agricultural tasks are demanded of youths in the villages and many opportunities exist for them to indulge in agro-based industries, men and women now prefer to emigrate to the town or city to look for regular salaried positions. The tendency to seek non-agricultural jobs varies considerably from region to region according to the availability of opportunities in land settlement schemes or salaried jobs in the vicinity of the village, but generally, added prestige is given to youths who have permanent town jobs, even if only as unskilled factory labourers.

In Mawang, and increasingly so in many other villages, mothers tend to seek out men with salaried positions as prospective grooms for their daughters because of the added security they can provide for their future family. This has created a new social differentiation pattern within the *teruna* group. Those who continue to be farmers feel ashamed for doing so and struggle to make themselves attractive to the opposite sex in other ways, while those who work in factories or who seek employment in the navy, army or police boast of new social and personal experiences and have little difficulty attracting women as potential spouses. Young farmers always complain that they find it difficult to get a good wife (*susah cari isteri*) unless they can compensate for their low position by producing the material symbols of success and achievement — a vehicle, preferably a motorcycle or a car, durables for their household and providing their potential wives with the kind of bridal wealth expected of men who 'have made it' (*sudah senang*, lit. 'already easy'). The anxiety to be economically independent and productive is closely linked to their pre-marital status. Already marginalized, they have to prove their capabilities to others much more than married men. Obviously, it is linked to their potential sexual and social role performance, for Malay women of both the younger and older generations seem to show a preference for working men with regular employment as potential spouses or sons-in-law.

However, although the Malays stress propriety and domesticity for unmarried women and productivity and independence for unmarried men, both sexes within the *kaum remaja* are bound by strict moral codes of behaviour based on rules of *adat* and Islam. Although few Islamic codes of ritual behaviour are observed, such as regular prayers and, for women, sexual modesty by concealment of hair and chest through veiling (*aurat*), sexual codes of behaviour relating to *adat* which have strong parallels in Islam are usually observed. Pre-marital sex, for example, is strictly forbidden though when it happens, attempts are quickly made to marry the couple before anyone gets to know of it. If it becomes a public issue, it is undoubtedly a source of shame (*malu*) and a major stigma for both the girl and boy and their parents. However, punishment according to Muslim law is unheard of.[15] In the rural areas in Malaysia, as in Mawang, courtship periods are often short and a close relationship with a man from the village invariably leads to marriage. Relationships which cannot be solemnized because of parental objections or individual differences are soon converted into close fictitious sibling relationships (*mengaku adik, abang*). The creation of these 'sister and brother' relationships between the *anak dara* and *teruna* categories immediately resolves situations of potential conflict between the concerned parties.

Tactile behaviour between sexes and open flirtation is discouraged, but in villages like Mawang where Islamic revivalist groups have not yet influenced the pattern of social relations amongst the youth, discreet flirtation between the sexes is a standard practice. Generally, in Malay rural society, flirtation and repartee between the sexes gets less discreet and distinctly more bawdy and obscene with increasing age and sexual experience. This in fact is quite contrary to conventional Islamic practices of social behaviour between men and women. However, it is practised with spontaneity and is regarded to be perfectly acceptable within the context of Malay norms of intersexual behaviour.

Dissonance in Socialization Forces in Rural Areas

In the village, the wider *dakwa* movements (particularly activities associated with the Darul Arqam or *tabliqh*) are viewed with suspicion by elders who generally believe that it is better to learn more about Islam on their own than through these movements. Though standards of religiosity vary from those who do not observe any of the fundamental rules (*wajib*) of *rukun* like praying, fasting, performing the *haj*, to those who observe the *rukun* and are also well versed with the Qur'an and its principles of *tafsir* or interpretation, *dakwa* activities are generally avoided by the elder generation. This is a consequence of the conflicting lines of leadership between the *ulama* (strongly backed by village elders) and the new generation of leaders in *dakwa*. The conflict is usually articulated in many different ways. Some of the comments of elders from Mawang deserve special attention and are listed below:

1. The leaders are not sincere (*ikhlas, jujur*) in their advancement of Islam; they employ Islam for their own personal gains. A frequent comment made of Arqam is that the profits derived from their sales is probably used to advance Arqam, not Islam in a broader sense.
2. The villagers and elders in particular are already well versed with Islam and do not need to learn more about it.
3. Such movements are a bad influence on the youth since those who became active have been known to turn against their parents or cease to heed their advice and reason. Rumours of children leaving their homes to live in communes in Kota Bharu and other cities create a real fear in older women and men who have adolescent children.
4. The movement is 'anti-government' and not supportive of government policies and programmes. Bearing in mind that Mawang is a Barisan Nasional stronghold, it is not surprising that *dakwa* is rejected because it is perceived to be 'anti-government'.
5. A number of 'deviant' or *songsang* (in the village it is simply referred to as *karut* or *merapu* (south *merepek* lit.'rubbish') activities are performed by the *dakwa* which has no place in village life. Amongst these are *mengatip* (compulsive utterances of the verses 'There is no God but Allah and Muhamad is the Messenger', with the purpose of producing 'trance states'); and the tendency for leaders to take on many wives which is seen to be an excuse for lust (*gatai/gatal*) and promiscuity; the use of principles of *menurun* (possession) to evoke genealogies of descent from sacred ancestors. In the latter, villagers probably hear about what takes place in the cities from kinsmen and friends since no one could quote particular examples of observing such acts.[16]

Although *dakwa* is not taken seriously by villagers in Mawang, informal pressure to conform to the practices of *dakwa* is exerted upon the young, by schoolteachers or friends within the school. Responses are varied and *ad hoc* and factors like family background, school performance and the extent of one's existing knowledge of Islam may effect the way in which young boys and girls respond to this pressure. The majority indicate that fear of alienation from friends commonly makes them observe the form of dressing upheld in *dakwa* though they do not affiliate or identify with any one particular *dakwa* group or organization. When these village girls wear the *telekung*, they state that they are merely conforming to a fundamental (*wajib*) requirement in the Qur'an while remaining dissociated from the mainline *dakwa* movement in the country. Some may quip with sarcasm, 'How can we be *dakwa*, we are not intellectual like those who go to university, we are stupid!' Though some genuinely feel that they can improve their personalities and mode of life by undergoing spiritual training through Islam, this is not accompanied by any attempt to understand the religion better through reading and discussion. A few are moved by the poetic expressions of the scriptures in the Qur'an and the eloquence and oratory skill of some of the popular speakers on Islam; for these young men and women, it is generally an awe-inspiring experience which makes them *khayal* (intoxicated, high). Hence, their interest in Islam is extremely personal and does not encourage them as such to join any particular *dakwa* group or organization.

It is difficult to argue that children with religious backgrounds whose parents or close kinsmen adhere closely to Islamic teachings have a greater tendency to participate in *dakwa* in some form or other. Indeed, in Mawang, it is these very parents who discourage them from doing so partly because they feel that they have already imparted sufficient religious knowledge to their children to prepare them for the future and also because they fear that they may lose the ability to control and discipline them in the manner to which they are accustomed. Intergenerational differences and mis-understandings have also emerged in families where parents have not bothered to bring their children up in the Islamic way and the children have decided to take their initiative to learn more about it themselves. As a result, some have accused their parents of not having performed their duty according to the Islamic tradition and have openly defied and criticized them, causing much unhappiness and tension within the family. In Mawang, the majority of parents do not have adequate knowledge of Islam but this has never been seen as a problem since children are normally placed under the tutelage of a religious teacher not only for Qur'anic lessons but also for religious instruction on the Hadith. Such conflicts between parents and children on religious issues were not formerly prevalent. These parents seriously believe that secular education is more important than religious education during the period of secondary school-ing and fear that religious activities may distract their children from attaining academic success and a good career.

Parents may resign themselves to overt changes in their children's dressing or social activities when they realize that the pressure from peer groups in the schools is too much for their children to resist or endure. In one such family in Mawang, the girl's parents, who were extremely religious, refused to allow her to wear the *telekung* at school. Her father was an *imam*. He said that it was an insult that someone else had influenced her into wearing it, particularly when he did not feel it was necessary. She was enrolled in a private secondary school in the town of Kulim, Kedah, where most of her friends had taken to veiling under the influence of an *ustazah* at school. For months, she had tearful exchanges with her parents stating that merely wearing the *telekung* did not indicate that she was following general religious trends, that it was only a convenience and an attempt to ward off criticisms from her friends. However, her father did not permit her to do so and the matter was left undiscussed. Afterwards, she obtained a Grade III in the Sijil Pelajaran Malaysia, Malaysian Certificate of Education examination (Ordinary Level), but was determined to reregister in another school to obtain a better grade. The only school available was one financed and administered by PAS, where it was essential for all the girls to wear the *telekung*. Her father, upon observing the daughter's desperation to obtain better grades, conceded after briefing her that he did so only because her new school required it. He also told her that she should not feel obliged to follow any of the group religious practices performed in the school, other than the usual daily prayers. A more detailed examination of school socialization processes revealed some ways in which *dakwa* has affected social relationships and intersexual behaviour amongst the young.

It is obvious that increasing conflicts are manifested in socialization forces derived from informal village institutions of learning and more formal academic institutions in towns. First, the social environment in the village is significantly different from the school. The average rural child no longer perceives the school as merely a place to obtain literacy before preparation for marriage or village work. Similar pressures of attainment and achievement are manifested as in urban school children. Increasing academic competition, interpersonal rivalries, jealousy and group pressure to conform to both formal and informal codes of academic attainment impose new strains upon the rural student. Furthermore, intersexual relationships and friendship ties have to be moulded differently, in and out of the village, creating extraordinary problems in adjustment to school life.

On the informal level, for academic and personal reasons, both sexes strive to be acceptable, popular and gather friends or 'members' with whom they can maintain relationships on a regular and intensive basis. A great amount of apprehension develops when these forms of relationships are not as easily developed or maintained as in the village, where homogeneity of background and experience introduces an immediate spontaneous selecting response in peer group membership. Peer group formation in villages is normally based on age cohorts, further differentiated according to gender. These develop into permanent age-sets where both sexes maintain distinct groups which interact now and again, informally and formally. In secondary schools or pre-university colleges in small towns, the majority of the students come from rural backgrounds. Peer group relationships formed with friends of both sexes from different villages tend to develop into categories of fictitious kinship relationships within and between different age-sets. These relationships tend to generate more tension than those formed in the village, mainly because the school environment is charged with competition and rivalry of both an academic and a personal nature. The formation of such relationships becomes an indicator of rank and prestige amongst schoolmates. The most humiliating position is not to have any fictitious sibling relationship at all and the best would be to have one which inspires both a personal friendship and a kind of study partner relationship.

The Extension of Sibling Relationships in Schools

Adat siblingship principles are extended to friends and acquaintances in schools to bring some of the support systems of the village to a place which is unfamiliar and potentially threatening. Immediately, unfamiliar relationships symbolically express the same kind of cohesion and solidarity generated within real siblingships in the village. McKinley (1983) argues that siblingship is the basis of Malay bilaterality within the kinship order. His argument would be even more significant if argued in the context of fictitious siblingship relationships. From adolescence to adulthood, these relationships are constantly created to mediate between the traditional and modern, the familiar and unfamiliar, the impersonal and personal. It observes no sexual boundaries and instead attempts to reorder new hierarchical relationships according to the familiar rules of age and seniority in the village. Fictitious siblingships enable Malay bilaterality to permeate modern urban institutions at all levels, functioning as a moderator of change and transformation.

The system is now rampant in secondary schools, universities and other institutions of higher learning. Within the sexes, a young girl or boy becomes an *adik* ('younger sister' or 'younger brother') to the elder who becomes a *kakak* or *abang* ('elder sister' or 'elder brother'). The relationship of a younger girl to her *kakak* or *kakak angkat* ('adopted sister') is based on adoration and respect; she looks upon the elder for advice and guidance on all matters pertaining to her education, family or personal problems which she may face from time to time in her relationship with her own peer group. The same kind of relationship is observed between an *abang angkat* and an *adik angkat*. These relationships of 'fictitious kin' in schools occur commonly between different sets, a situation which is not very common in the village since different age-sets tend to avoid one another, having little basis for social interaction. The school environment, however, allows opportunity for more interaction of this kind. Establishing close links with seniors is a way of advancing prestige within one's age-set, just as it is an added boost to a 'senior' to have a 'junior' taken under her wing. In this respect, the elder girl assumes a highly supportive role and very often becomes extremely possessive of her *adik*, particularly when other members of her own peer group attempt to bully the younger or intervene in the relationship in some way. Since it is extremely reassuring and flattering to have adoring younger girls at one's heels, it occasionally happens that a classmate or friend within one's peer group may attempt to break up such a relationship in order to win the attention and admiration of the younger girl.

One such case in the Adabi Secondary School at Bukit Mertajam concerned an extremely pretty young girl who had already declared (*mengaku*) an 'adoptive sister' relationship with a senior from Mawang. Since their parents knew each other, it was quite natural for the elder to protect the younger from rough teasing classmates, as well as assist her in her schoolwork. Unfortunately, another senior decided that she wanted to 'win' the younger girl over and told the latter malicious untruths about her *kakak*'s behaviour amongst her classmates. Soon the younger girl detached herself from her 'elder sister' and attached herself instead to the new girl. Her 'elder sister' was bitterly hurt and upset, especially as the senior was one of her friends and a 'member' from her own class. She cried for days and tried to coax her 'little sister' not to believe the awful things said about her, claiming that it was a case of *fitnah* ('malicious framing'), but to no avail. Finally, she was forced to admit that she had lost her 'little sister' permanently. The experience left her shaken and confused. She lost confidence in her friends and classmates, alienated herself from her peer group and eventually drifted out of circulation, mooning around her house for days, much to the anguish and despair of her mother. Finally she failed her Sijil Pelajaran Malaysia (Malaysian Certificate of Examination, Ordinary Level).

Relationships of this nature between older and younger age-grades in schools are taken very seriously. On a psychological level, the need to form fictitious siblingship ties reflect the traumas of the Malay youth devoid of value and status in the village and eager to compensate for it somehow in schools by consolidating relationships along kinship lines. Symbolically, the whole school is converted into a 'village' activated by a system of interlocking kindred and friendship ties. Furthermore, the highly competitive atmosphere in schools amongst girls and between girls and boys produces tensions that require immediate solutions. The creation of fictitious sibling relationships everywhere helps to channel these emotions in a positive direction. Students strive to prove their superiority and capabilities in some form and this is often difficult, unless they have leadership qualities or talent of some kind in sports, music, dance or drama or achieve a high academic performance level. Girls who are extremely talented or who are of a high intellectual calibre do not compete for friendship or admiration from others within or across age-sets. It is the ordinary 'run-of-the-mill' kind who is not particularly bright, pretty or talented who has academic and personal problems of this kind. From comments of adolescent boys in Mawang, it appears that male students also take such relationships seriously and compete with one another in establishing important or prestigious fictitious kinship ties. Often this is done by adopting a younger girl as an *adik angkat*. The *adik* and *abang angkat* system between the sexes implies that all in all, a person could have two or more types of fictitious siblingships:

1. with a younger or older member of one's sex;
2. with a younger or older member of the opposite sex;
3. with a peer of the opposite sex where a boy of the same age automatically becomes an *abang* and the girl, an *adik*.

As explained earlier, the attempt to integrate cultural norms of relationships into the school environment may facilitate greater academic achievement and reduce personal adjustment problems though the reverse effects of this system have been shown. This informal network of fictitious siblingship often contravenes the kinds of relationship which the school formally believes in promoting, particularly in religious-type schools.

On the formal level, gender relationships within a co-educational school or college are based on Islamic codes of morality which tend to be less compromising than those observed in the village. While it is proper for girls to interact with boys in group discussions, projects or extra-curricular activities, it is decidedly improper to establish personal relationships with them. Peer group support or enthusiasm for such relationships cannot overcome the rigid disapproval and acid comments of teachers so that these siblingships are seldom given the chance to develop openly or spontaneously. *Pantun*, verses in the form of quatrains, may be slipped in each other's schoolbags or desks. Letters may be exchanged through mutual friends. They normally contain friendly advice and verses of affection. These verses may get progressively romantic as the relationships are prolonged or if they extend into the higher grades, particularly in pre-university (Form Six) classes. Older girls may strive to meet their *abang angkat* in the town on the pretext of buying books or clothes or visiting a girlfriend, and may then sneak into a cinema-hall together or have food in a local restaurant or coffee-shop. The conversation is normally limited to school affairs, mutual friends or hobbies, and it is only when it develops into a really serious affair that the pair attempt to discuss their future together. If a girl has no ambition of carrying on with her studies upon completion of her secondary schooling, her parents may consider her ready for marriage and, provided the boy's parents approve, raise no objections to this idea. In this sense, fictitious siblingships develop into affinal relationships through marriage but they may also fade away as new potential candidates come into the picture. The potential sexual component of the siblingship may be curbed or nurtured, depending on the individual circumstances of the relationship.

It very often happens that parents want to see their children establish a proper career for themselves before they settle down and may discourage early marriage. Sometimes ambitious parents may deliberately break up such a relationship when it comes to deciding between future education for their sons and daughters and a new daughter- or son-in-law. On the other hand, families which are highly dependent on their children to bring home extra income to meet the basic needs of the household, may encourage early marriages when daughters appear to have little interest or potential in further studies. While it is important to marry off daughters to reduce the economic dependency on the family as soon as possible, it is necessary to delay the marriage of their sons till they are eligible for long term employment in the army, police or other areas in the public sector. The increasing trend to seek employment in processing industries such as electronics, textiles and food-manufacturing has deferred the marriageable age categories of both men and women so that even if parents are hard hit by poverty, it is preferable to allow daughters to seek employment in these factories to bring home extra cash earnings. Marriage is now less commonly used as a strategy to transfer the burden of economic responsibility to the son-in-law (Ong, 1987).

The kind of male and female behaviour expected of students of the *kaum remaja* varies according to the organizational principles of the school or pre-university college. If the school's administration imposes fundamental Islamic modes of administration, intersexual contact or communication is not as easily achieved as in the more cosmopolitant Christian Missionary or state-owned schools. Many of the schools attended by students from Mawang and neighbouring villages are either privately owned by the Islamic-based political party PAS (Adabi, Masyriah) or government-sponsored like the convent in Bukit Mertajam. Some attend schools which were originally religious schools but which have subsequently been upgraded and converted to State National schools.

On the formal level, in the private schools funded by PAS, male and female relationships are completely discouraged and the rules of behaviour based on sexual segregation and avoidance may even make it impossible for formal group discussions or meetings to be held between boys and girls. For example, all women, including Malay female teachers, observe the *aurat*. Direct eye contact between men and women is forbidden and male and female students are not allowed to speak to each other in or out of the classroom. Female students are placed at the rear end of the classroom while male students sit at the front. The latter are not allowed to turn around to look at the girls when they are called upon to make comments or to provide answers to questions posed on them. Prayers are strictly observed during school hours. Students are called upon for disciplinary action when they deliberately or unintentionally miss their prayers.

After school, boys and girls are not allowed to walk home together and if they attempt to get personally acquainted in the premises of the school or dormitory, may be liable for *khalwat*, which as explained earlier, is a state-imposed rule of sexual misconduct ('close proximity' or 'sexual intimacy') between an unmarried man and woman. In an Institute for pre-university students in Bukit Mertajam which is attended by a number of students from Mawang and its neighbouring villages, four *khalwat* cases were reported during the period of field research when the school reopened in March 1982. The students were not forced to marry, but in each case, both parties were suspended from school for a few weeks and the matter reported to their parents. None of these students were from Mawang but it appeared that the matter was merely hushed up in the village concerned and not discussed further. The students were also not further punished by their parents.

Islamic conformity in these schools and colleges reflect forms of symbolic acceptance and support as those found in local universities. Some of the students state that they adhere to the rules to be able to study peacefully there and do not really believe that they can abide by the same rules of social conduct when they ultimately graduate. Many girls, for example, do not wear their veil after school and although this is clearly forbidden, feel that as long as their parents do not mind, they should be free to do so. Some complain that there are a few school informants or 'spies', amongst whom are the schoolteachers themselves, who report such misconduct to the school authorities for the necessary disciplinary action to be imposed on the 'guilty' students. A girl student also complained that veiling heightened the boys' curiosity about the length and texture of their hair (whether it was straight, curly, or permed) and that she found this more disturbing than the normal teasing and flirtation that takes place in the village in the absence of elders (Karim, 1987 a, where this is discussed in greater detail). She was once confronted by a boy who whispered to her rather poetically, '*Alangkah indahnya jika kamu buka telekung supaya saya dapat renong mahkota kamu itu?*' ('Would it not be lovely if you could remove your veil for me to cast my eyes on your crowning glory?'). She said she was subdued to shocked silence and moved away quickly before he could say anything further. The boy merely looked amused and smiled know-ingly at her for several days afterwards. She said she could have converted this meeting to an *abang angkat* relationship and toned it down but she was furious (*dah naik steam*, colloquial) and was too 'hot' (to mean 'angry' rather than 'aroused' in the Western sense) with him and chose not to do so.

In schools which maintain Islamic ideology as the basis of socialization, sexual awareness and curiosity are not magically removed and under certain circumstances may even encourage greater sexual arousal within the *kaum remaja*. Significantly, a general complaint amongst students, including the boys, is that some of the teachers do not observe the very rule they preach. Male teachers may openly tease the girls in the class and even look at them directly, much to the annoyance of other students looking on. This form of conduct appears to be more common amongst junior rather than senior teachers but it may be said that regardless of seniority, only some of the teachers in these schools are sincerely committed to implementing Islamic rules of behaviour correctly. Many regard teaching as just another job and may decide to alleviate the boredom of teaching by teasing the students. A girl stated that her Geography teacher always insists on including 'nipples' on all mountain and hill tops he draws on the blackboard to elicit laughter from the students. Giggling and sniggering, unfortunately, is forbidden, and when the teacher encourages it, the class monitor usually attempts to stop it.

It also frequently happens that girls with pretty faces (hair remains concealed under the *telekung*) tend to get more attention from male teachers, including religious teachers. There are a few well-known cases of teachers who have married their students and it is not so much their marriage to these girls that have upset the students as the attention, open show of admiration and favouritism which these teachers bestow upon the girls during school hours. Students who are not very attractive or clever reveal their insecurity and resentment when such forms of favouritism are shown by avoiding contact with their teachers. While they do not care to be in the same position as the favoured girls, they do feel that it invariably affects the system of academic grading. They claim that favourites of teachers usually stand to benefit. Some, however, do feel a certain amount of sympathy for the favoured girls for they feel that without such forms of distraction, the girls could have continued with their education and carved out careers for themselves. Generally, both boys and girls form a low opinion of male teachers who show extra interest in female students. It is uncommon for female teachers to show similar interest in male students although this may happen occasionally.

The focus on the adolescent age group has been for a purpose. While the group appears to be receiving the direct pressures of religious revivalism, it is simultaneously geared towards academic achievement and urban employment. These trends introduce states of dissonance within socialization processes, ultimately pulling the *kaum remaja* into a different mode of life which serve to marginalize them even more in the family, peer group and village. School and college attendance encourages conformity to *dakwa* while urban employment in industry enhances modernity.

Wider religious movements maintain varying standards of social acceptability and conformity and as both boys and girlsof the *kaum remaja* waver from indigenous *adat* practices to religious fundamentalism, they become the indicators of the success and effectiveness of these new trends. The same pattern of use or abuse of women has been apparent in other societies where ecstatic cults, charismatic movements and fundamentalism have been widespread (Lewis, 1971; Mernissi, 1975; Waddy, 1980; Shahshahani, 1984). In Malaysia, the apparent conflict in responses and reactions to revivalism amongst the *kaum remaja* and the dominant rural population seem to suggest that *adat* values continue to seek recognition despite intervention from outside social forces.

Matrimony and Dakwa

The greater integration of older, married women in village community life shields them from the influences of *dakwa* to a great extent. The phenomenon of veiling, for example, has not caught on at all amongst them and women observe head covers in the same way as they used to do before, by wearing the *selendang* loosely around the head for formal ritual ceremonies, like weddings and funerals. For married village women who are gainfully employed in land schemes, estates or factories, head scarves may be worn at their place of work. They may also place their husbands and children before their careers, but there are indications of resilience and autonomy in their relationships with spouses or peer group. First, in relation to the observance of veiling, a husband may, under the current influences of Islam, request that his wife wear the veil, but the situation does not necessarily lead to one of male domination in marriage. There have been numerous instances where a woman takes to piety as a means of controlling her husband better. A man who requests that his wife wears a head scarf or *telekung* is in a sense declaring his state of religiosity before her. Her subsequent piety necessitates him to observe similar religious standards. It is uncommon to find men imposing Islamic standards of modesty through veiling or domesticity upon their wives merely as an excuse to indulge in extramarital relationships or other socially deviant activities. The more common scene is for both spouses to observe Islamic fundamentals together or not at all. Some women in the village confide that it is better to get a man to be religious because it becomes easier to control them. Extreme cases, of course, have been known to occur when men use Islamic principles of polygyny as an excuse to have a more varied sexual and social life but these are rare in villages. In both rural and urban centres, polygyny is more closely associated with class rather than adherence to Islamic revivalism.

On the subject of domesticity, new notions of the 'model mother' in Malaysian Islam or *Ummi Mithali* have not been received popularly. The concept of the 'model mother' as one who places husband and children before anything else, is a theoretical formulation of government sponsored religious groups like PERKIM or the *dakwa* bureau of the government.[17] In the village, married women, when questioned on this 'model mother' concept, scorn the government for implementing it, for it assumes that Muslim women have not been previously concerned for their spouses or children. As one woman puts it, 'Where is there a mother who is not concerned for her family? It is more important to get men to be more concerned for it. Let's have *ayah mitahli* ('model father').' Again, the number of Malay women giving up their careers for domesticity is negligible and national statistics of deployment amongst Malay women are usually attributed to retrenchment, rather than voluntary withdrawal. It may be assumed that one of the more important reasons for Malay women's continued employment is the encouragement given by spouses to be gainfully employed, probably to lessen their own burden of supporting the family.

Generally, female economic productivity and employment have been traditionally viewed as necessary and important in Malay rural society, encouraging women (married or single) to continue with gainful employment. In any case, the effects of Islamic revivalism on female domesticity have been obscured by other public media which stress the combination of education, career development and motherhood for Muslim women and non-Muslims alike. In fact, trends of postponement of matrimony accelerated by the pursuit of employment in the tertiary sector and public services has brought down the annual growth rate of the population from 3.1 per cent in the 1970 census to 2.4 per cent per annum between 1986 — 1990 (Fifth Malaysia Plan; 129).[18]

Movement of Young Women into Industry

In the decade after Independence in 1957, the Malayan government pursued economic strategies that aimed to improve the economic livelihood of the rural population, which was predominantly Malay, through a diverse range of rural development programmes. Agencies aimed to improve economic productivity and marketing techniques by encouraging resettlement in integrated land schemes and this led to vast displacements of Malay populations within the rural area. The expansion of multinational and local-based industries in the fringe of capital towns also encouraged rural and urban migration but this merely brought on urban poverty amongst Malay migrants. Jobs were scarce, poor-paying, irregular and workers were not well organized in trade unions to improve working conditions. The racial riots in Kuala Lumpur on 13 May 1969 in which Malays on the fringe of urban poverty vented their frustrations upon the more settled Chinese population, was an indicator that rural poverty was not easily resolved through integrated land development schemes, nor by encouraging rural Malays to migrate to the cities. A more viable infrastructural base was necessary and efforts to improve agriculture techniques, managerial skills and individual participation were accelerated under the 'New Economic Policy' implemented in 1970 under the Third Malaysia Plan.

Women have contributed significantly to waged employment in primary sectors of the economy, oriented around the production of rubber, coconut, oil-palm, tea and pineapple in smallholdings, estates and plantations. The 1985 figures in Table 6.1 demonstrate lower overall female employment in all sectors, compared to male employment, but within the primary sector, women's employment in agricultural activities surpasses other categories of work at 39.3 per cent. Trends in the estate sector have led to a gradual deployment of women between 1967 and 1980 with the exception of oil-palm production which has shown an increase in both male and female participation over the same period.

In the 1970s with the increasing urbanization and development of the tertiary sector, imbalances in rural and urban development became more discernible in the Peninsula. The manufacturing sector drew labour away from agriculture, mainly from the younger age category, an important source of labour for family smallholdings and farms. In the 1970s and 1980s in particular, the number of young men and women drifting into unskilled, low-paying jobs in the manufacturing sector has been significantly high. National statistics on the distribution of population reveal that the majority of the people continued to be concentrated in the rural areas. In 1980, 69.3 per cent. of the population were rural while 30.7 per cent resided in urban areas. Malays constituted 65.2 per cent of the rural population and only 32.8 per cent of the urban.[19] Significantly, with most of the regular (salaried) employment opportunities concentrated in urban areas, rural and urban drift was highest amongst the Malays. Reliable statistics on Malay rural and urban migration are not available but estimates indicate that between 1975 and 1980, the annual average growth rate of Malay migrant workers in urban centres was approximately 5.7 per cent (Ministry of Labour, 1982).

It is significant that the kind of industries encouraged by the Malaysian government also created a high demand for female labour. In the post-Independence period between 1960 and 1980 the Malaysian government promoted the development of labour-intensive industries, such as electronics, textiles and garment manufacture, and the assembly of electrical goods. The majority of these manufacturing concerns represented foreign multinational corporations from Japan, Korea, Europe and the United States. Significantly, these labour-intensive operations generated a high demand for unskilled female labour which was mainly obtained from the rural areas in the country. This implied that the majority of these young factory workers were Malays. The percentage of women in the secondary sector was 40 per cent in 1985 but this is likely to increase with the expansion of the electronic and textile industry in Malaysia (Table 6.1).[20] This significant increase in manufacturing created a labour shortage in the agricultural sector, particularly in labour-intensive activities relating to rubber tapping and rice cultivation.

Recent estimates show that in most Malaysian Free Trade Zones, it is the electronics and textile industries which have utilized female labour to the optimum, cashing in on what can be described as 'female orientalism'. Women become the ideal choice of foreign investors who seek a passive

TABLE 6.1   Malaysia: Employment Distribution of Women by Sector and Major Occupational Groups, 1985

	Total	(per cent)	Female	(per cent)
I. Primary Sector				
Professional and Technical Workers	7,663	100.00	609	7.9
Administrative and Managerial Workers	5,337	100.00	293	5.5
Clerical Workers	12,735	100.00	4,284	33.6
Sales Workers	1,114	100.00	80	7.2
Service Workers	11,614	100.00	3,277	28.2
Agricultural Workers	1,657,631	100.00	651,815	39.3
Production Workers	65,731	100.00	4,397	6.7
II. Secondary Sector				
Professional and Technical Workers	34,701	100.00	4,846	14.0
Administrative and Managerial Workers	52,916	100.00	2,184	4.1
Clerical Workers	79,217	100.00	48,050	60.7
Sales Workers	11,043	100.00	2,268	20.5
Service Workers	23,160	100.00	7,031	30.4
Agricultural Workers	6,043	100.00	779	12.2
Production Workers	1,062,352	100.00	329,215	40.0
III. Tertiary Sector				
Professional and Technical Workers	384,398	100.00	171,439	44.6
Administrative and Managerial Workers	51,725	100.00	8,681	16.8
Clerical Workers	340,431	100.00	217,399	63.9
Sales Workers	613,734	100.00	212,836	34.7
Service Workers	597,895	100.00	258,083	43.2
Agricultural Workers	55,677	100.00	4,644	8.3
Production Workers	270,525	100.00	10,801	4.0

Source: Statistics Department, Labour Force Surveys, 1985

and submissive workforce to ensure maximum productivity at this level (*New Straits Times*, 1 August 1985; Ong, 1987). The distribution of women's formal employment in the different occupational sectors is shown in Table 6.1. Significantly, only a very small percentage of women are employed in professional (7.9 per cent), administrative or managerial occupations (5.5 per cent); the vast majority are employed in the lower occupational categories. The 40 per cent engaged in production and related functions in the secondary sector in 1985 contrasts with a figure of less than 10 per cent in 1970. These women workers have recently been recruited from rural areas to form a massive labour force engaged in industry owned mainly by foreign multinationals including Hewlett Packard, Bosch, Intel, Audio Electronics, National Semiconductors, RUF, Hitachi, Mostek and Motorola. In accordance with the New Economic Policy (1970-1990), which attempts to diversify the economy even more through massive industrialization and urban development, increasing numbers of men and women will be engaged in economic occupations which will bring them directly into the scope of formal legislative and legal policies concerning manual workers.

Decision-making on the higher levels of management (Table 6.1) appears to be a male reserve, within the primary sector, recording only 5.5 per cent women. The secondary sector records 4.1 per cent and the tertiary sector 16.1 per cent. Yet, women's capacity for decision-making in industrial legislation and labour policy could indeed be improved if agricultural or production workers maintained a strong collaborative network through trade union activities and political participation. However, the contrary was truer to the picture where semi-literacy, rural traditions and an overtly oppressive male hierarchy in decision-making levels in industry has resulted in the reverse effect, encapsulating women even more into non-decision-making roles in the production process. Tables 6.2, 6.3 and 6.4 show recent membership in trade unions by numbers, sex and status.

TABLE 6.2 Trade Unions Membership, Malaysia, 1986 to 1988

Region/ State	No of Unions			Membership in Register			Membership in Benefit		
	1986	*1987*	*1988*	*1986*	*1987*	*1988*	*1986*	*1987*	*1988*
Peninsular Malaysia	305	311	322	560,952	561,248	568,893	526,659	528,820	534,406
Sabah	32	33	30	17,866	18,392	20,294	15,768	16,274	16,499
Sarawak	64	65	62	27,529	26,892	28,334	24,862	26,490	26,490
TOTAL	401	409	414	606,347	606,532	617,521	567,289	571,584	577,395

Source: Ministry of Human Resources, Malaysia, 1990

TABLE 6.3   Trade Unions Membership by Gender, Malaysia, 1982 to 1988

Year	Male		Female		Total	
	Number	*Per cent*	*Number*	*Per cent*	*Number*	*Per cent*
1982	388,753	73.5	140,293	26.5	529,046	100.0
1983	384,043	72.6	145,178	27.4	529,211	100.0
1984	373,346	73.0	137,898	27.0	511,244	100.0
1985	381,457	73.1	139,891	26.9	521,348	100.0
1986	382,355	72.8	142,736	27.2	525,091	100.0
1987	375,850	71.1	152,447	28.9	528,297	100.0
1988	374,465	70.1	159,456	29.9	533,921	100.0

Source: Ministry of Human Resources, Malaysia, 1990

It can be seen that although the number and membership of trade unions have increased over the years (from 401 in 1986 to 414 in 1988), female membership is significantly lower than male and in fact has not increased appreciably between 1982 and 1988 (from 26.5 per cent to 29.9 per cent). The figures contrast even more sharply in terms of status and leadership positions in the trade unions. In 1984, women constituted only 2.91 per cent of trade union leadership (Presidency). Their position as Secretary (1.82 per cent) and Treasurer (5.10 per cent) were equally dismal. These figures increased in 1988 to 4.04 per cent for the Presidency, 7.14 per cent and 10.25 per cent for Secretary and Treasurer, respectively. Increasingly, as a consequence of non-participation in formal leadership or more direct channels of communication, women tend to protest through the more coveted institutions of mass hysteria (Lee and Ackerman, 1981; Ong, 1987). Massive factory employment has had the final effect of hindering women's intellectual and mental advancement although a long term perspective might see this as an initiation into political conscientization (See Lewenhak, 1977 on British women in the trade union movement).

The Malay women who drift into these urban centres are mainly in the 18 to 25 age group and so are mostly unmarried, with the minimal qualifications of post-primary education. They represent, for the most, women from the *anak dara sunti* age group who have postponed their marriages to enjoy economic and social independence for a while. As far as they are concerned, they are better off earning a living in the town than staying at home in preparation for marriage. What is really being appreciated is the new purchasing power they now enjoy, the release from traditional social controls, and the ability to socialize freely with men and women and to enjoy the bright lights of the city.

TABLE 6.4 Principal Officers of Trade Unions by Gender, Malaysia, 1984 to 1988

Year	President				Secretary				Treasure			
	Male	Female	Total	Per cent	Male	Female	Total	Per cent	Male	Female	Total	Per cent
1984	267	8	275	2.91	270	5	275	1.82	261	14	275	5.10
1985	278	4	282	1.42	273	9	282	3.19	254	28	282	9.93
1986	286	6	292	2.05	279	13	292	4.45	265	27	292	9.25
1987	286	12	298	4.03	283	15	298	5.03	269	29	298	9.73
1988	309	13	322	4.04	299	23	322	7.14	289	33	322	10.25

Source: Ministry of Human Resources, Malaysia, 1990

The New Working Environment

Generally, young women who seek employment outside the village either commute daily to their place of work or live in the towns permanently. In Mawang and other neighbouring villages, the majority of the young men and women commute since companies in Butterworth provide transport to and from the villages. Those who seek employment in Penang live within the Free Trade Zone area of Bayan Lepas.

For those who choose the latter, a new way of life is experienced which is radically different from that in the village. They are able to socialize freely with male employees and develop regular relationships with other young men and women in the area. They tend to nucleate in subsidized or private dwellings within the Free Trade Zone areas so that most of their social activities are concentrated around their place of work.[21] Their visual and physical impact on the local scene is dramatic. They are constantly seen waiting for buses, walking, laughing and chatting together, unveiled and clad in attractive modern uniforms, conveying images of youth, abandonment and vitality. Malay and non-Malay men often form liaisons with these girls, not so much for the purpose of marriage but merely to establish temporary sexual relationships. However, despite their image of heightened sexuality, these girls essentially maintain Malay values of marriage and normally assume that such relationships lead to long term commitment and security.

Such differences in rural and urban value systems in urban centres have led to the formation of loose, irregular attachments which rarely crystallize into marriages because of the negative sexual image they portray. Furthermore, the situation is extremely different from the village where kinsmen and elders monitor romantic attachments very closely and hasten matrimony when the couple appear to be very involved with each other. Malay female workers often express anxiety and concern for the future, feelings which periodically surface in nervous breakdowns, drug addiction, smoking and hysteria.[22] It is significant that these working girls are categorically referred to by the term *'Minah Karan'* (lit. 'Minah, the Electronic Lady'), which in Malaysia has come to convey wantonness and promiscuity and render a derogatory image of women hired on the assembly line (Fatimah Daud, 1985). Malay men in similar levels of employment are likewise labelled *'Ahmad Spaner'* ('Ahmad, with the spanner') but this joking reference only evokes images of a low-paying job; it is not a reference point for sexual immorality. Such men certainly are important candidates for mothers seeking spouses for their daughters in the village.

For those who commute, similar images of women as modern and hence, promiscuous are produced though in a lesser degree. To the women and men in the village they symbolize modernity, liberation and open sexuality and are consequently subject to more moral censure than other unmarried girls of their own age group or young men who are gainfully employed in urban areas. Elders complain that they have become irreligious, disrespectful, over-independent and generally unconcerned about communal social affairs. In reality, their irregular working hours, based on the shift system and increasing difficulty in coping with domestic responsibilities have significantly contributed to their disinterest in participating in village affairs.

The working conditions of female migrant workers in the Free Trade Zone are also radically different from agricultural or agro-based village occupations. The factories demand regular attendance, consistent hard work and concentration in assembling and processing minute parts of electrical or electronic commodities. The work environment is completely opposed to the more casual and irregular work pattern in the village. Agricultural and agro-based activities may be labour-intensive and time-consuming but they are often seasonal activities performed within a personal and informal social environment which accommodates individual and social preferences and interests.

In Mawang, a career as an unskilled factory worker is usually the last resort for village girls who seek employment in urban centres. They constantly express their desire to be trained as teachers, nurses or secretaries or to obtain clerical positions within government agencies. There is a definite preference for these more conventional careers which offer greater long term economic security than factory work. More specifically, they are concerned for their low promotional prospects, fixed or maximum wages, limited opportunities for further training and the likelihood of retrenchment. It is also known that women obtain lower salaries than men in the factories. The latter are mainly employed to handle machines which is said to require more skill and physical effort. Obviously here for women, the intense need for concentration in micro-assembling occupations and physical or psychological stress resulting from 'high-space' work and close supervision in the assembly-line have not been given much value in job renumeration. Generally, it can be seen that *anak dara* women more than the *teruna* have been marginalized by employment in the tertiary sector, not only in terms of their social stigmatization but also in relation to the hierarchical formation of male and female, higher skilled and lower skilled categories of work which are maintained in the manufacturing sector.

The problem is further aggravated by their marginal participation in union activities. For this part of the study, fifty interviews were conducted with Malay women production workers from Mawang and as a comparison, sixty with Malay production women workers from Bayan Lepas in Penang. The former group comprised only unmarried women while the latter contained both single and married women.

The right to union representation, although enshrined in the labour laws, is one which has not been forthcoming for many workers in the manufacturing industry. This contrasts with the participatory spirit of corporateness and group enterprise set out in the New Economic Policy. Furthermore, the Malaysian government's 'Look East Policy' of emulating labour and managerial designs from Japan in particular, its attempts to encourage small in-house unions and Quality Control Circles (QCCs) has been effective in preventing the large unions from negotiating for better wages and working conditions for all workers engaged in the same industry. This, combined with the fact that the workforce is largely female, lacking corporate leadership or access to information about representation or unionization, creates a vicious circle of passive acceptance amongst female workers about work conditions.

Reviewing the problems in history, since the time unions were officiated under the Trade Unions Enactment of 1940, female leadership in trade unionization has been conspicuously absent. Ironically, as shown earlier, although female employment in estates and plantations has been significantly high, the majority (mostly Tamils) have been satisfied with providing support to their male counterparts. Within the patriarchal confinements of estate life, this would in any case have been discouraged by both family members and union officials. Since the 1960s, with the increasing employment of women in manufacturing industries, the problem of female participation or representation has taken a step for the worse, with the government's own policy of discouraging large-scale collective representation for fear of deployment of capital and investment by foreign multinationals. Bureaucratic controls and red-tape, for example, have prevented electronic workers from forming their own union; this has been aggravated by the principle that collective representation is possible only when homogeneity in the kind of commodities produced has been established. Hence, workers in both electronic and electrical companies have had problems in establishing a joint union because of some of these technical obstacles. The recognition for an *en bloc* union representation in the electronics industry began as early as 1974 but even to the present time, the government and formation of a trade union for electronic workers has not been realized.

The sixty young women who were randomly selected from Bayan Lepas in Penang were asked to respond to questions on trade union activities. All had working experience of more than a year in the electronics industry. When asked about their participation in trade unions, almost all (55) said that they found it too time-consuming and could not be as active as they would like to be. Trade union meetings kept them away from their families, and domestic chores could not be attended to properly. Some added that their families (or spouses) did not approve of their involvement in unions while others felt that union work was probably more suitable for men with their limited domestic responsibilities and chores. Finally, a few claimed that union leaders were usually charismatic and aggressive once they reached the top and that even if they could compete with men in this sector, would probably not be able to rally enough support from fellow women workers.

It was found that women in this group were not fully committed to the activities of their union. In fact, many were of the opinion that unions were anti-management organizations and believed that active involvement would lead to retrenchment. Reviewing the situation objectively, it was quite obvious that the limited choices of work for young rural and urban women with only secondary school qualification was a real deterrent to union participation. The fear to make demands over and above what was received acted as an added psychological barrier to unionization.

When the fifty girls from Mawang were interviewed about their working conditions in the security of their villages, the majority (48) expressed a sense of frustration and despair over their life situation and working conditions, particularly their wages. They said that as factory workers, they were *pengemis dalam negeri sendiri* ('beggars in one's own country'), subject to inferior occupational status, low wages and moral censure and stigmatization by community and society. There was not much else they could do except to be domestically employed. The fear of having little freedom in domestic work (house help) was a reason why many refrained from seeking work in private homes.

Significantly, these girls believed that it was better to seek employment in companies which had been unionized for it ensured protection against unfair retrenchment. This view indicated a learning experience based on their observations of production workers who had been easily dismissed because they had not been unionized. Many indicated that they had been forced to change their place of work to seek better wages or working conditions elsewhere. These women differed significantly in their views of unionization from the former group, who were possibly more aware of the hard realities of unionization, described earlier. These village girls, however, still viewed unions in rosy terms — strong and powerful, equivalent to a system of male leadership and providing a necessary support system. The other group, however, were more cynical than grateful and considered their work as part of their life predicament. They did not feel that a male-dominated union could help them. Their overriding mistrust of male domination in management was extended to unions. The feeling was that if women had to fight for their own rights, they had to have greater participation in unionization, but structural constraints of work and marriage prevented them from taking a more active role in decision-making. Both groups, however, confirmed the finding that factory work was the last resort for any form of formal employment for young women. They all preferred to be professionally oriented to embark on better careers such as teaching, nursing and even clerical positions.

This feeling was reinforced by village elders who openly condemned factory work for the social independence and moral laxity it appeared to bring Malay youth, particularly women. Unfortunately, since factory work is associated with family poverty (necessitating these young girls to seek quick ready-made jobs immediately after the completion of secondary school, or sometimes even before), a new social hierarchy is created in the village with rural elites censuring impoverished families for encouraging their young to be employed in occupations leading to 'moral depravity'. Class values become solidly entrenched through further modes of social differentiation. 'Moral depravity' is associated with the young and poor and progress and respectability with the young and elite. It appears that only the latter can now afford to conform to the traditions of *adat*. Modernity and the adoption of Western culture in young Malay women through factory employment is as dissociated from *adat* as Islamic revivalism. Revivalism does not encourage women to participate in waged employment and productive work which can generate a fair amount of economic independence and self-reliance. *Adat* does so but only if it preserves women's modesty and femininity (*kehalusan, manis*). Industrialization and religious revivalism help young women retain their traditionally marginal and inferior status rather than get rid of it. Symbolically, through opposing patterns of self-representation in work and attire, industrialization and revivalism have reinforced the marginality of the *anak dara sunti*.

Since only a small percentage of Malay youths have managed to detach themselves from the periphery, to enjoy a better position through education and professionalism, Malay cultural forms of distributing power from the 'core' to the 'periphery' (based on seniority, eldership, marriage., etc.) are not significantly altered by processes of class formation, formal education and development. These processes merely add on to it, enriching the ingredients of the cake. Rural adolescent single women can improve their position only if greater value is placed on their work through better renumeration or if they can attain better political or union participation. Even so, they can only elevate their position to that of their male counterparts of the same generation, a position similar to their position in the village before.

In Malaysia in 1960, the Benham Committee recommended equal pay for women in certain occupations where women tended to predominate — but it also recommended lower wage scales for women in certain service categories. Generally, it is well-known that despite the presence of legislation advocating equal pay or its equivalent, there is little evidence that equal pay is actually received in many countries. For example, in the

United States the ratio of male to female earnings varies considerably from occupation to occupation but rarely do women approach anything like parity. Information collected on median weekly earnings of full-time employees (whether wages or salaries) indicated that women's pay cheques are on average only 65 per cent those of men (ILO, 1982). In the United Kingdom, even with the Equal Opportunities Act of 1975, it is reported that employers continue to find ways and means of avoiding this legality by introducing a wage structure which places women in lower-paid occupations or by paying men extra for merit, long service or willingness to work overtime.

In Malaysia, the differential pay structure for women in government service sectors was a source of general dissatisfaction resulting in massive strike action. Women teachers in particular were vociferous and by 1969, the government accepted the principle of equal pay for men and women in equivalent grades of occupations. However, women in the private sector continued to lag behind their counterparts in the public sector. In 1980, the average monthly wage paid to women workers was M$90.00 to M$209.00 less than that paid to male workers. This was a marginal improvement since 1974, when wage differentials were between M$27.00 and M$243.00. In the case of daily paid workers, women received only between 74 per cent and 79 per cent of the rates paid to male counterparts (Ministry of Labour and Manpower, Occupational Wage Surveys 1980). The Employment Act also did not specify on the minimum wage rate to be received from any employer according to the system laid down by the ILO in Convention 131 and Recommendation 135 of 1940 (ILO, 1982 a). However, under the Wage Council Act, 1947, the minimum wage for shop-assistants, employees in coffee-shops, restaurants, hotels, bars, Penang stevedores, cargo-handlers and lightermen, and cinema workers was to be M$250.00 per month. Industrial workers were left out of this Act and their wages continued to be fixed by labour market supply-and-demand mechanisms. The government's reluctance to pursue this act of legislation again reflects its acute dependence on foreign investment in industry with cheap labour as its main source of inducement. Any imposed minimum wage, particularly if it is higher than the prevailing rates, may encourage them to relocate their industries elsewhere. Hence, young rural and urban women continue to be at a disadvantage politically, economically and socially until and unless they realize their potential power in the modern labour force.

Young Production Workers and the Controls of Adat

If greater social differentiation is now discerned among Malay young single women, this has been greatly contributed by industrial employment based on paternalism and misogyny. The problem is aggravated by the stigmatization of production work by both rural and urban Malays of the older generation. Not only is production work associated with unskilled employment, it is also believed to be another form of Westernization which threatens traditional ways. Steady employment is sought and hard work and enterprise are valued as long as they do not produce seemingly similar standards of behaviour as those perceived in the West. Significantly, the image of the young Malay girl as one who is comely and 'cultured' (berbudi bahasa) and who 'does not kill an ant when she steps on it' (pijak semut pun tak mati) to indicate gentility and decorum somehow does not materialize in the urban social milieu. The preferred standard of behaviour of being provocative yet inaccessible is badly shaken when a girl adorns Western clothing and socializes freely with men. Personal communication with these girls indicate that they certainly value their newly-found freedom and sometimes take full advantage of it. New items of social value relating to dressing and beautification are taken advantage of by men and women who go to the dormitories to sell them cloth and cosmetics on a monthly instalment basis. In the township of Bayan Baru in Penang, for example, where many factory workers live, the girls wait for the event when an old Chinese man, referred to as apek (respectful, for a Chinese elder) takes them to scenic spots to have their photographs taken. Accumulating and exchanging snapshots and taking them back to the village creates much excitement. The apek sells these photographs to the girls at an extremely high price, but they do not mind since they say that he is actually doing them a favour.

The local religious authorities occasionally send an ustazah (female religious teacher) to preach to them on Islam but she is not very popular. Seldom are religious activities considered to be of great importance. Some wear the short veil telekung but claim that they do so to avoid male advances. The majority have many male associates with whom they may go on 'dates' but group events are usually favoured and picnics and trips to the beaches and hills of Penang are important group activities. Some of the prettier girls also speak of part-time 'modelling' and 'escorting' activities. They chose to be extremely vague about this but these activities seem to be linked to invitations by supervisors or other staff to attend dinners and functions. Party dresses are supplied and the girls are paid to accompany and socialize with senior managerial staff, usually ex-patriates. Although data on pre-marital relations is hard to obtain, it is nevertheless a problem, judging from the number of illegal abortion clinics which have sprung up in Bayan Lepas and Bayan Baru around and outside the Free Trade Zone. Obviously, these clinics are also patronized by girls from the other ethnic groups but illegal abortions among Malay girls has been known to occur in the smaller towns and fringe villages. While it is cheaper to abort a pregnancy through a traditional midwife (bidan kam-

pung), they are not trained to carry out abortions and merely administer potions which are not always successful.

The experience of these girls may be said to be radically different from those in the village and it is for this reason that social stigmatization develops. The experience of their counterparts attending secondary schools — modern or religious, pre-university classes and other tertiary school programmes are also different, not so much because they are embedded in village or small town social networks but because they have come under the influence of Islamic revivalist forces. As explained earlier, Islamic revivalism has a similar effect of reproducing the peripheral status of young women in this age category. Women's sexuality is diminished rather than enhanced through external symbols of dressing and social behaviour. This is also perceived by many to be contrary to Malay values (since the symbolic manifestations of Islamic revivalism are derived from local interpretations of Arab or West Asian culture). Finally, both forms of social behaviour, Western or revivalist, are regarded as undesirable to the extreme and are rejected by the majority. This seems to suggest that the Malays constantly attempt to steer towards a 'cultural core' — *adat* codes and values of basic religiosity (non-*dakwa*) which are felt to be in keeping with tradition.

This 'cultural core' is increasingly articulated in the notion of *syarat* — the system of interpretation of common rules of *adat* and Islam and/or merging sunna institutions in Islam with the ritual regalia of Malay *adat*. The principle of *syarat* ideologically and ritually fuses practices which are compatible and discards those which are not, so that the 'cultural core' expresses what is fundamentally necessary or proper for the regeneration of the society.

Syarat *as a Principle of Mediation*

The interpretation of behaviour by *syarat* generally defines processes of ritual mediation between *adat* and Islam. This is justified by the comment that Malays have to comply with the ritual basics of culture or *syarat* (from Arabic *sarala*, meaning 'to prescribe', 'make law'). By this is implied that there are certain basic procedures in *adat* and in Islam which have to be upheld, to make a situation or event 'acceptable' or 'proper'. The contents, however, cannot be predecided — they are subject to local interpretations at a given time of what is *syarat*. Indeed, what is 'proper' and 'acceptable' varies from one time to another, place to place and interpreter to interpreter. As long as a person complies with the minimum requirements of custom and religion at that particular time and place, he or she has followed the order of the 'proper' and 'acceptable'. Compliance with *syarat* Islam and *adat* distinguishes the practising Muslim from the infidel and the 'cultured' individual from the 'common' (*orang beradat/orang tidak beradat*).

Generally, the principle of *syarat* in Malay culture follows certain basic rules. First, procedures of Sunna are usually considered over and above *syarat*. In this category of ritual activity *dakwa* Muslims attempt to leave their mark by rejecting wasteful, lavish ceremonies derived from Arab traditions and pre-Islamic rituals. However, certain Sunna practices are kept, particularly those relating to dress and this is mainly to distinguish themselves from the majority of Muslims in the country (for example, wearing green robes, wrapping the head cover in the way of the Prophet, or wearing wooden shoes instead of leather). Second in *syarat*, is that things which symbolize origins, parentage, and ethnicity should be continued. Here, certain *adat* practices may gain new ground amongst urban Malays anxious to show proof of origin and parentage. In many instances, these involve local interpretations of *adat-istiadat Melayu*, some of which are derived from Sunna traditions which are now simply referred to as *adat* and symbolically categorized as 'Malay' rather than 'Islamic'. The resurgence of *akikah* ('sacrifice of a goat or lamb at the birth of a child') and *berendui* (or *naik buayan*) a ritual of rocking a newborn baby to welcome it to the world demonstrates this trend. The third rule is that rituals may carry on being practised if they bring goodwill and entertainment to the community. One of these is the *bersanding* (public display of a bride and bridegroom in ornamental clothing). Another is the tradition of feasting (*kenduri-kendara*) on occasions of birth, marriage, death and departure for the haj. Fourthly, even if a ritual is known to be animistic, it may still be performed if it ensures continuity of good health, safety in child birth or alleviation of illness. This, involves ritual baths (*mandi sintok limau*), 'cradling of the womb' (*lenggang perut*) for the first pregnancy, taboos or *pantang-larang* during pregnancy and after the birth and a host of other rituals which concern the *bomoh* and the midwife.

The compromising message of *ikutlah syarat* or 'follow the basics' is subject to so much variance that sometimes one can only know what is 'proper' or 'acceptable' after a spontaneous interpretation by an elder or specialist. It is a process of 'thinking aloud culture', where legitimacy and justification are constantly sought by people according to convenience and practical reasons. It is this flexibility and spontaneity in interpreting boundaries and categories which enable Malay bilaterality to triumph in the long term. An example of how a particular *akikah* ceremony may be conducted will explain some of the finer points of *syarat*.

The ritual of *akikah* or the sacrifice (*qur'ban*) of a goat or lamb for a newly-born child (usually two for a boy and one for a girl) on the seventh day of birth, or later, is theoretically contained within the category of Sunna rituals in Islam. It is usually accompanied by the ceremony of *cukur rambut* or 'shaving the head' (also Sunna) and an additional *berendui* (*naik buayan*) ceremony. The infant is rocked to sleep to the tunes of *berzanji*, individual singing of selected verses from the Qur'an, a preamble to the *Murhaban* (songs of praise for Muhamad the Prophet) sung in chorus. Songs of love and epical history (*sya'er*) may also be sung during this ritual. These rituals form a series of interrelated cultural and religious activities which are performed within the same day or separately over a few days. Malays believe that it is proper and perfectly acceptable to do all of them, or at least to make an effort at holding some of them, particularly for the firstborn child (male or female). Holding all of them would imply conformity to *adat-istiadat* to the extreme (full ritual regalia) while holding the basic *cukur rambut* and the sacrificial act of slaying a goat or lamb would be to comply with *syarat* in Islam.

Currently, the relevance of *berendui* within *akikah* has been questioned. While many believe that *berendui* is in keeping with the spirit of festivity and rejoicing at the birth of an infant, a manifestation of collective sentiments which is Sunna in Islam, others believe that is essentially non-Islamic (leaning more heavily to Arab or local custom than to the Qur'an) and should be removed. The festive spirit of *akikah* surfacing in *berzanji*, *murhaban* or *sya'er* in fact is prevalent in other Muslim cultures in Saudi Arabia, Pakistan and Morocco, so the Malay situation is by no means unique. Most of these *murhaban* and *sya'er* sung contain similar themes of praise of the Prophet and God, and stories of the feats of the Prophet and his daughter, Siti Fatimah (*Sya'er* Siti Fatimah). In Malaysia, however, in keeping with Malay traditions of flexibility, some of these songs have become parochialized and refer to local epical events like the Japanese occupation of Malaya (*Sya'er Jepun langgar Malaya*) or the burning of the fort of Kuala Kedah (*Sya'er Kuala Kedah terbakar*). However, these intrusions of local Malay epics in the *sya'er* is taken for granted. To the Malays, it is more important to preserve the spirit of entertainment (*berseronok*) than worry about the finer details of authencity, composition and contents.

Within the context of Islamic revivalism, a recent *akikah* ceremony in which I participated, again raised the issue of interpretation between the 'proper' and 'improper' — the search for 'true' differences in meaning between custom and religion. The *akikah* to be performed was entirely organized by a group of women who were affiliated to one another through their membership in the Women's Institute (Perkumpulan Perempuan) and Wanita UMNO (the women's division of the United Malay National Organization). The point of controversy was whether one or two goats should be sacrificed (*qur'ban*) for the newly-born boy. If Islamic Sunna values are closely observed, two goats should be sacrificed for a male and one for a female infant, but if Malay *adat* requirements are to be met, one goat would suffice for either, following the principle that an infant 'girl' is valued equally to a boy. The organizer or 'ritual consultant' for the host was a veteran of Malay *adat-istiadat* and extremely knowledgeable in

Islamic rituals. She decided that it was not necessary to discriminate between the sexes, that one goat would suffice for the boy. She added that two goats or lambs for a boy was Sunna but one was the *syarat*. What was important, she stated, was that the host complied with *syarat* in Islam. This implied that one goat would do as well. It was not so much a question of waste but discrimination.

The decision merged with the spirit of Malay *adat*. According to her interpretation of *qur'ban* for infants, two goats were preferable but not essential. The second issue was whether *berendui* should be performed or discarded and if it was in any way vital for the proper performance of *akikah*. After some discussion, she told the host that it was customary but not necessary. Besides, it was extremely difficult to organize a group which could sing the relevant *sya'er*. Finally, the *berendui* was not performed since the performers could not be found on time, but the sleeping baby was placed in a cradle in the centre of the room, encircled by the women who performed the *berzanji* and *murhaban* for several hours.

The *cukur rambut* was then performed and this was followed by a lavish feast (*kenduri*). During the preparation for the *cukur rambut* ceremony, the women spontaneously prepared ritual items which were important in *adat* and mainly derived from Malay pre- Islamic animistic ideas of 'sympathetic magic' — a basket of boiled eggs, decorated with fresh flowers and shoots, signifying continued fertility; a young coconut filled with coconut juice (*air kelapa*) to contain the hair of the infant, a symbol of good health and eternal prosperity; and a tray of ten-dollar bills folded in the shape of birds, to be given to the women participants as a gesture of generosity and reciprocity.

The ritual process of the *cukur rambut* performed before the *murhaban* was also highly animistic in procedure. The infant was passed from the arms of a young nubile to that of a blossoming teenager, and finally to a betrothed young woman, symbolically representing the smooth transition from childhood to adolescence and womanhood. The sleeping baby was then carried around to have bits of its hair snipped off by all the women present. The hair was placed in the coconut and was later floated down the river with messages of hope that the infant would journey to distant lands in search of knowledge and wealth. Usually, women who are barren or who have problems in childbirth compete to carry the baby for this ceremony since it is believed that the act will increase their fertility. In this particular ceremony, the baby was carried by a childless woman who had been married for several years.

The *akikah*-related set of rituals demonstrate one of the many ways in which, on the level of interpersonal and group behaviour, Islam and *adat* become fused and undifferentiated in accordance with processes of '*adatization* of Islam'. Significantly, interpretations are not necessarily biased towards Islam but may lean on *adat* traditions which are not only impartial to gender but comprise elaborate ritual procedures oriented around animistic notions of fertility and prosperity. In this case, the *akikah* ceremony was symbolically ordered through *adat* practices. The reverse process, the 'Islamization of *adat*', may suggest an *akikah* of sexual discrimination in *qur'ban* (two goats for a boy and one for a girl) accompanied by a kind of 'ritual bareness' — the sacrifice is quietly made without much fuss and bother and the meat distributed to poor Muslims. Muslim fundamentalists in fact advocate this procedure. In the example described, the 'ritual bareness' of the act of *qur'ban*, which is *syarat* in Islam, was glorified and expanded through *adat* which brings along with it more colour, activity, community participation and festivity.

Eventually, *adat*, through elaborate ritualization procedures, manages to dominate a religious ceremony by making it conform to the domain of 'traditional cultural Malay practices', or *adat-istiadat Melayu*. In this sense, though Islam and Islamic fundamentalism may impose new meanings and definitions of 'right' and 'wrong', the cultural system, through *adat*, also attempts to reproduce its own set of ideas of the 'proper' and 'improper'. Consequently, ritual activity based on Islam or principles of Sunna very often become subsumed under or extended into elaborate *adat* practices. Often, this occurs when women are the important ritual bearers of the occasion and can perform the ceremony independently from men. In this context, as long as they can control the show, they tend to 'publicize' their skills even more dramatically, making full use of the occasion to demonstrate their expertise and sense of participation and fun.

This phenomenon extends into other important areas of celebration and feasting, particularly engagements and weddings. The *bersanding* cere-mony in marriage, involving the public display of a married pair in fine ostentatious attire after the performance of *aqad* ('solemnizing a marriage') is considered improper to revivalists since it goes against Islam (*maksiat*-'wasteful', 'extravagant'). However, despite the existing climate of Islamic revivalism, elders continue to see it as necessary and 'proper' and resistance on the part of young *dakwa* couples to *bersanding* leads to public censure.[23] I observed a young Muslim who refused to go through the *bersanding* ceremony on account of his *dakwa* activities. He was criticized by his parents and some elders but they gave in to his wishes. The boy was referred to as disrespectful (*biadap, kurang ajar*) and arrogant in his disregard for custom. He did not know *adat* (*tidak tahu adat*) was the general opinion of the crowd. In another case, the refusal to undergo the *bersanding* by the couple did not lead to any conflict with the parents, but friends and relatives who were invited said that it was disappointing. The wedding ceased to have an 'enjoyable atmosphere' (*tidak seronok*). Guests came and had some food, went into the house, viewed the bride and left. Other than the lack of tradition, such wedding were significantly different in the way they discouraged merriment and a close sense of community participation.

Processes of Islamization may under certain circumstances be subsumed under processes of acculturation through *adat*, which maintains an elaborate ritual system of its own. Islam provides alternative modes of thinking and behaviour from *adat* but it is not always successful in displaying it independently outside the frills and fancies of *adat*. In this context, as long as *adat* rituals continue to be important, Malay women's roles as ritual specialists and performers can be maintained, since it is *adat* rather than Islam which gives them this privilege.

On a more general level of analysis, *adat* and Islam seem to be in symbolic conformity to one another through the mediatory notion of *syarat*. *Syarat* acts as a measurement for 'ritual basics' in culture and Islam — minimal levels of conformity to both *adat* and Islamic practices. In *adat*, the basic rules which are explained by *syarat* express the core value system of the Malays and this concerns behaviour and relationships which are regarded as essentially proper and correct and which form the basic ingredients of Malay socialization processes. It includes procedures and rituals which are regarded as essential in conception, childbirth and marriage, involving certain individuals or a section of the village or kindred group. Though all *adat* practices are considered proper, those which are obviously animistic, wasteful or extravagant are said to contradict Islam. The trend in *dakwa* is to discourage such practices from being observed. For non-revivalists, the dilemma between 'proper Islam' and 'proper *adat*' is often mediated by explanations of 'ritual basics' for both so that any extra activity, if performed, is encouraged and welcomed. Women tend to welcome those activities which demonstrate their own sphere of ritual specialization, a vital source of power and autonomy for the Malay women in both rural and urban society. The domain of extensive ritual activities concerned with engagements and weddings and feasting, rites in preparation for the birth of a firstborn, celebrations on the birth of a son or daughter, shamanistic seances for women 'possessed' — these are the ritual spheres of women. These events blur distinctions between the domestic and political, private and public. Ritual monopoly makes them the bearers of heritage and tradition. As long as *adat* remains a basic source of Malay heritage, they can use it to their advantage to compete with men in Islam.

Men had a monopoly in pre-Islamic rituals of healing and curing which continue to be practised privately although such rituals are out of favour officially. In a sense, the men have lost an important source of public activity. This is compensated through Islam where certain groups assert their power by reducing these rituals to the realm of the undesirable, the 'surplus' of ritual activity in animism which is not essential to Muslims. Malay revivalists interpret *syarat* as a necessary activity in Islam and one which does not compromise with the practice of *adat*. This inevitably creates a split in opinion about things necessary and acceptable in Malay

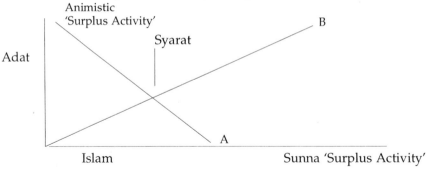

FIGURE 6.1 *Syarat* and the Relationship between *Adat* and Islam

social life, but as shown earlier, it does not obliterate the trend towards the *'adatization'* of Islam. (Figure 6.1)

Despite the prevalence of interpersonal and group dissonance over the maintenance of both *adat* and Islamic practices, the two systems of ideas comprise different value preferences which appeal to different sets of people in time and place. The trend towards revivalism, however, does not obliterate *adat* from social activity. While earlier forms of animism may be gradually removed (A), *adat* permeates Islamic-Sunna traditions through the ritual mode, dramatizing public ceremonies with animistic ideas where gender differentiation is absent. Finally, *adat* is reproduced through the fusion of culture and religion (A and B), in women's activity. It attempts to neutralize trends of revivalism (B) which encourage only Arab or Sunna traditions and which prioritize gender through male power and authority.

Notes

1. Marina Merican's unpublished BA Honours Thesis, University of Malaya, 1961, was an analysis of Sayyid Shaykh's work. It is entitled 'Syed Sheikh Al-Hadi dan Pendapat-Pendapatnya Mengenai Kemajuan Kaum Perempuan'.

2. British intervention to a certain extent prevented this conflict from spreading further but not before a wave of anti-British sentiment spread amongst intellectuals and professionals throughout the Peninsula. See Mohammad Sarim Haji Mustajab's essay on the *Islah Islamiyyah* Movement (1979).

3. Refer to the *New Straits Times*, July 1986, which deals with this issue in some depth. *Tariqat* in its traditional sense means 'the way to perform the finest prayer or the best performance in the way of Truth'.

4. He was said to have led an austere life despite belonging to a wealthy merchant family in Java. Before coming to Malaysia, he was invited to be *Imam* of Masjid Ma'ruf near North Bridge Road in Singapore.

5. In the village where this study was conducted, a woman whose son joined the Tabliqh movement said that she was annoyed with him for doing so, because he neglected his wife and children for many months while he went preaching. In one sermon given by a Tabliqh member in the village, a man challenged the speaker by commenting that even the Prophet brought his wife, Aishah, and children to Mount Hiraq when he went to meditate. The Tabliqh Preacher replied that he had to sacrifice family duties for the sake of Allah *(kerana Allah)*, a reply which was thought to be all too convenient by some men and women present.

6. Membership of the Tabliqh amongst university lecturers, medical doctors, bank officers and accountants is increasing, showing the movement to be following the same direction as Arqam in tapping Muslims who are not only economically self-reliant but who can also contribute a certain amount of welfare and economic assistance to other members.

7. Certain 'pop' shows have been banned in some universities because they are believed to be *maksiat*, but this has not been without dispute amongst Malay students who do not prescribe to preachings of their religious counterparts.

8. Nagata (1984), focuses on formal and informal Islamic organizations and groups, including cult movements, personalities and leaders, without describing the current participation of the masses in *dakwa* where participation is more symbolic or situational. Frequently, the book gives a good review of organizational behaviour within Islam but dynamic intervention of cultural forces in religious organizations and cults is not highlighted.

9. These forms of extreme dressing are commonly seen in colleges and universities in Malaysia. In Universiti Sains Malaysia in 1984, three Malay girls, covered from head to toe in black, with black veils over their faces, were labelled as 'freakish'*(sudah menyeleweng)* and were the butt of jokes from both Malays and non-Malays, such as, that these women constantly fell into drains, could easily rob banks, and felt that they were the chosen few. Since they were medical 'freshmen', conversation focussed on how they performed in laboratory conditions and when these girls eventually dropped out of the course, it was taken as added confirmation that such practices has no place in formal education. By 1985, the number of girls wearing the *parda* had increased to twenty-three. In February 1985, the University implemented the government ruling that the *parda* be banned from government establishment and institutions.

10. Nagata (1984: 177) states that the percentage of students involved in *dakwa* movement are as follows: 20 per cent of the students of the University of Malaya, 40 per cent at Universiti Kebangsaan Malaysia (the National University), 10 per cent at Universiti Pertanian Malaysia (Agricultural University of Malaysia) and Universiti Teknologi Malaysia (Technological University of Malaysia) and less than 10 per cent at Universiti Sains Malaysia (the Science University of Malaysia in Penang). It is not stated whether these figures are the result of a comprehensive survey of students supporting *dakwa* activities in some form, but if it is merely based on a head count of dressing and veiling, the figures are very much higher particularly in Universiti Pertanian Malaysia and Universiti Teknologi Malaysia where almost all Muslim girls are veiled.

11. The term *anak dara* is more commonly used today than *anak dara sunti*. While *anak dara* implies 'to be of age' or sexually mature *(sudah cukup umur)*, the term

anak dara sunti associates young girls with virginity, symbolically 'unopened flowers', conveying images of youth, chastity and purity. The term *teruna* for young men also implies chastity, virginity and vitality.

12. Again to reflect, Malay marriages take place in the age category of 18 and 25 although it would be considered unusual for a girl of less than 18 to be married. Young men, however, tend to marry in their early twenties and to be married in their adolescence is today considered unusual.

13. The term 'member', adopted from English, is now a common pidgin expression for a close friend, and has replaced older terms of expression like *geng* (gang) or *sahabat karib*, the latter of which continues to be standard expression in formal Bahasa Malaysia.

14. Formal political definitions of youth stretch the *belia* age group to about 35, which includes a large majority of married men. This loose definition is devised entirely for political purposes — the convenience of controlling the activities of the younger generation and are contradictory to cultural definitions of youth. For this reason, the term *kaum remaja* has been used instead of *belia*.

15. Involving death through public stoning for women and hundred lashes for men in public execution. The statement implements a rule called *khalwat* whereby a couple found in close proximity is fined but this is a Malaysian adaptation of Islamic law on pre-marital relations and adultery. There has been no known cases of *khalwat* in the village of Mawang. A girl who socialized freely with her boyfriend from Bukit Mertajam was the target of village gossip but the only action taken by her parents was to arrange for a speedy marriage, which both parties agreed to.

16. The tendency to evoke these genealogies is rather common in Kuala Lumpur, particularly amongst Malays of Arab and Indian (Tamil) descent. I witnessed one such case when the son of a prominent ex-senator went into a trance to assist his good friend in tracing his descent back ten generations in Madras. He finally made contact with this ancestor who had been extremely religious, and a renowned scholar, and who was now upset that the house he had been called into had not been spiritually blessed before *(doa selamat)* such a ceremony was performed. The ancestor is now referred to as *wali*. This mystical experience has made this person extremely respectful amongst his friends.

17. Documentaries on the 'ideal mother' or *ibu mithali* images are flashed on television now and again for the attention of millions of viewers in the country. The focus is on the domestic roles of Muslim women and the emulation of these roles by daughters to the exclusion of husband and sons, not only contradicts the notions of 'sharing' and 'complementarity' in spouse and parent and child relationships in Islam but also the long term cohesive efforts of women's groups and organizations in the country to encourage more sharing of domestic roles between women and men and to decrease women's problems of domesticity and 'dual-day' work. Numerous Malay women have come forward with the statement that the Malay-Islamic notion of *anak mithali* ('the ideal child') accompanying the expression *syurga itu di tapak kaki ibu* ('heaven lies at the feet of mother') should in fact be regarded more important, stressing the care, concern and loyalty of children to their mothers. Also, notions of *'suami mithali'* ('the ideal husband') should be given as much value and relevance as *'isteri mithali'* ('the ideal wife').

18. Malaysia's population growth is now viewed with disfavour by the Prime

Minister's Department which issued an official statement *(New Straits Times,* 15 April 1984; 12 June 1984) that Malaysia's current population of 16 million should increase to 70 million (period of growth not specified) with a mean average of five children per family. It accompanied a comment that as local industrial growth superseded tertiary development, Malaysia would be short of skilled human resources. Hence, family sizes should increase. Women who were deployed from manufacturing should get married and produce babies. The statement, quoted to have come from the Prime Minister's Department, produced shock waves amongst women's groups, particularly the National Council of Women's Organizations. More negative reactions were heard amongst women and men in villages, who expressed confusion because they were earlier told to plan for smaller families. Finally, the government issued another statement saying that the population projections included Sabah and Sarawak and covered a time span of 115 years. If this was so, then the 70 million figure projected a modest growth rate.

19. Figures obtained from the General Report Population Census, 1980.

20. Primary Sector includes agriculture, forestry, fishing, and mining and quarrying while the Secondary Sector includes manufacturing and construction. The Tertiary Sector includes electricity, gas and retail trade; hotels and restaurants; finance, insurance, real estates and business; and services. The major occupational groups are classified according to that of the Dictionary of Occupational Classification, 1979 (Manpower Department, Ministry of Human Resources, formerly Ministry of Labour). The data is taken from the annual Labour Force Surveys conducted primarily to collect information on the structure and distribution of the labour force, employment and unemployment. Since surveys cover only 1.5 per cent of the population, any form of analysis at a more detailed level of disaggregation, example, by occupation, sector and sex must be done with some caution, as the margin of error could be quite wide. As such, the data presented above is to be seen in this light, and treated as indicative.

21. The largest of these Free Trade Zone areas is in Bayan Lepas in Penang which employed approximately 12,000 women before the massive retrenchment policy in early 1985 during the trade recession. In 1989 and 1990, the same companies conducted 'walk in interviews' for women operators and complained of shortage of new workers.

22. Individual hysteria which occurs in the factory invariably leads to mass hysteria, a phenomenon which is partly attributed to new stress states experienced by rural girls in a robotic working environment. See, Lee and Ackerman, 1981 and Ong, 1987 for some new sociological perspectives into the problem. The difficulty of reconciling rural and modern needs and values is also an important contributing factor to the development of such mental states in Malay women. Non-malay women are not known to get into mass hysterical states in factories in Malaysia.

23. The Malay *nikah gantung* ('a hanging' marriage) suggests a state of ritual incompletion when a *bersanding* and *kenduri* (feast) are not performed.

7

Conclusion

Biduk Lalu, Kiambang Bertaut
As the boat passes, the water cress parts only to rejoin
— *Malay proverb*

The Gender of Politics and Public Life

The view of male dominance as 'natural' introduces universalities without suggesting that processes of history, both global and local, invariably contribute towards the powerlessness of women. Scholars who advocate this universal view imply that differences in biological and reproductive functions, always lead to gender differentiation within the milieu of 'culture' either structurally or within the framework of social transformation. In what way and to what extent do these differences maintain hierarchies between men and women? How do they reinforce the distribution of power between men and women and how do institutional structures develop to regulate and legitimize these differences? In this context, is it sociologically valid to assume that gender differentiation invariably contributes towards the subjugation or undevelopment of women in all important arenas of social activity? To what extent does a culture prevent domestic roles monopolized by women, to develop a 'public' value, in the sense that these roles may be, formally and informally, linked with the advancement of women's power? In politics and government, does female exclusion from the formal public sphere of authority imply that women are social actors who cannot determine trends of development in the political process or make major contributions to social and political history?

Many of these questions in the 'gender debate' have yet to be answered. A major weakness in anthropological research on women lies in fact in the regeneration of academic dichotomies between culture and nature, domestic and politic, private and public, informal and formal. Female invisibility may be an explanation for a certain kind of power rather than powerlessness. Informal power or influence may also be less easily destroyed than the 'formal'. When informal power surfaces into the public, it becomes more dramatically visible and threatening. Such is the history of the Western feminist movement, the female ecstatic cults of the Muslim world, women's militancy in Islam or massive adolescent hysteria in religious schools in Malaysia. A young Malay girl confided after a bout of hysteria, 'We do not want to be put away or hidden. We are as important as the men and as our teachers. Our parents value us no differently.'

This study of Malay women, through *adat* and Islam, attempts to review some of these problematic areas in gender relations, by examining both historical and contemporary evidence. More specifically, the dominant view upheld in this study is that throughout history, Malay culture, in *adat*, has ensured women a position equal to men and that *adat* constructions of gender regularly attempt to redefine and reaffirm women's social contributions in the long term. Hence, despite former and current patriarchal developments in thinking through Islam and religious orthodoxy, the religion is often operationalized according to these indigenous reconstructions of culture and gender. In this sense, Malay *adat* as an 'equalizer' actively attempts to formulate women's position vis-a-vis men in non-hierarchical ways despite Islamization and other allied processes (capitalism, industrialization and modern bureaucracy) which become subject to male interpretations which are usually made to favour men rather than women. Islam in Malaysia is culturalistic rather than fundamentalistic, a Geertzian originale of Southeast Asian Islam. Despite prevailing trends in rooting Islam more firmly in Malay society by both the government and religious groups, the Malay *umma* is increasingly split and divided by political and cultish *ad hoc* religious groups. Divergent trends in interpretation and implementation serve to cancel out rather than advance the contribution of Islam to Malay everyday life. The problem is indeed accelerated by the infinite creation of power cells amongst religious specialists who struggle with one another for monopoly and control in disseminating knowledge and information on Islam.

Over history, it was shown that the variant of Islam which was practised in early Malaya was more ritualistic in meaning and form. Ideologically, it did little to change or develop the cultural system in any significant way, or safely enrich it with a new form of ethnocentrism and unity. The structures of power and authority in kingships were tailored from Malay values of reciprocity between unequals rather than from Islam. The Islamization of the Malay States and the Malay social system did not introduce significant radical changes in institutions. It merely provided alternative modes of thinking and decision-making in certain matters like marriage, property and inheritance without threatening existing forms of action and behaviour.

Though Islam established new sources of authority through literacy and scholarship, the class of *ulama* did not succeed in taking over the existing political scene. They merely added more leverage to the existing political system in terms off criteria of leadership and its sources of legitimacy. The political structure appeared to retain its own characteristic mould. State formation through Malay kingship was achieved by rules of matrilateral filiation between 'stranger-kings' and commoners. This gave the indigenous Malays a firm control in formal political affairs, eventually enabling them to establish a class of Malay aristocrats.

Malay women who married kings were able to exert their influence in state political affairs and in the case of Tun Fatimah, the last consort of Melaka, even assume control of the kingship. Generally, although the trend of development of royal customs and procedures or *adat-istiadat di Raja* reinforced ritual and symbolic separation between rulers and the peasant masses, the integration of peasant-based values of reciprocity (*budi/jasa*) and justice (*keadilan*) within the political order was notably apparent. Also, Malay women in history were not passive receivers of authority; they were active participants of the political process and demonstrated a fair amount of competition and control in political decision-making.

With the crystallization of the Malay ego-centred kindred structure, the domestic unit, comprising the nuclear or extended family, became the most fundamental principle of social grouping and social interaction. The resulting networks did not place significant differences in women's role as public or private, formal or informal. Consequently, they were able to procure numerous social roles outside the domestic sphere. Within this system of social relations, the boundaries of domestic and non-domestic were not clearly discerned. Women's domestic roles as wives and mothers had a 'public' content in the sense that marital status and motherhood formed the basis of expansion and extension of social roles within the community, transcending at times differences in class and social ranking.

With bilaterality maintaining its own continuity in the present, the diversity of women's social roles and multiplicity of alternatives and choices available in performing them make Malay social relations rather different from those found in other Muslim societies in Asia. Where Malay women's sphere of influence is limited, as in Islamic rituals or politics featuring on Islam, customary rights in *adat* attempt to mediate the problem by giving women dominant roles in *rites de passage*. Indeed, in urban areas where Malay women have opportunities to organize themselves inde-pendently from men through membership in women's organizations like the Women's Institute, women's branch of national political parties like

Wanita UMNO or smaller neighbourhood groupings organized through the system of *usrah*, Malay women conduct both cultural and religious feasts and ceremonies independently from men. Numerous ritual ceremonies have been observed (*do'a selamat* [thanksgiving], *tah'lil*, *murhaban*) where prayers are led by women in an all-female congregation. The few husbands who attend do not have any ritual function and only come to partake of the feast.

In Malay society, as in other Southeast Asian systems, tradition also safeguards the autonomy of Malay women to a significant extent in the way in which they attempt to compete with men and other women to establish a niche for themselves in politics and government. Here, Malays differ significantly from their Muslim counterparts in West and South Asia. Despite the prevailing forces of revivalism and in spite of the more rapid acquisition of modern or Western values by Chinese and Indians, Malay women more than any other ethnic group in Malaysia have been successful in defending their rights for political representation. Doubtless they have also been used by their male counterparts in party politics and have become the 'hands and feet' of the government (Barisan Nasional or National Front), campaigning obsessively for votes in the villages. This has curbed their ability to compete equally with men on the national arena of politics but it has created a group of highly politically conscious rural and urban women who are actively involved in political decision-making at the grassroots, state and national levels. In this sense, Islam has not seriously curbed existing venues for political participation and communication.

Generally, amongst the older women, adaptation to changes in religious orientation, modernization and development follow egalitarian principles of gender developed within the indigenous system of social relations. Marital status, seniority and class continue to be the base for defining social position and status. Once this is determined, formal education, professionalism and successful penetration of the modern bureaucratic system ensure their continued participation in modern society. Since modern bureaucracy does not have rules of gender like *adat*, Malay women find it difficult to advance forward in the same sphere of public activity as men. Men generally find it easier to penetrate and manipulate modern bureaucratic political structures to their advantage, and hence fair better than women in public life. Also, if Malay kinship systems become subject to greater individualism and personal gain as has been suggested before (Banks, 1972), men may gain 'more than women by anchoring these values more firmly in gender'. A decline in the preference for applying rules of bilaterality may undermine women's position.

The idea that trends of development have actually transformed or restructured the indigenous order to the extent that existing rules of relationships become irrelevant or inoperable need to be carefully substantiated. Evidence in the present study points that none of these 'trends' or 'changes' are conclusive. An important part of Malay history has been women's contributions to the development of culture and society where overt structures of kingship leaned more heavily on patriarchy. In contemporary Islam, reconceptualization of order and relationships take a longer time to crystallize than changes of a symbolic form. Veiling, for example, may reduce the public image of Malay women in relation to both *adat* and modern values of gender but it does not necessarily lead to the devaluation of Malay women if their important contribution to social, economic and political life remains preserved. There is no conclusive evidence that the *dakwa* movement has succeeded in doing this, other than sharpening symbols of gender differentiation in a visible way. Furthermore, if certain cultish activities in Islam have reduced women's participation in public life, these are isolated *ad hoc* examples, not a massive movement legitimized by law. In any case, for the majority, symbolic conformity seems to be the preferred mode of adaptation to contemporary Islam.

In Islam, gender may always be a useful basis for operationalizing new roles and relationships but the important factor is to review it in a temporal perspective, to differentiate short term adjustments from the long term. Naipaul's 'Among the Believers' (1981) is a fine example of how a writer can confuse these two levels. He describes Malay village life as a paradise rapidly destroyed by modernism and resurrected by Islam. Writing from the 'Holiday Inn', it seemed horrific, uncivilized and permanent. In perspective, the situation shows a new Malay alternative to self-containment, a stop-gap attempt to control modernism and urbanism, at least for those who see tradition as paradise.

In the light of current trends of Islamic revivalism affecting urban Malays, the trends of development of *adat* need to be understood very carefully, particularly in relation to gender values. Malay *adat* upholds, amongst other things, egalitarian principles of ordering relationships between men and women in the context of the family, kinship and wider systems of relations based in the village and beyond. Age, siblingship, seniority and generational differences are given priority over gender in the household and wider social system.

Public policy, however, has credited men with greater value than women, since public and private corporations tend to locate and validify the sources of power and decision-making in men rather than women. Yet in rural households, women control farming and other agro-based activities, sometimes entirely on their own. In rural society, women derive a wider public importance through economic roles although statisticians and economists review them differently. Women's contribution to the economic system in terms of organization, management and physical labour provides them with a wider range of control over fundamental decision-making processes that reflect their value and power. Furthermore, they maintain vital primary and intermediary roles in formal rituals and ceremonies, derived from culture and custom, and these provide them with a significant degree of role specialization and professionalism. The kindred system naturally allows domestic roles to be extended into the more formal, public sphere in the absence of rigid boundaries of descent, corporate membership and ownership and inheritance rules. In evaluating the value of women in the rural economy, one has clearly to sort out differences between indigenous constructs of productivity and those developed by planners and economists from without (Rogers, 1980).

Although Malays have been Islamized for approximately five centuries, animistic and Hindu beliefs and rituals have dominated personal, group and communal activities in both rural and urban areas. Furthermore, these pre-Islamic ideologies have often been given added legitimacy in the context of a Muslim world through the employment of Arabic rhetorics and Qur'anic verses which symbolically convey conformity to religious orthodoxy. Anti-animistic movements expressed generally in the rejection of *syirik* practices in Islam have only successfully removed shamanistic rituals and seances from ritual spheres in the last few decades or so, and even so, only in formal, public rituals. The *pawang* or village shaman no longer performs community rituals to propitiate spirits and evil influences from the village but personal utilization of the village traditional healer or *bomoh* is still extremely rampant in rural areas.

However, it is in the context of the difficulties and trials of urban life that shamanism and animism demonstrate their full potential. Everywhere in towns and cities, *bomoh* are summoned to bless new housing sites and houses (*menawar tapak rumah, rumah*), to obtain job promotions or to ensure that employers succumb to the employee's will (*tangkal naik pangkat, tangkal penunduk, penian*), to obtain a spouse easily (*tangkal pengasih*), to protect oneself against a rival or business opponent (*tangkal pelindung*), and in more pragmatic situations, access to 'state' or 'national' *bomoh* to ward off rain during football matches, parades, open rallies and political campaigns. Even Islamic revivalism enjoys its moments of *syirik* melodramas in the invocation of ancestors to create or produce genealogies of descent from religious or charismatic leaders (*wali*), in the same vein as the cults of '*walism*' in North Africa, Morocco and Pakistan.

Islam in Culture

In defining the roles of women, the Qur'an begins with the premise that women are biologically different from men and so should be treated accordingly; to be economically provided for, sheltered and protected within the confinements of the home, reciprocating in moral virtue, modesty and domesticity. However, the principle of *ijtihad* in Islam or logical reasoning provides room for the evaluation of the roles of Muslim women and their corresponding position in society, in terms of cultural specifications. Thus, modernists like Fazlur Rahman (1983) suggest that the position of Muslim women should be perceived in terms of their economic and social contributions to marriage, family and society, for the Qur'an was produced in historic times as a reformist ideology against the rampant inhuman treatment of debtors, slaves and women. His argument suggests that the religion was deliberately developed to uplift rather than reduce the value of women in the same way as the equal rights movement in the West was motivated to assist women understand their rights. However, the pre-Islamic Arab treatment of women and the distinctions between cultural and Islamic practices in the Arab-Muslim world need to be carefully analysed, particularly since they differ so much from the practices in Muslim Southeast Asia.

Reviewing traditional Malay gender relationships outside Islam, it is quite apparent that even here, social institutions are not comparable with those found in other cultures which have adopted Islam. Kiddie and Beck (1978: 25) writing on Muslim women, observed that 'the basic patterns of male domination, the virginity fidelity son producing ethos, a sexual double standard and so on existed in the Middle East and in other parts of the world long before Islam was born'. These patterns of male dominance were not discernible in Malay culture though they have become progressively apparent in Islamic cult groups or political parties which use Islam as their political manifesto.

Significantly, according to the law of Syariah, polygyny, inheritance shares of family members which decree that women get only half the share of men, obedience, chastity, modesty in dressing, male guardianship for women, and the rule that women's testimony is worth half that of men, are essential to Islam. Societies which already advocate rules of sexual differentiation which undermine women may find it easier than others to implement Qur'anic laws. In Southeast Asian Muslim societies like Malaysia, Indonesia and Mindanao in southern Philippines, such rules are more difficult to implement and the result is usually a bric brac of procedures, situationally implemented with diverse regional modes of interpretation (for example, rural to urban, and state to state). Here, the image of Islam contrasts sharply with West or South Asia.

The Southeast Asian example does not support the idea of Islam 'wiping off' earlier structures and replacing them with a more worldly orthodox tradition. What is important to understand, however, is the way in which indigenous and Islamic institutions permeate the thought process and behaviour of the population. Models of operationalizing dual or multi-structures seem to be the general concern of the Muslim populace, rather than the rejection or substitution of one system for another.

In some Arab-speaking Muslim countries, formal employment is discouraged amongst single and married women, particularly those of the higher classes. Women who exercise their economic independence are socially stigmatized, for they are believed to possess the moral laxity attributed to career-minded Western women. Dwyer's (1978) study of Moroccan women in Taroundant reveals that such distinctions are more clearly borne out in married women. A married women enjoys her status as a wife and mother by virtue of her predominantly 'private' life and to become 'public' through economic independence or employment implies a decision to forgo rights and obligations of marriage and motherhood. Marriage and motherhood bring on the ultimate in sex segregation. Distinctions between the private and public in spheres of social activity reveals a social system characterized by male dominance and female subordination. As she (1978: 22) states, 'sex segregation, of course, does not necessarily imply the subordination of women, nor indeed, must it imply the subordination of either sex. There is always the theoretical possibility of separate but equal existences. In the Moroccan setting, however, the separation of the sexes is part of a male-female relational system in which women are markedly subordinate'.

Shahshani's study of women's movement's in Iran (1984) shows how male manipulation of women as a politically powerful force has been obvious in two contrasting scenes, the drive towards modernization during the Pahlavi regime, when women opposed custom, superstition and forms of female segregation, and later in the Islamic movement, when women voluntarily donned the veil or *hejab* to protest against Reza Shah's anti-Islamic movement. In this sense, reviewing several decades of Iranian social history, the patriarchal order has remained unchanged since values of gender differentiation and segregation have not been significantly restructured. Wikan's research on the women of Sohar in Omani Society (1982) demonstrates similar norms of sexual differentiation and segregation with both married and unmarried women. Women remain subsumed in the sphere of domesticity while men maintained the public sector. Professionalism, waged-employment, and geographical mobility remain the privileges of men rather than women. Some studies of social systems in Asia do not even attempt to mention women as participants of the system, whether passively or actively. Akhbar Ahmed's (1983) study of the Wazirs of Waziristan, for example, does not discuss women's role in relation to tribal politics and Islam. His introductory comment is revealing, that Waziristan society is male dominated and that 'women enjoy almost no rights and do not inherit land or property though they work from sunrise to sunset, fetching water, collecting firewood and looking after the home, children and animals'(p.27).

Viewed comparatively, systems of separation of role, rights and status according to gender are not significantly evident among the Malays, safe what has developed in urban industrial employment or recent Islamic movements (either Western or Arabic norms have been applied in ordering roles and positions respectively). Married Malay women may derive high status from formal employment particularly if they are also professionally trained and are able to maintain well-paying jobs in the public and private sectors or compete in public political life. They are not physically segregated from men and even those who are involved in *dakwa* in some form do not surrender their careers for motherhood, unless their employment leads to other problems like difficulty in obtaining domestic help or alternate care services for children or elderly parents. Women who have given up their careers in response to *dakwa* are too few yet to suggest a possible trend towards domestication. In this sense, principles of economic productivity, independence and a sense of work ethics in women have not been removed in any significant way. Traditionally, the Malay cultural system is able to generate a wide range of economic and social activities for men and women without apparent discrimination in values attributed to any category of work. However, women's participation in the capitalistic system, accompanied by new definitions of work and productivity has been significantly disadvantageous to women's advancement.

Generally then, despite Islamic revivalism, norms of socialization that govern Malay men and women continue to be influenced by the bilaterality of *adat* on which Malaysian Islam rests comfortably. The conversion of women from family-based occupations in agriculture to waged-employment and the imposition of rules of sexual differentiation through Islamic revivalism have affected single and married women in different ways. A significant consequence of revivalism is that through participation in Islamic activities, the 'peripheral' status of single women has been reinforced even more strongly. From a theoretical point of view, it seems as if these shifts have merely followed 'lines of least resistance' in pre-existing social hierarchies within the Malay tradition. Hence, the new gender hierarchies created in revivalist groups are in fact extensions of pre-existing relationships where young and single women suffer marginality almost in the same way as young men. It is for this reason that women and, to a lesser extent, men of the younger generation have not protested against these new developments in Islam. As emphasized before, despite the obvious contributions of young women to the *dakwa* movement, their position is structurally similar to their former role in the village — socially marginal and ritually unimportant.

Malaysian Islamic Revivalism as Anti-Westernization
Rather Than Anti-*Adat*

In the climate of Malaysian Islamic revivalism, the *dakwa* movement, introduced as an anti-Western strategy, employs gender as one of its more important symbols of differentiating between Westernization and traditionalism. Veiling becomes associated with indigenous ways, in contrast to unveiling which is associated with modernism and Westernization. Keddie more recently confirms this argument by stating that Islamists see Western attitudes towards women and Western clothing and behaviour as part of a Western cultural and political offensive (1990: 10). In Malaysia, though these differences are more symbolic than real, in the sense that veiling is often an expression of peer group conformity and acceptance rather than a response to new knowledge on Islam, the movement has ignored Malay women's important contributions to social and public life. The emphasis on domesticity, moral virtue and modesty through veiling seems to suggest that women have been the victims of moral denigration through Westernization processes. Thus, through overt symbols of behaviour and activity, as in the emphasis on 'the redressing of women' (as against the 'undressing of women' in Westernization), Islam is made to oppose capitalism and the world order through employing new strategies of gender which have little relevance in Malay culture. Inter-personal relationships between women and men have not been seriously affected, mainly because the modes of gender differentiation are maintained symbolically, as discussed earlier. Banks (1990: 533) adopts a similar argument of revivalism being more anti-West than anti- *adat* (read cultural traditions). His analysis of four Malay novels suggest that their anti-West and pro-Islamic stand is a movement towards a central cultural model.

Malay culture through *adat* continues to integrate the public and private and formal and informal distinctions of gender roles rather successfully despite attempts from leaders of the *dakwa* movement to undo this integrative function by introducing Arab cultural values through Islamic reform. This complex interplay of Islam in support of indigenization (anti-West) and against tradition (*adat*, in particular animistic tradition and bilaterality) needs further elaboration. While on the macro-level the *dakwa* movement projects itself as an indigenous response to cultural destabilization and an attempt to reconsolidate Malay values in the wake of increasing Westernization and class hierarchies, it seems to oppose culture and *adat* on the level of inter-personal gender relationships. Yet, in view of the situational pragmatic responses of men and women towards *dakwa* and the cultish coveted forms of leadership which have developed in *dakwa*, it is apparent that it has only barely scratched the surface of the indigenous order. This implies that it is the massive symbolic appeal of *dakwa* as a strategy of social opposition to Westernization, urbanization and capitalism which is sociologically more important. In *dakwa*, the benefits appear to be channelled to an ethnic group as a whole although women seem to be the ploys of movement. Thus, in the conflict between Islamic revivalism and modernism, it is the spirit of opposition which counts, not so much the way in which the system is being opposed.

Cultural Splitting Through Westernization and Revivalism

Predictably, both Islamic revivalism and capitalism have shown their mark on the younger generation of Malays rather than the older. Forms of development amongst Muslim women workers reveal the opposite effects of adaptation to industrialization and modernity. Even in early 1985, during the period of massive retrenchment of electronic and garment production workers, the majority of girls who lost their jobs did not return to the villages to resume agricultural work. They argued that town conditions were more favourable on account of the great freedom they enjoyed and the opportunities available for socializing with members of their own peer group. They believed that they could also have freer social relationships and contract better marriages with urban Muslims. Indeed, these girls often became victims of preying men who promised marriage in return for sex. These attachments did not lead to marriage, causing heartache and misery.

If the problem of female tertiary employment is analysed in greater detail, it will be apparent that these girls have been placed in situations similar to their female counterparts in the *dakwa* movement. The Malaysian government encourages the establishment of Free Trade Zones for the effective utilization of pioneer status schemes, local infrastructural resources and readily available cheap female labour, mainly from the rural areas. Simultaneously, multinationals, conduct massive campaigns to lure these girls into waged employment, providing bus services to and from the villages, dormitories and other incentives to keep them at work such as, colourful uniforms, music in the cafeteria, first-name terms between the management and the worker, beauty competitions, outings by the sea, and staff dinners. The acquisition of a new sense of freedom, impersonal forms of communication, repartee and open flirtation have been deliberately contrived in the courtship period of recruitment. The success of multinationals has depended mainly on this massive movement of young women into Free Trade Zones. Towards the end of the period of tax relief or during trade recessions, the very same girls are dismissed, locked out or forced to opt for 'voluntary retrenchment'.[1]

All in all, it appears that these young women have been victimized by their participation in industrial development in the same way as others have been by supporting social movements in Islam. The trends of victimization and marginalization are similar though they represent opposite sides of the coin. Reviewing these developments in the light of indigenous values of *adat*, these young women are experiencing a new form of marginalization relating to earlier experiences in the village. Unfortunately, in the context of the class and patriarchally structured milieu of industry, their marginality is accompanied by a new form of moral stigmatization or public censure. Thus, though their economic contributions are now more visible in terms of productivity and revenue, they have not advanced their social position in any way.

To reflect, the Malaysian-Islamic movement has produced new power bases for men at the expense of the female participants of the movement. However, so far, it appears to have affected the younger generation of women more than the older. Significantly, it is also this generation which does not derive much status from *adat*. This suggests a continuity in tradition when young unmarried women become more easily subsumed under autocratic structures than their married counterparts. Conclusively, earlier hierarchies of age, seniority and eldership are being recreated in a new form.

Culture in the Short and the Long Term

In the humanities and social sciences, few studies on women have bypassed the attempt to establish some kind of statement or generalization on women's 'power'. Rousseau's argument of domination through sexuality (skilfully discussed by J. Schwartz, 1984) highlights differences in male-female psyche, suggesting a possible universality that intersexual domination is an inherent feature of mankind. Everywhere, women appear to be subjugated and controlled by men, though in reality, women struggle to control intersexual relationships or free themselves from male domination.

In history, many strategies of successful male domination have been shown, revealed in the perpetuation of ideologies of misogyny, male cults or fascism. Simone de Beauvoir's description of the Second Sex (1953), and Foucault's idea of 'the politics of sex' highlight male domination in terms of historical processes. Rousseau's or Foucault's notion of sexual relations as expressions of men's and women's respective desires to rule or women's submission to male bigotry, respectively, is re-explained by some social scientists in terms of theories of socialization and cultural conditioning. Psychologists move to deeper levels of explanations and meanings by viewing this in terms of self-fulfilling prophecies when men uphold misogyny through conceptions of women's inferiority and immorality while women internalize these ideas and justify their own exclusion from power and politics. However, these conclusions cannot be universal. Where women have transcended domestic and political or public and private dichotomies of role and function, they have managed to maintain inter-sexual relationships of mutual dependency that reduce competition and rivalry.

Male domination only becomes absolute when women have, through history, come to accept the limitations of their own power in relation to men. This is not evident in the histories of some Western and non-Western societies where women's concern for political and social recognition has always surfaced in some form or another. Nationalist movements in the Muslim world converted women to a militant force. Historical processes relating to conditions of state formation, colonization, industrialization and development can diminish female public participation and respon-sibility but alternative systems of ideas which support female autonomy or mutual dependency and reciprocity between the sexes are also evident. Indeed, cultural institutions which seemingly support patriliny or patriar-chy do not automatically reflect female passivism or women's acceptance of subjugation, nor do matrilineal or bilaterality-ordered systems automat-ically provide infinite venues for female activity and power. What is more important for a social scientist to study is the system of 'checks and balances' between incompatible or conflicting ideological systems which culturally determine the distribution of power and responsibility between the sexes. In Malay society, for example, bilaterality within the system of social relations facilitates women's active participation in ritual and community relations, though it is not rules of bilaterality which attempt to moderate relationships between men and women but Malay concep-tualization of these rules which makes them effective functionally.

Malay *adat* operationalizes rules of bilaterality in a way which is advantageous to women. In history, it was the way in which the total *adat* system moved forward to establish itself despite counter-fundamental strains in Islam that guaranteed Malay women their continued value in society. Currently, cultural processes maintain a dialectic between *adat* and Islam and although compromises are less easily arrived at in the wake of a new religious revivalism, the public intuitively selects *adat* as the moderator.

Bilaterality has been the principle of defining women's relationship with men and in history, it has been operationalized in ways which have secured women's position in society in the short and the long term. In the contemporary situation, processes of Westernization or its antithesis, Islam, have so far not overcome established values and codes of intersexual behaviour mainly because Malay populations, both rural and urban, continue to seek middle-level approaches to change and development through *adat*. Cultural splitting through revivalism or Westernization is believed to weaken the society. Avoidance of extreme or reactionary behaviour lead the majority to seek moderate approaches. Conceptualization of ideal-type behaviour through moderate approaches are usually redefinitions of *adat*.

The anti-modernist or anti-Western ethos of *dakwa* in Malaysia is consistent with Islamic reform movements which have surfaced in numerous countries with Muslim populations since the turn of the century. These movements have usually corresponded with pivotal points of change or transformation in the histories of different nations and assume many forms, from fundamentalism or a return to the scriptures referred to as 'scripturalism' by Geertz (1968) to a political nationalist movement which is distinctly anti-West. The Qur'an and authentic Sunna texts have been utilized time and again as the basis for nationalism or social reform providing women with considerably more power than what they had before. On the other hand, revivalist movements of spiritualism and charisma also invoke Muslim patriarchy and female domesticity — sainthoods, *Mahadism, Walism, Ratu Adil* and *Keramah*.[2]

In the modern context, the expression of *dakwa* in Malaysia seems to be more in keeping with global trends of anti-Westernization rather than concrete social reforms. It attempts to deorientalize culture and society through raising various concepts like the Islamic community or *Umma* and the *bai'tumal* (central treasury). In the process of doing so, it removes some women to the periphery, but as explained earlier, this process reinforces the earlier minimal status of adolescent women. For the most, however, it expresses itself mainly in veiling. This phenomenon has a symbolic appeal in that it is seldom accompanied by knowledge of the scriptures. Veiling suggests a pointed rejection of Westernization and a return to tradition.[3] Symbolically, it reinforces cultural values by fusing *adat* and Islam in a bold display of self-identity. The consequences of this is dramatic. Women become the symbols of self-containment and self-definition of a culture which is fast changing.

Culture in the long term is its own equalizer. It produces its own strategies of 'checks and controls' through both self-criticism and self-containment. It defines peoples's own internal dilemma of adaptation and adjustment by moderating trends of change from one period to another. Over history, it reacts against new ideas while it absorbs others in its efforts to reaffirm old and establish new meanings within existing spheres of relations. In the long term, an understanding of some of these processes of self-criticism and self-containment not only elucidates relations of power in gender but also provides a useful methodology for analysing culture itself as a volatile system actively seeking self-definition.

Notes

1. Most of the girls who were affected worked in the electronics industry, signifying the untimely death of *Minah Karan* or the 'Electronic Minah' as these girls have been labelled. The streamlining of the electronics industry through new technology has been one of the reasons for the retrenchment of female workers. Other reports have been made that multinational companies had decided to wind up their business after the expiry of their ten-year tax holiday, as an attempt to force the government to concede to further tax reliefs.

2. In Malaysia, Muslim women have been dissociated from cults of *Mahadism* or *Walism* but women having been linked to the *keramat (keramah)*. Most of these concern unusual happenings like women 'giving birth' to snakes (obviously untrue but the myth alone is enough to make a *Keramat (keramah)* last for a few months); giving birth to a baby with a complete set of teeth, or sudden ability to recite the Qur'an. In most cases, these forms of *Keramat (keramah)* are a temporary commercial venture, led by husbands or fathers who have witnessed these 'miracles'.

3. Tradition here implies ways which seem to be more in keeping with the 'Malay way of life' or *adat*.

Bibliography

A. Ghani Ismail, (1986), 'Bigger Problems Facing Islam and Ulama than Kassim's Book', *New Straits Times*, 26 June.

Ahmad, P. (1982), *Development Plan: Karyaneka 1982*, Kuala Lumpur.

Akhbar Ahmad, (1983), *Religion and Politics in Muslim Society: Order and Conflict in Pakistan*, Cambridge: Cambridge University Press.

Al-Faruqi, I. (1986), 'Bringing Back the Great Vision in Islam's Followers', New Straits Times, 22, 23, and 24 August; Originally published, *The Inquiry*, London.

Almagor, U. (1978), 'Gerontocracy, Polygamy and Scarce Resources', Le Fontaine ed., *Sex and Age as Principles of Social Differentiation*, London: Academic Press.

Althusser, L. (1973), *Essays in Self-Criticism*, London: Humanities Press.

Amin, S. (1974), *Accumulation on a World Scale: A Critique of the Theory of Underdevelopment*, Vol. I and II, New York: Monthly Review Press.

Aminuddin Baki, (1983), 'The Institution of Debt-Slavery in Perak', *Malaysia in History*, Vol. 26, Kuala Lumpur: Malaysian History Society; First published in *Peninjau Sejarah*, 1(1), 1966.

Andaya, L. Y. (1975 a), *The Kingdom of Johore, 1641-1728: Economic and Political Development*, Kuala Lumpur: Oxford University Press.

_____ (1975 b), 'The Structure of Power in Seventeenth Century Johore', in *Pre-Colonial State Systems in South East Asia*, Monographs of the Malaysian Branch of the Royal Asiatic Society, 6: 1-11.

_____ (1984), 'Historical Links Between the Aquatic Populations and the Coastal Peoples of the Malay World and Celebes', Muhammad Abu Bakar, Amarjit Kaur, Abdullah Lakana Shazali, eds., *Historia*, Kuala lumpur: The Malaysian Historical Society.

Anonymous, (1989), 'A New Japan: The Left Wins an Election', *Asiaweek*, 4 August.

'Anti-Abortion Campaign News Letter', (1984), National Organization for Women, Hyde Park, Chicago, 22 July.

Ariffin Nopiah, (1979), *A Brief Introduction to the Orang Seletar of the Johor Coast with Special Reference to Kampung Simpang Arang*, Research Report No. 8, School of Social Sciences, Universiti Sains Malaysia, Penang.

Ashaari Muhammad, Ustaz Hj. (1986), *Aurad Muhammadiah Pegangan Darul Arqam*, Kuala Lumpur: Penerangan Al-Arqam.

Asia Week, (1990), 'Eye Witness: Coming Down the Mountain', 9 February, 35-41.

Ayse Nurlifer Narli, (1986), *Malay Women in Tertiary Education: Trends of Change in Female Role-Ideology*, unpublished Doctoral Thesis, Penang: Department of Sociology and Anthropology, School of Social Sciences, Universiti Sains Malaysia.

Aziz, A. (undated), *Dang Anum*, Kuala Lumpur: Pustaka Antara.

Banks, D.J. (1972), 'Changing Kinship in North Malaya', *American Anthropologist*, 74(5): 1254-75.

_____ (1976), 'Islam and Inheritance in Malaya: Cultural Conflict or Islamic Revolution', *American Ethnologist*, 3: 4, Nov. 573-586.

_____ (1983), *Malay Kinship*, Philadelphia: Institute for the Study of Human Issues.

_____ (1990), 'Resurgent Islam and Malay Rural Culture: Malay Novelists and the Invention of Culture, *American Ethnologist*, August 17: 3, 531-548.

Barth, F. (1973), 'Descent and Marriage Reconsidered', J. Goody, ed., *The Character of Kinship*, Cambridge: Cambridge University Press, 3-20.

Beck, L. and Keddie, K. (1978), *Women in the Muslim World*, Cambridge: Harvard University Press.

Benda-Beckmann, K. Von (1984), *The Broken Stairways to Concensus: Village Justice and State Courts in Minangkabau*, Dordrecht-Cinnaminion: Foris Publication.

_____ (1988), 'Development, Law and Gender-Skewing: An Examination of the Impact of Development on the Socio-Legal Position of Indonesian Women, with Special Reference to Minangkabau' Paper Presented at the Seminar on 'The Socio-Legal Position of Women in Changing Society', IUAES Commission on 'Folk Law and Legal Pluralism', Zagreb.

Berar, A. (1981), Arab Convention No. 5 of 1979 Respecting Women Workers (1978), Law No.35.

_____ Kuwait Law No. 38, Concerning Work in the Private Sector, 1964.

Bird, I. L. (1967), *The Golden Chersonese: Travels in Malaya in 1879*, Oxford: Oxford University Press; Kuala Lumpur: Originally published, 1883.

Blagden, C. D. (1897), 'An Account of the Cultivation of Rice in Malacca', *Journal of the Straits Branch of the Royal Asiatic Society*, July, 30(2): 285-304.

_____ (1917), 'Memorandum on the Aborigines in the Jasin District of Malacca, dated 1892', *State Branch of the Royal Asiatic Society*, 77: 177-180.

Blagden, C. D. (1918), 'The Canibal King in the "Kedah Annals"', *Journal of the Straits Branch of the Royal Asiatic Society*, 79: 47-48.

_____ (1930), 'Minangkabau Custom in Malacca', *Journal of the Malayan Branch of the Royal Asiatic Society*, 8(2): 307-313.

Blaxall, M. and Reagan, B. (1976), *Women and the Workplace: The Implications of Occupational Segregation*, Chicago: University of Chicago Press.

Boserup, E. (1970), *Women's Role in Economic Development*, New York: St. Martin's Press.

Bouhdiba, A. (1985), *Sexuality in Islam*, London: Routledge and Kegan Paul, Translated from the French by Allan Sheridan, Orginal Edition, Press Universitaires de France 1975.

Bourdieu, P. (1980), *Le Sens Pratique*, Paris: Edition Minuit.

Bowen, J. R. (1983), 'Cultural Models for Historical Genealogies: The Case of the Melaka Sultanate', K. S. Sandhu and P. Wheatley, eds., *Melaka*, Institute of Southeast Asian Studies, Singapore, and Oxford University Press, Kuala Lumpur, 1: 162-179.

Braddell, R. (1980), 'The Study of Ancient Times in the Malay Peninsula and Straits of Malacca', *Journal of Malayan Branch of Royal Asiatic Society*, 7; Originally published, Singapore, 13(2), 1935.

Caldecott, A. (1971), 'Jelebu: Its History and Constitution', R. J. Wilkinson, ed., *Papers on Malay Subjects*, Kuala Lumpur: Oxford University Press; First published, Kuala Lumpur: Goverment Press, 1912.

Carsten, J. F. (1987), *Women, Kinship and Community in a Malay Fishing Village on Pulau Langkawi, Kedah, Malaysia*, unpublished Doctoral Thesis, London School of Economics and Political Science.

Chandra Muzaffar, (1979), *Protector: An Analysis of the Concept and Practice of Loyalty in Leader-Led Relationships within Malay Society,* Penang: Aliran.

_____ (1986), 'Malaysia: Islamic Resurgence and the Question of Development', *SOJOURN,* Singapore: Institute of Southeast Asian Studies, 1(1): 57-75.

Cheah Boon Kheng (1981), 'Social Banditry and Rural Crime in Northern Kedah, 1909-1927', *Journal of the Malayan Branch of the Royal Asiatic Society,* 54(2): 98-130.

Cohen, A. (1969), 'Political Anthropology: The Analysis of the Symbolism of Power Relations', *MAN,* 4(2): 215-233.

Cohen, R. (1976), 'Comments on Winzeler's "Ecology, Culture, Social Organization and State Formation in Southeast Asia"', *Current Anthropology,* December 17(4): 632.

Crocker, L. G. ed. (——), J. J. Rousseau, *The Social Contract and Discourse on the Origin of Inequality,* New York: Pocket Books.

D'Almeida, W. B. (1876), 'Geography of Perak and Selangor, and Brief Sketch of Some of the Adjacent Malay States', *Journal of the Royal Geographical Society,* 45: 358-80.

Dancz, V.H. (1981), 'Women's Auxillaries and Party Politics in Western Malaysia', PhD. Dissertation, Ann Arbor: University Micro Films International.

Davenport, W. (1959), 'Non-Unilinear Descent and Descent Groups', *American Anthropologist,* 61: 557-69.

Deyo, F. C. (1976), 'Marital Status, Job Orientation and Work Commitment among Semi-skilled Female Workers in Singapore', Working Paper 54, Department of Sociology, University of Singapore.

de Beauvoir, S. (1953), *The Second Sex,* translated and edited by H. M. Parshley, 1st American ed., New York: Knopf.

de Jong, P. E., de Josselin, (1952), *Minangkabau and Negeri Sembilan Socio-political Structure in Indonesia,* Hague: Martinus Nijhoff.

_____ (1960), 'Islam Versus Adat in Negeri Sembilan (Malaya)', in *Bijdragen Tot de Taal Land en VolkenKunde,* 116: 158-203.

Department of Statistics, (1970), General Report of the Population Census, Kuala Lumpur: Government Printers.

_____ (1980), General Report of the Population Census, Kuala Lumpur: Government Printers.

Djamour, J. (1959), *Malay Kinship and Marriage,* London: Athlone Press.

Dumont, L. (1968), 'Marriage Alliance', O. L. Sills, ed., *International Encyclopedia of the Social Sciences,* New York: Macmillan Co. and Free Press, 10: 79-83.

Dwyer, D. H. (1978), *Images and Self-Images: Male and Female in Morocco,* New York: Columbia University Press.

Eberhardt, N. ed. (1988), *Gender, Power and the Construction of the Moral Order: Studies from the Thai Periphery,* Monograph No. 4, Madison: Center for Southeast Asian Studies, University of Wisconsin.

Engels, (1884), *Rise of the Family, Private Property and the State,* Chicago: Charles H. Kerr.

Enriquez, C. M. (1927), *Malaya: An Account of its People, Flora, Fauna,* London: Hurst and Blackett Ltd.

Equal Opportunities Commission, (1982), 'Code of Practice: Equal Opportunities, Policies, Procedures and Practices in Employment', *Social and Labour Bulletin,* 3, Manchester: International Labour Organization.

Evans-Pritchard, E. E. (1965), *The Position of Women in Primitive Societies and Other Essays in Social Anthropology*, London: Faber and Faber Ltd.

Fabian, J. (1983), *Time and the Other*, New York: Columbia University Press.

Fanon, F. (1967), *The Wretched of the Earth*, London: Penguin Books.

Fatimah Daud, (1985), *Minah Karan: The Truth About Malaysian Factory Girls*, Kuala Lumpur: Berita Publishing Sdn. Bhd.

Fazlur Rahman, (1979), *Islam*, Chicago: University of Chicago Press; Originally published in 1966.

_____ (1982), *Islam and Modernity: Transformation of an Intellectual Tradition*, Chicago: University of Chicago Press.

_____ (1983), 'The Status of Women in Islam: A Modernist Interpretation', H. Papanek and G. Minault, eds., *Separate Worlds: Studies of Purdah in South Asia*, Columbia: Chanakya Publications, and Delhi: South Asia Books, 285-309.

Fifth Malaysia Plan, 1986-1990, (1986), Kuala Lumpur: National Printing Department.

Firth, Raymond, (1930), 'General Observations upon the Classificatory System', *Journal of the Royal Anthropological Institute*, 60: 266-68.

_____ (1957), 'A Note on Descent Groups in Polynesia', *MAN*, 57: 4-8.

_____ (1963), 'Bilateral Descent Groups: An Operational Viewpoint', I.S. Chapera, ed., *Studies in Kinship and Marriage*, R.A.C. Paper 16.

Firth, Rosemary, (1966), *Housekeeping among Malay Peasants*, London School of Economics, Monographs on Social Anthropology, London: The Athlone Press.

Fong, M. (1975), *Female Labour Force Participation in a Modernising Society: Malaya and Singapore, 1921-1957*, Hawaii: East-West Institute.

Fook Seng Loh, P. (1975) *Seeds of Separation: Educational Policy in Malaya, 1927-1940*, Kuala Lumpur: Oxford University Press.

Fortes, M. (1945), *The Dynamics of Clanship among the Tallensi*, London: Oxford University Press.

_____ (1949), 'Time and the Social Structure', M. Fortes, ed., *Social Structure: Essays Presented to Radcliffe-Brown*, Oxford: Clarendon Press, 54-84.

_____ (1953), 'Structure of Unilineal Descent Groups', *American Anthropologist*, 55: 17-41.

Fortes, M. and Evans Pritchard, E. eds. (1940), *African Political Systems* (Introduction), London: Oxford University Press.

Foucault, M. (1978), *The History of Sexuality*, Vol. 1, New York: Pantheon Books.

Fox, R. (1967), *Kinship and Marriage*, Harmondsworth: Penguin Books.

Frazer, J. (1959), *The New Golden Bough*, Abridged by T. H. Gaster, New York: Mentor Books.

Freeman, D. (1961), 'On the Concept of the Kindred', *Journal of the Royal Anthropological Institute*, 91: 192-220.

Fried, M. H. (1967), *The Evolution of Political Society: An Essay in Political Anthropology*, New York: Random House Inc.

Geertz, H. and Geertz, C. (1961), *Kinship in Bali*, Chicago: University of Chicago Press.

Geertz, C. (1968), *Islam Observed: Religious Development in Morocco and Indonesia*, Chicago: University of Chicago Press.

_____ (1980), *Negara: The Theatre State in Nineteenth Century Bali*, Princeton: Princeton University Press.

Gender Statistics in Malaysia, (1990), Women and Human Resource Studies Unit, Universiti Sains Malaysia, Penang.

Goodenough, (1955), 'A Problem in Malayo-Polynesian Social Organization', *American Anthropologist*, 55: 71-83.

Goody, K. (1961), 'Polygyny, Economy and the Role of Women', J. Goody, ed., *The Character of Kinship*, Chicago: Chicago University Press.

Gough, K. (1975), 'The Origin of the Family', R. R. Reiter, ed., *Towards an Anthropology of Women*, New York: Monthly Review Press.

Gullick, J. M. (1965), *Indigenous Political Systems of Western Malaya*, London: Athlone Press; First Published 1958.

_____ (1984), 'The Entrepreneur in Late Nineteenth Century Malay society', the Third James C. Jackson Memorial Lecture, 1984, Asian Studies Association of Australia; republished in *Journal of the Malayan Branch of the Royal Asiatic Society*, 58(1), 1985.

Hafiz Ghulam Sarwar, (1985), *Philosophy of the Qur'an*, Lahore: Sh. Muhammad Ashraf (10th edition); First published 1938.

Hamdani, H. (1967), *Tun Kudu*, Kuala Lumpur: Pustaka Antara.

_____ (1977), *Tun Fatimah: Sri Kandi Melaka*, Kuala Lumpur: Syarikat Buku Uni-Text.

Harris, O. (1978), 'Complementary and Conflict: An Andean View of Women and Men', La Fontaine ed., *Sex and Age as Principles of Social Differentiation*, London: Academic Press.

Heyzer, N. (1986), *Working Women in Southeast Asia: Development Subordination and Emancipation*, Stratford: Open University Press.

Hill, R. D. (1977), *Rice in Malaya: A Study in Historical Geography*, Kuala Lumpur: Oxford University Press.

Hing Ai Yun, Rokiah Talib and Nik Safiah Karim, (1984), *Women in Malaysia*, Petaling Jaya: Pelanduk Publications.

Hooker, M. B. ed. (1970), *Readings in Malay Adat Laws*, Singapore: Singapore University Press.

_____ (1978), *Adat Law in Modern Indonesia*, Kuala Lumpur: Oxford University Press.

Howe, R. W. (1990), 'Women in the Court of President Bush', *The Observer Magazine;* reprinted in *The New Straits Times*, 21-22 January.

Hughes, T. D. (1935), 'A Portuguese Account of Johore', *Journal of the Straits Branch of the Royal Asiatic Society*, October, 13(2): 115-156 (translated from 'The Journey of Antonio de Alburquerque Coelho', by Captain Joao Javares de Vellez Guerreiro, 1732).

Hutheesing, O. (1981), *Pros and Cons of a Government Programme for Women*, Penang: KANITA Report.

Ikmal Said, M. (1985), *The Evolution of Large Paddy Farms in the Muda Area, Kedah*, Rural Poverty Study Series Vol. 2, Monograph No. 8, Penang: Centre of Policy Research.

Innes, E. (1974), *The Golden Chersonese with the Gilding off*, Kuala Lumpur: Oxford University Press; Originally published 1879.

International Labour Organization, (1982a), 'Introduction to I.L.O. Standards Concerning Women Workers', *Women at Work*, No.1, Geneva.

_____ (1982b), 'Promotion of Equality', *Women at Work*, No.2.

238

_____ (1982c), 'Equal Pay', *Women at Work*, No.2.

Jain, D. (1980), *Women's Quest for Power*, New Delhi: Institute of Social Studies.

Jamilah Karim Khan, (1989), 'Isu-Isu Sosiologikal dalam Pembahagian Harta Pesaka dan Harta Sepencarian di Pulau Pinang dan Kedah', Workshop 'Syariah and Civil Laws: Developments, Implementation and the Position of Muslim Women', Penang: KANITA, Universiti Sains Malaysia.

Jeanniere, A. (1964), *The Anthropology of Sex*, New York: Harper and Row.

Johns, A. H. (1976), 'Islam in Southeast Asia: Problems of Perspectives', C. D. Cowan and O. W. Wolters, eds., *Southeast Asian History and Historiography*, Ithaca: Cornell University Press.

Kaberry, P. M. (1939), *Aboriginal Women: Sacred and Profane*, Philadelphia: The Blakeston Company.

Kahn, J. (1976), 'Tradition, Matriliny and Change among the Minangkabau of Indonesia', *Bidjragen Tot de Taal*, 132(1): 64-95.

Karim, W. J. (1980), 'Children of the Garden: Concepts of Size, Space and Time in Child Socialization among the Ma' Betisek and the Malays', *Federation Museum Journal*, 25: 151-58.

_____ (1981), *Ma' Betisek Concepts of Living Things*, London: Athlone Press.

_____ (1982), *The KANITA Project: Past Policies and Future Trends*, Penang: KANITA Report.

_____ (1983), 'Malay Women's Movements: Leadership and Processes of Change', *International Social Science Journal*, 35(4): 719-731.

_____ (1984), 'Malay Midwives and Witches', *Social Science and Medicine*, 18(22): 159-66.

_____ (1985 a), 'History and the Interpretation of Culture: A Commentary on the Sullivan-Milner Debate', *Kajian Malaysia*, (Journal of the Malaysian Studies), June, 3(1): 163-68.

_____ (1985 b), 'Women in Industry: Electronic Women', *Inside Asia*, November-December, 6: 20-21.

_____ (1987 a), 'The Status of Malay Women in Malaysia: From Culture to Islam and Industrialization', *International Journal of Sociology of the Family*, Spring, 17(1): 41-55.

_____ (1987 b), *Women's Work and Status Production Process*, Penang: KANITA/Ford Foundation.

_____ (1990), 'Prelude to Madness: The Language of Emotion in Courtship and Early Marriage', W. J. Karim ed., *Emotions of Culture*, Singapore: Oxford University Press.

_____ (1991), 'Sociological Observations on the Division of Property at Divorce and Death', in Karim, W. J. ed. *Sociological and Legal Implication of the Implementation of Islamic Family Law in Malaysia*, The KANITA Project Report for Ford Foundation, Penang; 84-115.

Kartini, R. A. (1976), *Letters of a Javanese Princess*, Kuala Lumpur: Oxford University Press; translated from the Dutch by Agnes Louise Symmers, edited and with an Introduction by H. Geertz, Hong Kong: Heinemann Educational Books (Asia).

Kartodirjo, S. (1973), *Protest Movements in Rural Java: A Study of Agrarian Unrest in the Nineteenth and Early Twentieth Centuries*, Singapore: Oxford University Press.

Kassim Ahmad, (1986), *Hadis: Suatu Penilaian Semula*, Petaling Jaya: Media Intelek.

Kassim Ahmad, ed. (1973), *Hikayat Hang Tuah*, Kuala Lumpur: Dewan Bahasa dan Pustaka.

Keddie, N. (1990), 'Women in a Bind: Female Subordination in a Muslim World', Summary of Lecture at 'Women's History Week '90', Harvard and Radcliffe, *Radcliffe News*, Summer, 10-11.

Kessler, C. S. (1980), 'Malaysia: Islamic Revivalism and Political Disaffection in a Divided Society', *Southeast Asian Chronicle*, 75.

Khoo Khay Kim, (1972), *The Western Malay States, 1850-1873, The Effects of Commercial Development on Malay Politics*, Kuala Lumpur.

Kiefer, T. M. (1972), *The Tausuq: Violence and Law in a Philippine Moslem Society*, New York: Holt, Rinehart and Winston.

Kuchiba, M., Tsubouchi, Y. and Maeda, N. (1979), *Three Malay Villages: A Sociology of Paddy Growers in West Malaysia*, Monograph of the Center for SEA Studies, Kyoto University, Honolulu: University Press of Hawaii.

Laderman, C. (1983), *Wives and Midwives: Childbirth and Nutrition in Rural Malaysia*, Berkeley: University of California Press.

Lamphere, L. (1975), 'Women and Domestic Power: Political and Economic Strategies in Domestic Groups', D. Raphael, ed., *Being Female: Reproduction, Power and Change*, The Hague: Mouton Publishers, 117-130.

Landes, R. (1938), *The Ojibwa Women*, New York: Columbia University Press.

Leach, E. (1970), *Political Systems of Highland Burma: A Study of Kachin Social Structure*, London: Athlone Press; First Published 1954.

_____ (1973), 'Complementary Filiation and Bilateral Kinship', J. Goody, ed., *The Character of Kinship*, Cambridge: Cambridge University Press, 53-58.

Leacock, E. (1981a) 'Introduction: Engels and the History of Women's Oppression', New York: Monthly Review Press, 13-32.

_____ (1981b) 'Status among the Montagnais-Naskapi of Labrador', New York: Monthly Review Press, 39-62.

_____ (1981c) 'Women's Status in Egalitarian Society: Implications for Social Evaluation', *Myths of Male Dominance: Collected Articles on Women Cross-culturally*, New York: Monthly Review Press, 138-187.

Lee, D. (1979), 'Population Planning in Malaysia: Some Policy Considerations', *Malaysia: Some Contemporary Issues in Socio-economic Development*, Kuala Lumpur: Pesatuan Ekonomi Malaysia and The Asia Foundation.

Lee Kuan Yew, (1983), 'National Day Speech', 14 August, Excerpts of Speech as it appears in 'The Education of Women and Patterns of Procreation', *Regional Institute of Higher Education and Development Bulletin*, July-September, 10(3): 1-7.

Lee R. L. M. and Ackerman, S. E. (1980), 'The Sociocultural Dynamics of Mass Hysteria: A Case of Social Conflict in West Malaysia, *Psychiatry*, 43: 78-88.

Lee, R. (1982), 'Politics, Sexual and Non-equal in an Egalitarian Society', E. Leacock and R. Lee, eds., *Politics and History in Band Society*, Cambridge: Cambridge University Press, 37-59.

Leith, G. (1804), *A Short Account of the Settlement, Produce and Commerce of Prince Wales Island in the Straits of Malacca*, London: J. Booth.

Leontiev, A. (1981), *Problems of the Development of the Mind*, Moscow: Progress Publishers.

Levi-Strauss, C. (1969), *The Elementary Structures of Kinship*, London: Eyre and Spottiswoode.

Lewenhak, S. (1974), *Women and Trade Unions*, London: Ernest Benn Ltd.

_____ (1980), *Women at Work*, Glasgow: Fontana Paperbacks.

Lewis, M. (1971), *Ecstatic Religion*, Harmondsworth, Penguin Books.

_____ (1986), *Religion in Context*, Cambridge: Cambridge University Press.

Liaw, Y. F. (1975), *Sejarah Kesusasteraan Melayu Klasik*, Singapore: Pustaka Nasional.

Linehan, W. (1947), 'The Kings of Fourteenth Century Singapore', *Journal of the Malayan Branch of the Royal Asiatic Society*, 20(2): 117-127.

Lister, M. (1890), 'Malay Law in Negeri Sembilan', *Journal of the Straits Branch of the Royal Asiatic Society*, 22(2): 299-320.

Lochhead, J. and Ramachandran, V. (1983), *Income-generating Activities for Women: A Case Study of Malaysia*, Penang: KANITA, Universiti Sains Malaysia, Commonwealth Secretariat Report.

_____ (1983), *Women and Employment: A Case Study of Malaysia*, Penang: KANITA, Universiti Sains Malaysia.

Logan, J. R. (1855), 'A Translation of the Malayan Laws of the Principality of Johore', *Journal of the Indian Archipelago and East Asia*, 9: 71-95.

_____ (1887), 'Journal of an Excursion from Singapore to Malacca and Penang', *Miscellaneous Papers relating to Indo-China and the Indian Archipelago*, London, 1(2): 1-20.

Logan, (1955), *Malaysian Employment Ordinance*, Personal Management Consultant, Penang (Incorporating Amendments up to 15 September, 1981), Kuala Lumpur.

Loh Fook Seng, (1975), *Seeds of Separatism: Educational Policy in Malaya, 1874-1940*, Kuala Lumpur: Oxford University Press.

Low, H. (1878), 'Letter to Colonial Secretary, Straits Settlements', Kuala Kangsar, 14 December; Reprinted in Innes, Appendix c, No. 1.

Low, J. (1972), *The British Settlement of Penang*, Singapore: Oxford University Press; reprinted from Dissertation by Captain James Low on the Soil and Agriculture of the British Settlement of Penang, Singapore: Singapore Free Press Office, 1836.

MacCormack, C. P. and Strathern, M. eds. (1980), *Nature, Culture and Gender*, Cambridge: Cambridge University Press.

Majlis Muzakarah Sheikhul Arqam, (1988), 'Ustaz Hj. Ashaari Muhammad dengan Para Pensyarah Universiti Sains Malaysia', 28 March, Penang: School of Social Sciences, Universiti Sains Malaysia.

Malaysian Centre for Development Studies, (1975), 'Labour Turnover Study of Penang Electronics Factories', Kuala Lumpur.

Malaysian Law Conference, (1975), Proceedings of the Seminar 'Current Legislation in Peninsular Malaysia: Some Thoughts for International Women's Year', October, Kuala Lumpur.

Manderson, L. (1980), *Women, Politics and Change: The Kaum Ibu UMNO, Malaysia, 1945-1972*, Kuala Lumpur: Oxford University Press.

Marmaduke, M., Pickthall, (1953), *The Meaning of the Glorious Koran*, New York: Mentor Books.

Masefield, J. (1967), *The Travels of Marco Polo*, with Introduction by Masefield, J., London: Everyman's Library.

Maxwell, W. E. (1884), 'The Law and Custom of the Malays with Reference to the Tenure of Law', *Journal of the Straits Branch of the Royal Asiatic Society*, 13: 75-80, 103-106.

_____ (1890), 'The Ruling Family of Selangor', *Journal of the Straits Branch of the Royal Society*, 22: 321-324.

McKinley, R. (1983), 'Cain and Abel on the Malay Peninsula', *Siblingship in Ocenia: Studies in the Meaning of Kin Relations*, ASAO Monograph No.8, Lanham: University Press of America; Originally published 1979, Ann Arbor, University of Michigan Press.

Mernissi, F. (1975), *Beyond the Veil: Male - Female Dynamics in a Modern Muslim Society*, Cambridge, Massachusetts: Halsted Press.

Milner, A. C. (1982), *Kerajaan: Malay Political Culture on the Eve of Colonial Rule*, Tucson: The University Arizona Press.

Ministry of Labour, (1980), *Occupational Wage Surveys*, Kuala Lumpur.

Ministry of Labour, (1990), *Monthly Labour Statistics*, Kuala Lumpur.

Mohammad Sarim Hj. Mustajab, (1979), 'Gerakan Islamiyah di Tanah Melayu, 1906 hingga 1948', *Malaysia: Sejarah dan Process Pembangunan*, Kuala Lumpur: Malaysian Historical Society.

Moore, H., (1988), *Feminism and Anthropology*, Cambridge: Polity Press.

Morgan, L. (1870), *Systems of Consanguinity and Affinity in the Human Family*, Smithsonian Institute, Contributions to Knowledge, 17.

Morris, B. (1982), 'The Family, Group Structuring and Trade among South Indian Hunters and Gatherers', E. Leacock and R. Lee, eds., *Politics and History in Band Society*, Cambridge: Cambridge University Press, 171-180.

Murdock, G. P. (1960), 'Cognatic Forms of Social Organization', G. P. Murdock, ed., *Social Structure in Southeast Asia*, Viking Fund Publication in Anthropology, No. 29.

Nagata, J. (1984), *The Reflowering of Malaysian Islam*, Vancouver: University of British Columbia Press.

Naipaul, V. S. (1981), *Amongst the Believers*, New York: Vintage Books.

New Straits Times, (1984), 13 July.

_____ (1985), 1 August.

_____ (1986), 17 September.

_____ (1987), 30 June; 3 August; 10 August.

_____ (1988), 14 February.

_____ (1989), 11 August.

Ng, C. (1987), 'Agricultural Modernization and Gender Differentiation in a Rural Malay Community 1983-87', C. Ng, ed., *Technology and Gender: Women's Work in Asia*, Serdang: Women's Studies Unit, Universiti Pertanian Malaysia.

O'Brien, N. L. (1979), *Class, Sex and Ethnic Stratification in West Malaysia, with particular reference to Women in the Professions*, Doctoral Thesis, Monash University.

Ong, A. (1987), *Spirits of Resistance and Capitalist Discipline*, New York: State University of New York Press.

Ortner, S. B. (1974), 'Is Female to Male as Nature is to Culture?', M. Z. Rosaldo and L. Lamphere, eds., *Women, Culture and Society*, Stanford: Stanford University Press, 67-88.

Ortner, S. B. and Whithead, H., eds. (1981), *Sexual Meanings: The Cultural Construction of Gender and Sexuality*, Cambridge: Cambridge University Press.

Osman, T. (1982), 'Cultural History and the Documentation of Folk Culture', *Purba*, Journal of the Association of the National Museum of Malaysia, 1.

Overing, J. (1986), 'Men Control Women? The Catch 22 in the Analysis of Gender', *International Journal of Moral and Social Studies*, Summer, (2).

Papanek, H. (1979), 'Family Status Production: The "Work" and "Non-work" of Women', *SIGNS, Journal of Women in Culture and Society,* 4(4): 775-781.

Parnickel, B. (1960), *An Attempt at Interpretation of the Main Characters of the Malay Hikayat Hang Tuah,* Moscow: Oriental Literature Publishing House.

Parr, C. W. C. and MacCray, W. H. (1910), 'Rembau: Its History, Constitution and Customs', *Journal of the Straits Branch of the Royal Asiatic Society,* 56: 1-157.

Peacock, J. L. (1973), *Indonesia: An Anthropological Perspective,* Pacific Polisades, California: Goodyear Pub. Co.

Pehrson, R. N. (1971), 'Bilateral Kin Groupings as a Structural Type: A Preliminary Statement', M. Glaburn, ed., *Reading in Kinship and Social Structure,* New York: Harper and Row.

Peletz, M. G. (1981), *Social History and Evolution in the Interrelationship of Adat and Islam in Rembau, Negeri Sembilan,* Institute of Sotheast Asian Studies, Singapore; Paper No. 27.

Pires, T. (1967), *The Suma Oriental of Tome Pires: An Account of the East from the Red Sea to Japan,* written in Malacca and India in 1512-1515 and the Book of Francisco Rodrigues Rutter of a voyage in the Red Sea, Nendeln: Liechenstein Kraus Reprint.

Rabinow, P. (1975), *Symbolic Domination: Cultural Form and Historical Change in Morocco,* Chicago: University of Chicago Press.

Radcliffe-Brown, (1952), *Structure and Function in Primitive Society: Essay and Address,* New York: The Free Press.

Raja Chulan, (1966), *Misa Melayu,* Kuala Lumpur: Pustaka Antara.

Raphael, D. (1975), 'Women and Power: Introductory Notes', D. Raphael, ed., *Being Female,* The Hague, Mounton Publishers, 111-16.

Razha Rashid, (1990), *On the Subject of Malay Kings: A Study of the Bases and Process of Legitimacy and Legitimation of Leadership in a Malay Village,* Unpublished Doctoral Thesis, Toronto: University of Toronto.

Reid, A. (1984), 'The Islamization of Southeast Asia', Muhammad Abu Bakar, Amarjit Kaur, Abdullah Zakaria Ghazali, eds., *Historia,* Kuala Lumpur: The Malaysian Historical Society.

Reiter, R. (1975), *Towards an Anthropology of Women,* New York: Monthly Review Press.

Ricoeur, P. (1979), 'The Model of the Text: Meaningful Action Considered as a Text', P. Rabinow and W. M. Sullivan, eds., *Interpretive Social Science: A Reader,* Berkeley: University of California Press.

_____ (1981), *Hermeneutics and the Human Sciences: Essays on Language, Action and Interpretation,* Cambridge: Cambridge University Press.

Rigby, J. (1970), 'The Ninety-Nine Laws of Perak', M. B. Hooker, ed., *Readings in Adat Laws,* Singapore: Singapore University Press.

Roff, W. R. (1974), *The Origins of Malay Nationalism,* University of Malaya Press, Kuala Lumpur.

Rogers, B. (1980), *The Domestication of Women: Discrimination in Developing Societies,* New York: St. Martin's Press.

Rosaldo, M. Z. and Lamphere, L. (1974), 'Introduction', *Women, Cultural and Society,* Stanford: Stanford University Press, 1-6.

_____ (1974), 'Women Culture and Society: A Theoretical Overview', *Women, Culture and Society,* Stanford: Stanford University Press, 17-42.

Sabbah, F.A (1988), *Women in the Muslim Unconscious*, New York: Pergamon Press, 17-42.

Sacks, K. (1975), 'Engels Revisited: Women, the Organization of Production and Private Property', R. Reiter, ed., *Towards an Anthropology of Women*, New York: Monthly Review Press, 11-19.

Sahlins, M. (1976), *Culture and Practical Reason*, Chicago: University of Chicago Press.

_____ (1981 a), *Historical Metaphors and Mythical Realities: Structure in the Early History of the Sandwich Islands Kingdom*, Ann Arbor: University of Michigan Press.

_____ (1981 b), 'Stranger-King or Dumezil among the Fijians', *Journal of Pacific Affairs*, 16: 107-132.

_____ (1987), *Islands of History*, Chicago: University of Chicago Press.

Said, E. (1978), *Orientalism*, New York: Vintage Books.

Samad Ahmad, A. (1963), *Sejarah Kesusasteraan Melayu II*, Kuala Lumpur: Dewan Bahasa dan Pustaka.

_____ (1979), *Sulalatus Salatin (Sejarah Melayu)*, Kuala Lumpur: Dewan Bahasa dan Pustaka.

Sansom, S. (1978), 'Sex, Age and Social Control in Mobs of the Darwin Hinterland', La Fontaine, ed., *Sex and Age as Principles of Social Differentiation*, London: Academic Press.

Sarina A. Rani, (1990), *Perlaksanaan Undang-Undang Keluarga Syarak dalam konteks Perkahwinan, Poligami dan Penceraian di Negeri Kelantan*, Graduate Exercise, School of Social Sciences, Department of Anthropology and Sociology, Universiti Sains Malaysia.

Schwartz, J. (1984), *The Sexual Politics of Jean-Jacques Rousseau*, Chicago: University of Chicago Press.

Scott, J. C. (1985 a), 'Resistance without Protest and without Organization: Peasant Opposition to the Islamic Zakat and the Christian Tithe', *Kajian Malaysia*, June, 3(1).

_____ (1985 b), *Weapons of the Weak: Everyday Forms of Peasant Resistance*, New Haven, Yale University Press, with Kuala Lumpur: University of Malaya Press.

Shaharuddin Maaruf, (1984), *Concept of a Hero in Malay Society*, Singapore: Eastern Universities Press.

Shahshahani, S. (1984), 'Religion, Politics and Society: A Historical Perspective on the Women's Movement in Iran', *Samya Shakti, Journal of Women's Studies*, Centre for Women's Development Studies, New Delhi, 1(2).

Shaw, W (1972), 'Amuk', *Federation Museum Journal*, 17: 1-29.

Shellabear, W. G. (1952), *Sejarah Melayu*, or the Malay Annals, Singapore: Malaya Publishing House; Originally published 1909.

Siegel, J. T. (1969), *The Rope of God*, Berkeley, University of California Press.

Sinha, C. (1989), 'Evolution, Development and the Social Production of Mind', *Cultural Dynamic*, 2:2, 188-205.

Skeat, W. W. (1967), *Malay Magic: Being an Introduction to the Folklore and Popular Religion of the Malay Peninsula*, New York: Dover Press; First published, London: Macmillan, 1900.

Slocum, S. (1975), 'Women the Gatherer: Male Bias in Anthropology', R. Reiter, ed., *Towards an Anthropology of Women*, New York: Monthly Review Press, 36-50.

Stivens, M. (1981), 'Women, Kinship and Capitalist Development', Young, Wolkwitz and Mc Cullagh, eds., *Of Marriage and Market*, London: CSE Books.

Strange, H. (1981), *Rural Malay Women in Tradition and Transition*, New York: Praeger Publications.

Strathern, M. (1987), *Dealing with Inequality: Analyzing Gender Relations in Melanesia and Beyond*, Cambridge: Cambridge University Press.

Sullivan, P. (1982), *Social Relations of Dependence in a Malay State: in Nineteenth Century Perak*, Kuala Lumpur: Malayan Branch of the Royal Asiatic Society, Monograph No. 10.

Sunday Star, (1990), 'Men still dominate top posts: Survey', August 19; 14.

_____ (1990), 'Women set to tear down more barriers', August 19; 3.

Swettenham, F. (1906), *British Malaya: An Account of the Origin and Progress of British Influence in Malaya*, London:George Allen and Unwin Ltd.

_____ (1942), *Footprints in Malaya*, London:Hutchinson and Co. Ltd.

Swift, M. G. (1965), *Peasant Society in Jelebu*, London: Athlone Press.

Syed Husin Ali, (1975), *Malay Peasant Society and Leadership*, Kuala Lumpur: Oxford University Press.

The New York Times, (1984), 13 July.

The Star, (1986), 16 August.

Tylor, E. N. (1937), 'Malay Family Law: An Essay on the Law and Custom Relating to the Distribution of Property on Dissolution of Marriage among Peninsula Malays with Illustrative Cases', *Journal of the Malayan Branch of the Royal Asiatic Society*, 15(1): 1-78.

_____ (1948), 'Aspects of Customary Inheritance in Negri Sembilan', *Journal of the Malayan Branch of the Royal Asiatic Society*, 21(2): 41-130.

_____ (1970), 'The Customary Law of Rembau', M. B. Hooker, ed., *Readings in Malay Adat Laws*, Singapore: Singapore University Press; First published 1929.

Unauthored, (1970), *The Woman Question: Selection from the Writings of Karl Marx, Frederick Engels, V. I. Lenin and Joseph Stalin*, New York: International Publishers; Originally published 1951.

Vygotsky, L. S. (1978), *Mind in Society: The Development of Higher Mental Processes*, Cambridge, Massachusetts: Harvard University Press.

_____ (1986), *Thought and Language*, Cambridge, Massachusetts: MIT Press.

Waddy, C. (1980), *Women in Muslim History*, New York: Longmans.

Wagner, R. (1981), *The Invention of Culture*, Chicago: University of Chicago Press.

Ward, S. (1980), 'Women in Education', J. Lebra and J. Paulson, eds., *Chinese Women in Southeast Asia*, Singapore: Times Book International.

Wheatley, P. (1964), *Impressions of the Malay Peninsula in Ancient Times*, Singapore: Eastern Universities Press Ltd.

Wikan, U. (1982), *Behind the Veil in Arabia: Women in Oman*, Baltimore: Johns Hopkins University Press.

Wilder, W. D. (1970), 'Socialization and Social Structure in a Malay Village', P. Mayer, ed., *Socialization: The Approach from Social Anthropology*, ASA Monograph 8, London: Tavistock Publication, 215-68.

_____ (1982), *Communication, Social Structure and Development in Rural Malaysia: A Study of Kampung Kuala Bera*, London: Athlone Press.

Wilken, G. A. (1921), *The Sociology of Malayan Peoples, Being Three Essays on Kinship, Marriage and Inheritance in Indonesia*, Committee for Malay States, Kuala Lumpur.

Wilkinson, R. J. (1971), 'Malay law', R. J. Wilkinson, ed., *Papers on Malay Subjects*, Kuala Lumpur: Oxford University Press, 1-45; First published 1908.

_____ (1935 b), 'The Fall of Malacca', *Journal of the Straits Branch of the Royal Asiatic Society*, October, 13(2): 68-69.

_____ (1935 c), 'Old Singapore', *Journal of the Straits Branch of the Royal Asiatic Society*, October, 13(1): 17-21.

_____ (1971), 'Malay law', R. J. Wilkinson, ed., *Papers on Malay Subjects*, Kuala Lumpur: Oxford University Press, 1-45; First published 1908.

Wilson, P. J. (1967), *A Malay Village and Malaysia: Social Values and Rural Development*, New Haven: Human Relations Area, Files Inc.

Winstedt, R. O. (1920), 'History of Kedah', *Journal of the Straits Branch of the Royal Asiatic Society*, March, 8: 29-35.

_____ (1932 a), 'The Bendaharas and Temenggong', *Journal of the Malayan Branch of the Royal Asiatic Society*, January, 10(1): 55-66.

_____ (1932 b), 'The Early Rulers of Perak, Pahang and Achch', *Journal of the Malayan Branch of the Royal Asiatic Society*, January, 10(1): 32-44.

_____ (1932 c), 'Mother-right among Khasis and Malays' *Journal of the Malayan Branch of the Royal Asiatic Society*, January, 10(1): 9-13.

_____ (1935),'A History of Malaya', *Journal of the Malayan Branch of the Royal Asiatic Society*, March, 13(1): 18-270.

_____ (1940), 'Alexander the Great and the Mount Meru and Chula Legends', *Journal of the Malayan Branch of the Royal Asiatic Society*, August, 18(2): 153.

_____ (1947), 'Kingship and Enthronement in Malaya', *Journal of the Straits Branch of the Royal Asiatic Society*, 20(1): 129-139.

_____ (1961), *The Malay Magician: Being Shaman, Shiva and Sufi*, London: Routledge and Kegan Paul.

_____ (1969), *Start from Alif: Count from One, An Anthropological Memoire*, Kuala Lumpur: Oxford University Press.

Winstedt, R. O. and Wilkinson, R. J. (1972), *A History of Perak*, Malayan Branch of the Royal Asiatic Society, Kuala Lumpur; Originally published 1878, 1882 and 1883, in Vols. 2, 9, and 12 of the *Journal of the Straits Branch of the Royal Asiatic Society*.

Winzeler, R. L. (1974), 'Sex Role Equality, Wet Rice Cultivation and the State in Southeast Asia', *American Anthropologist*, 76: 563-671.

_____ (1976), 'Ecology, Culture, Social Organization and State Formation in Southeast Asia', *Current Anthropology*, December, 17(4): 623-32.

Yayasan Al-Arqam, (1985), 'A Struggle to uphold the Tradition of the Early Prophet', Kuala Lumpur: Al-Arqam Information Services.

Glossary of Malay Terms

Adat	custom; customary; a way of life
Adil	just, *keadilan*, justice
Akal	reason (Ar.)
Bendahara	family of Prime Ministers or advisers to the King
Bersanding	public display of the bride and bridegroom in ornamental clothing
Budi	good deeds
Baraka	the manifestation of God's grace on earth
Bisan	co-parents in law
Dakwa	revivalist movements
Haji and Hajjah	man or woman respectively, who have completed the *Haji* or Pilgrimage to Mecca
Hadis	texts of the sayings and behaviour of Prophet Mohammad used as books of instructions for implementing the Qur'an
Ikrar-kata	a convenant; oath
Imam	head of a mosque
Iddah	a period of reconciliation or trial separation after divorce of 100 days for a Muslim couple
Ijtihad	principle of reasoning in Islam
Jawi	script using Arabic characters, developed for *Bahasa Melayu* before the Romanized *(Rumi)* version was introduced
Janji	to agree
Jemaah	group prayers
Kaum Muda	young faction ⎫ pertaining to the Islamic reformist movement in
Kaum Tua	old faction ⎭ Malaya, 1900 — 1940 s.
Kris	jagged-edged Malay knife, used by Malay warriors or kept as part of family heritage
Kelamin	household
Kerah	forced labour, traditionally directed by Sultan
Kafir	pagan
Kurtah	Indian, or Pakistani outfit for women
Keramah	with exceptional qualities, like saint

Laksamana	Chief Commander of the Navy, traditional title
Mentah	literally 'raw', term of reference for the young and unmarried
Pantun	four verse poem, with heoric couplets
Pakat	consensual decision-making
Pinglipor lara	storytellers who conveyed a pedagogy of the feats and fame of the rulers and his courtesans
Penghulu	village chief or head, now a public appointment
Pusaka	heritage
Pantang	taboo
Penyelewengan	deviance
Rumi	romanized script
Ratu Adil	a messiah, Indonesian
Seri Kandi	(Sanskrit-SRI, 'Majesty', 'Holiness-Kandi'), generally female heroines
Syahbandar	traditional title of 'Habour Master' in the Melaka Sultanate
Sya'er	a poetic verse
Sindiran	a way of communicating a negative comment about someone, through belittling oneself
Salafiyya	traditionalism in Islam
Surat Tauliah	letter of authority
Selendang	a long scarf wrapped around the head loosely and worn in numerous skilful and attractive styles
Tanah Terbiar	uncultivated land, usually ricelands
Tawhid	to make it work for the good of all
Teruna	young unmarried male; a bachelor
Tariqat	the way to perform the finest prayer or the best performance in the way of truth
Umma	(lit 'Muhammad's community')
Ulama	a religious leader, a man knowledgeable in Islam
Ulubalang	followers of traditional chiefs
Usrah	religious classes sermons
Ustaz and Ustazah	a male and a female teacher, respectively (generic; not necessarily a teacher versed in Islam)
Wakaf Keluarga	family group ownership
Wali	a pious Muslim; with extraordinary qualities of leadership in Islam, (*walism* — sainthood)

Index